# The Karen People Of Burma: A Study In Anthropology And Ethnology, Issue 8

## Harry Ignatius Marshall

**Nabu Public Domain Reprints:**

You are holding a reproduction of an original work published before 1923 that is in the public domain in the United States of America, and possibly other countries. You may freely copy and distribute this work as no entity (individual or corporate) has a copyright on the body of the work. This book may contain prior copyright references, and library stamps (as most of these works were scanned from library copies). These have been scanned and retained as part of the historical artifact.

This book may have occasional imperfections such as missing or blurred pages, poor pictures, errant marks, etc. that were either part of the original artifact, or were introduced by the scanning process. We believe this work is culturally important, and despite the imperfections, have elected to bring it back into print as part of our continuing commitment to the preservation of printed works worldwide. We appreciate your understanding of the imperfections in the preservation process, and hope you enjoy this valuable book.

**A Sgaw Karen Youth with His Harp**

In the olden days every youth loved his harp and carried it with him constantly. On such instruments as these they played the accompaniments to their old epic "htas," which have been preserved for generations. The boar's tusk comb hangs down behind this boy's ear.

The Ohio State University Bulletin
VOLUME 26          APRIL 29, 1922          NUMBER 13
CONTRIBUTIONS IN HISTORY AND POLITICAL SCIENCE    NUMBER 8

# The Karen People of Burma:
## A Study in Anthropology and Ethnology

BY

REV. HARRY IGNATIUS MARSHALL, M.A.

*Missionary of the American Baptist Foreign Mission Society,
Member of the Royal Asiatic Society of Great Britain
and Ireland, and of the American Oriental Society*

PUBLISHED BY THE UNIVERSITY AT COLUMBUS

Entered as second-class matter November 17, 1905, at the postoffice at Columbus, Ohio, under Act of Congress, July 16, 1894. Acceptance for mailing at special rate of postage provided for in Section 1103, Act of October 3, 1917. Authorized July 10, 1918.

Copyright, 1922
By The Ohio State University

# PREFACE

To many a visitor to Burma, who views the country from the deck of an Irrawaddy River steamer or from the window of a railway carriage, there appears to be little difference between the Karen and the Burman. This is not strange, for many individuals of the non-Burman tribes wear the Burmese costume and speak the Burmese language; and they present no markedly different characteristics in feature or color of skin. I have often heard the remark that "there is no difference between the Burman and the Karen." It is doubtless because the Government of Burma recognizes that there is a difference in the tribal characteristics, customs, and religion that it has adopted the wise policy of publishing a series of complete studies, of which this purports to be one, of these various peoples. If the reader will have the patience to read these pages, it is hoped that he will realize that, though the Karen have lived for generations in the closest proximity to the Burmese, they preserve their own racial traits, which are quite distinct from those of their more volatile neighbors with whom they have had little in common.

This work deals more particularly with the Sgaw branch of the Karen people. My own acquaintance has been more intimate with this tribe, though I have known many of the other groups. This circumstance, together with the fact that the Bwe and Taungthu peoples have already been described in the *Upper Burma Gazetteer*, as well as the limitations of space, has led me to limit my discussion to brief references to the other tribes. But I am convinced that in the main the Sgaw exhibit the general characteristics that are truly Karen in the broadest sense of the term. I have also omitted any detailed study of the large mass of Karen folklore, which may possibly be incorporated in some future study.

The reader may notice that I have used the term "Karen," instead of the more usual plural form "Karens," when referring to the tribal name. This is more accurate, for to add the "s" is as misleading in this case as in that of the Lao, who are often mistakenly spoken of as the "Laos." In the transliteration of Karen words I have followed the continental system of spelling, adopting "x" for the guttural which is pronounced like the "ch" in the Scotch "loch," and the dipthong "eu" for the sound which closely resembles the common pronunciation of "er" as in "her." I have accepted the simplified spelling for the tribal names, Pwo and Bwe, in place of the more cumbersome "Pgho" and "Bghai."

It is not without some misgivings that I allow these sheets to go to the publisher. The notes were collected at such intervals as could be taken from my labors as a district missionary, and that at a time when increasing administrative duties precluded my giving such attention to them as I could wish. The return to America on furlough necessitated the completion of the work on the opposite side of the world from the sources of my material, and where, though I enjoyed the privileges of a Graduate Fellowship at the Ohio State University, I had to depend largely on my personal collections, there being no department of Ethnology there.

I wish to acknowledge the assistance which I have had from my wife, whose sympathetic interest and accurate knowledge have been of untold value, and also the help I have received from my missionary colleagues, among whom I should mention my father-in-law, Rev. D. A. W. Smith, D.D.; Rev. C. A. Nichols, D.D., who was first to ask me to undertake the preparation of this work, and Rev. E. N. Harris. Among the many Karen members of the mission staff who have helped in the gathering of materials, I can only mention Thras San Gyi San Kwe, Po Myaing, and Shwe Thee, of Tharrawaddy; Thra Pan Ya Se, of Shwegyin; and Thra Aung Gaing, of Insein, who gave me a full account of the Karen of Siam. The sketches signed "D. P." are the work of a Karen schoolboy from Tavoy, Saw Day Po, who, to his credit it should be said, drew them without having had any instruction in drawing whatever. My thanks are also due to Drs. B. Laufer and Fay Cooper-Cole, of the Field Museum of Natural History, Chicago, for many valuable suggestions, and to Professors J. A. Leighton and W. H. Siebert, of the Ohio State University, for many kindnesses. To Professor Siebert I am especially indebted for a most painstaking review of my entire manuscript, for its acceptance for publication, and for seeing it through the press of the Ohio State University. Finally, I desire to express my gratitude to the Government of Burma for the privilege of undertaking this work. The necessity for careful observation and thorough investigation has not been without its benefits to me. The undertaking has been exacting and quite instructive, even if it had benefited no one but myself.

This book is, after all, but another by-product of the great missionary enterprise, which seeks to lift the less fortunate peoples of the world to a higher plane of life and enjoyment, and to bring to them the best of our Christian civilization. If this work should help to make the Karen better known and understood and in any way assist them along their upward path, the writer will feel that it has all been a part of the great task to which he has dedicated his life. May the blessing of God rest upon it.

COLUMBUS, OHIO
AUGUST 30, 1920

# CONTENTS

## PART I. GENERAL TOPICS

| CHAPTER | | |
|---|---|---|
| I. | Habitat and Tribal Distribution of the Karen | 1 |
| II. | The Origin of the Karen | 5 |
| III. | Physical Characteristics | 16 |
| IV. | Mental and Moral Characteristics | 22 |
| V. | Language | 31 |
| VI. | Dress and Ornaments | 35 |
| VII. | Measures of Time and Space. Karen Astronomy | 48 |

## PART II. DOMESTIC LIFE

| VIII. | The Karen Village-House | 56 |
|---|---|---|
| IX. | Food and Its Preparation | 66 |
| X. | Agricultural Pursuits and Other Occupations | 75 |
| XI. | Hunting and Fishing | 96 |
| XII. | Spinning, Dyeing, and Weaving. Mat-making and Basketry | 108 |
| XIII. | Bronze Drums | 115 |

## PART III. SOCIAL LIFE

| XIV. | Social Conditions | 127 |
|---|---|---|
| XV. | Laws and Precepts | 143 |
| XVI. | Warfare and Weapons | 152 |
| XVII. | Music, Musical Instruments, and Dancing | 161 |
| XVIII. | Birth Customs. Childhood | 168 |
| XIX. | Marriage Customs | 176 |
| XX. | Funeral Customs | 193 |

## PART IV. RELIGIOUS LIFE

| XXI. | Religious Conceptions | 210 |
|---|---|---|
| XXII. | Supernatural and Mythical Beings | 223 |
| XXIII. | Propitiatory Sacrifices and Healing Offerings | 234 |
| XXIV. | Feasts to the "Bgha" | 248 |
| XXV. | Mount "Thaw Thi." Religious Cults | 262 |
| XXVI. | Magic | 267 |
| XXVII. | Divinations | 279 |
| XXVIII. | Tabu | 286 |

## PART V. DEVELOPMENT OF THE KAREN PEOPLE

| XXIX. | Growth of Christianity Among the Karen | 296 |
|---|---|---|
| XXX. | Progress of the Karen Race | 304 |

## APPENDIXES

| A. | Glossary of Karen Words | 315 |
|---|---|---|
| B. | Bibliography | 321 |
| | Index | 325 |

## ILLUSTRATIONS

| | |
|---|---:|
| A Sgaw Karen Youth with His Harp . . . . . . . *Frontispiece* | |
| | PAGE |
| A Creek of the Irrawaddy Delta . . . . . . . . . | 2 |
| A Mountain Stream in Burma . . . . . . . . . | 2 |
| A Path through the Bamboo Jungle, Pegua Hills . . . . . | 7 |
| The Morning Mist in the Toungoo Hills . . . . . . . | 7 |
| Karen Hill Men Coming Down to the Plains . . . . . . | 13 |
| Karen Men from the Hills, Tharrawaddy District . . . . . | 15 |
| Karen Family with Traces of Negrito Blood . . . . . . | 17 |
| Sgaw Karen Young Bloods, Ngape Eh Village, Tharrawaddy Hills . . | 20 |
| Karen Boys . . . . . . . . . . . . . | 24 |
| Playmates: Karen Boys and the Sons of the Author . . . . | 24 |
| A Paku Schoolgirl, Toungoo . . . . . . . . . | 28 |
| A Karen Belle . . . . . . . . . . . . | 34 |
| A Bwe Karen Man's Suit . . . . . . . . . . | 36 |
| A Karen Bamboo Comb . . . . . . . . . . | 37 |
| Women's Garments . . . . . . . . . . . | 39 |
| Women's Head-dress . . . . . . . . . . . | 41 |
| Karen Skirts and Bags . . . . . . . . . . | 42 |
| A Padaung Couple, the Wife with Neck-rings and Leg-rings . . | 45 |
| Women's Earrings . . . . . . . . . . . | 46 |
| A Boar's Tusk Comb . . . . . . . . . . . | 47 |
| Karen Girls in Burmese Costume . . . . . . . . | 47 |
| Two Sgaw Karen Maidens . . . . . . . . . . | 52 |
| The Gateway of a Village Stockade . . . . . . . . | 55 |
| Part of a Mountain Karen Village, Tharrawaddy District . . . | 57 |
| Stockade and Gateway of the Village, Re Tho, Tharrawaddy District . | 57 |
| Plan of Shataw Village, Tharrawaddy District . . . . . | 59 |
| A Torch with Its Stand . . . . . . . . . . | 61 |
| Plan of a Karen Family-room . . . . . . . . . | 62 |
| A Hill Village in Transition . . . . . . . . . | 63 |
| Sideview of a Bamboo Karen House, Kaindagyi . . . . . | 65 |
| Pounding Paddy in a Mortar . . . . . . . . . | 68 |
| The Fireplace in a Hill Karen House . . . . . . . | 69 |
| Karen Tobacco Pipes and a Piston for Breaking Betel-nut . . . | 73 |
| Offerings and Traps on the Edge of a Field . . . . . . | 74 |

|                                                                                      | PAGE |
|--------------------------------------------------------------------------------------|------|
| A Hillside Plot Cut Ready for Burning                                                | 77   |
| A Paddy-bin for Storing Grain in the Field                                           | 77   |
| Off for the Fields with Baskets and Bags                                             | 80   |
| Plowing a Paddy Field in Lower Burma                                                 | 83   |
| Women Transplanting Paddy                                                            | 83   |
| Reaping Paddy with Sickles                                                           | 89   |
| A Threshing-floor on the Plains                                                      | 89   |
| Winnowing Paddy                                                                      | 91   |
| Fanning Paddy                                                                        | 91   |
| Sgaw Karen Women Carrying Grain in Large Baskets                                     | 94   |
| Karen Houses on the Plains                                                           | 94   |
| Turning the Buffaloes Out to Graze                                                   | 95   |
| Setting a Spring-trap, Pegu Hills                                                    | 100  |
| A Box Trap for Catching Birds                                                        | 100  |
| A Large Fish-trap                                                                    | 103  |
| Climbing the Toddy-palm                                                              | 103  |
| Cylindrical Fish-traps                                                               | 105  |
| Bottle-shaped Fish-trap                                                              | 105  |
| Ginning Cotton in the Pegu Hills                                                     | 109  |
| Batting Cotton into Smooth Layers with a Bow                                         | 109  |
| A Karen Girl at a Burmese Loom                                                       | 112  |
| The Karen Loom                                                                       | 112  |
| A Karen Matron Weaving under Her House                                               | 114  |
| Karen Bronze Drum, Nabaain Village, Tharrawaddy District                             | 119  |
| A "Rubbing" Showing the Pattern of the Head of the Nabaain Drum                      | 119  |
| Bronze Drum from Kondagyi, Tharrawaddy District                                      | 122  |
| Head of the Kondagyi Drum                                                            | 122  |
| Bronze Drum Owned by Rev. A. V. B. Crumb                                             | 125  |
| Head of Mr. Crumb's Drum                                                             | 125  |
| Bringing Water for the Visitor, Nabaain Village, Tharrawaddy District                | 128  |
| Young Women Bringing in Bamboo Fuel, Tharrawaddy Hills                               | 132  |
| Plains Women Bathing in the Irrawaddy, in the Lee of the High-sterned Burmese Boat   | 132  |
| Carrying Water in Bamboo Joints                                                      | 140  |
| Dipping Water from a Shallow Stream                                                  | 146  |
| Buffaloes at Their Daily Bath                                                        | 151  |
| Karens of Three Generations on the Plains                                            | 155  |
| Karen Girls of the Plains Carrying Water in Earthen Pots                             | 155  |
| A Sgaw Karen Orchestra, Tharrawaddy Hills                                            | 160  |
| Karen Jew's-harps                                                                    | 163  |

# ILLUSTRATIONS

|  | PAGE |
|---|---|
| A Karen Guitar | 163 |
| Playing the "Paw Ku" or Karen Xylophone | 165 |
| An Exhibition Performance on the Xylophone | 165 |
| Musical Score of a Karen "Hta" or Poem | 166 |
| A Child Riding on Its Mother's Hip | 172 |
| The Friends of the Bridegroom | 179 |
| The Bridegroom's Company Entering the Bride's Village | 185 |
| The Wedding Party | 185 |
| Karen Girls of the Plains, Tharawaddy District | 191 |
| Christian Converts, Ngape Eh Village, Tharrawaddy District | 191 |
| Sgaw Karen Young Women | 196 |
| Arrangement of Pestles for a Funeral Game | 200 |
| Another Arrangement of Pestles for a Funeral Game | 201 |
| A Sketch of a Tree Used in the Funeral Games | 203 |
| Climbing the Cocoanut-palm | 214 |
| A Hill Village in Transition | 220 |
| A Karen Village on the Plains | 220 |
| A Bwe Karen Christian Village, Toungoo District | 227 |
| Karen Girls Pounding Paddy in a Mortar Out-of-doors | 238 |
| A Bwe Karen Prophet | 246 |
| A Hut Erected in a Forest Clearing by a Self-styled Prophet as the Center of a New Karen Religious Cult of Short Duration | 246 |
| A Sgaw Karen Grandmother | 251 |
| Karen Villagers, Tharrawaddy District | 256 |
| Utensils for the Sacred "Bgha" Feast of a Pwo Karen Family, Bassein District | 260 |
| Village School-children with Their Teacher | 266 |
| Paku Karen Schoolgirls | 272 |
| Field-day, Tharrawaddy Karen High School | 281 |
| Chicken Bones Used in Divination | 282 |
| A Christian Karen Village School, Tharrawaddy District | 293 |
| Two Karen Christian Pastors | 295 |
| Karen Theological Students | 299 |
| A Christian Village School, Prome District | 302 |
| The Chapel and Schoolhouse of the American Baptist Mission High School, Tharrawaddy District | 302 |
| Schoolgirls at Calisthenics, Tharrawaddy Karen High School | 305 |
| Schoolboys Lined up for Drill | 305 |
| A Karen Teacher and Lahu Boys | 308 |
| Rev. Thra Maung Yin, of Bassein | 311 |
| Karen Military Police | 313 |

CHAPTER I

HABITAT AND TRIBAL DISTRIBUTION OF THE KAREN

The Karen are a group of Indo-Chinese tribes living principally in Burma, the easternmost province of the British Indian Empire, in the Indo-Chinese peninsula, and in the adjoining country of Siam to the east. They are found between the tenth and twenty-first degrees of north latitude and between the ninety-fourth and one hundredth degrees of east longitude. The greater part of this territory they occupy in connection with the other peoples of the country, namely, the Burmese, Shan, Siamese, and Chin. The only exclusively Karen country is the hilly region of the Toungoo district and the Karenni subdivision, where the Karen chiefs of five states, comprising 4,830 square miles and a population of 42,240, are still in power under the Advisory Council of the British Government. There is also a Karen chief ruling one of the Shan States, and five other states in that section are ruled by Taungthu chiefs. In all these latter districts we find a mixed population.[1]

The whole group of Karen tribes can be divided into three divisions, according to their language or dialect differences. These are the Sgaw, Pwo, and Bwe groups.

The Sgaw group is the largest and most widely scattered. They are found all through the Irrawaddy Delta, from the vicinity of Prome southward, and from the Arracan coast eastward to the neighborhood of Lakong in Siam and southward to the lowest point of the British possessions. The Paku and Mawnepgha tribes of the southern Toungoo Hills belong to this group. One dialect, with only slight variations, is used throughout this region.

The Pwo group comprises, besides the Pwo Karen, the Taungthu tribe, who call themselves the Pao. The Pwo are found along the seacoast from Arracan to Mergui and are said to be found nowhere more than fifty miles inland. However, I think that some of the Pwo villages in the Henzada district may be a little farther inland than that. The Taungthu are found in a section of country

---

[1] J. S. Scott: *Burma*, Appendix, pp. 470–481.

A Creek of the Irrawaddy River Delta, Bassein District
These streams form the highways of this district.

A Mountain Stream in Burma
The Karen build their villages along these streams of swift-running water.

running northward from Thaton into the Shan States beyond Taunggyi.

The Bwe tribes are found in the vicinity of Toungoo, in the territory extending from the foothills east of that city throughout the Karenni subdivision. This is a very mountainous region, and we find the people broken up into small tribes differing from one another in dialect, dress, and customs. Nine of these tribes were enumerated in the last Government census. The tendency of the present time is to consider these tribes more closely related than was formerly the case.

In the *Census Report* of the Government of India for the year 1911 we have the first enumeration of all Karens in the British territory. In former reports the Karenni territory was not included in the enumeration. The returns in 1911 showed a population of 1,102,695. This was an increase of 199,334 over the previous count in 1901, due in part to the increased extent of the territory covered. The enumeration, however, did not clearly distinguish between the Pwo and Sgaw branches of the race, due, as the *Report* says, to the fact that many returned themselves simply as Karens, without specifying to which branch they belonged. The total number of Pwos and Sgaws increased from 717,859 souls in 1901 to 872,825 in 1911, a gain of 154,966. This represents a real increase in population, for these tribes are all in Burma proper. The Pwo dialect is less persistent than the Sgaw, for more of its members are using Burmese to a much greater degree than the Sgaws, although the latter are also giving up their language where they are living in close contact with the Burmans. The Sgaw dialect is not "driving out the Pwo" as rumor says, but is merely holding its own better against the Burmese. Probably there are about half a million Sgaws in Burma and perhaps another 50,000 in Siam,[2] which would make them the most numerous branch of the race. The Taungthu were enumerated by themselves and, as has been said above, belong to the Pwo group. There were 183,054 of them in 1911. During the decade previous to that enumeration they had made an increase of 14,753 souls. The Pwo group would probably include altogether about 350,000 members and would stand second in point of numbers.[3]

---

[2] W. A. Graham, in the *Handbook of Siam*, estimates the Karen of that country at 30,000, but I think this estimate rather low.

[3] These citations are all from the *Census of India*, 1911, Vol. IX, pp. 275, ff.

The Bwe group is more definitely treated in the *Census Report*, for in this group each tribe is enumerated separately, as follows:

| | |
|---|---:|
| Karenni | 19,008 |
| Karennet | 3,721 |
| Karenbyu | 790 |
| Zayein | 4,981 |
| Sinsin | 533 |
| Bre | 6,911 |
| Mano | 1,445 |
| Yinbaw | 911 |
| Padaung | 8,516 |
| Total | 46,816 |

These tribes,[4] dwelling in the heart of the Karen country where they have been secure in the fastnesses of their native hills, have never before been counted with enough exactness to allow us to estimate their increase in numbers. There is no doubt that the general impression that they are really increasing is correct. Further investigation may show that some of these tribes as, for example, the Zayein, may be allied to non-Karen stock, such as the Wa of the Shan States.[5]

These Bwe tribes form a distinct group, but it is beyond the purpose of this present work to deal in particular with them, especially since they have already formed the subject of a study incorporated in the *Upper Burma Gazetteer*.[6]

---

[4] Karenni means literally Red Karen, in Burmese. It has been used of the tribe dwelling in the country now called by that name, because they wear red clothing. Similarly some writers have spoken of the White Karen and the Black Karen, "Karenbyu" and "Karennet."

[5] Rev. W. H. Young, formerly of Kenteung, tells me that the Wa language resembles the Karen in structure but not in vocabulary, while the Lahu and Pwo Karen have similar customs and vocabulary but a different sentence structure.

[6] Vol. I, Pt. I, Chapter IX.

## CHAPTER II

## THE ORIGIN OF THE KAREN

The traditions of the Karen clearly indicate that they have not always lived in their present home. The most striking story is that of "Htaw Meh Pa," the mythical founder of the Karen race, who lived with his numerous family in some unknown land to the North, where their fields were ravaged by a great boar. The patriarch went out and killed the boar; but when the sons went to bring in the carcass, they could find only one tusk which had been broken off in the fray. The old man made a comb out of this, which surprised them all by its power of conveying eternal youth to all who used it. Soon their country became overpopulated, and they set out to seek a new and better land. They traveled together till they came to a river called in Karen "Hti Seh Meh Ywa." Here the old man became impatient at the long time it took the members of the family to cook shellfish and went on ahead, promising to blaze his path that they might follow him through the jungle. After a while the Chinese came along and told them how to open the shells to get out the meat; and then, having eaten, they followed the old man, only to find that the plantain stalks he had cut off had shot up so high that it seemed impossible to overtake him. They, therefore, settled down in the vicinity. The patriarch went on, taking with him the magic comb which has never been discovered to this day.

While this tradition is not confined to the Karen,[1] it has a bearing, I believe, on their origin. A great deal has been written about the "Hti Seh Meh Ywa" or, as Dr. Mason called it, the "River of Running Sand,"[2] which is, as he thinks, the Gobi Desert. This opinion of Dr. Mason is derived from Fa Hien's description of his travels across that desert. However, the Karen name of the river means not only "flowing sand," but also a "river of

---
[1] This tradition is found among the Lahu and also, according to Thra Ba Te, among the Chin in the northwest of Burma.

MacMahon, in *The Karens of the Golden Chersonese*, p. 106, refers to a different version of this story, in which the Chinese go ahead instead of "Htaw Meh Pa," and on p. 104 MacMahon says he found traditions indicating that the Karen formed part of a Chinese expedition into Burma and that they were left behind because of their sluggish movements. These all point to early relations with the Chinese.

[2] Mason, *British Burma*, p. 831.

water flowing with sand."³ The reference to the Gobi Desert seems rather far-fetched and has, therefore, been abandoned by scholars. Dr. D. C. Gilmore suggests the Salween as being a river that fulfils the requirements of the tradition, but bases his conclusions largely on the reference to the early home of "Htaw Meh Pa" as located on Mount "Thaw Thi," the Olympus of the Karen, which is mentioned in Dr. Vinton's version of the story, from which he quotes.⁴ This reference is not found in other versions of the story and was probably not a part of it in its earliest form. It seems reasonable, therefore, to look further for the sandy river. Dr. Laufer⁵ asserts that the early home of the peoples of eastern Asia was in the upper reaches of the Hoang-ho or Yellow River, of China, and that from this center the Tibetans migrated westward; the early tribes of Indo-China, southward; and the Chinese, southeastward. According to this view, the progenitors of the Karen probably formed a part of the southward migration and, at some stage of their march, stopped on the banks of the Yellow River which, as its name suggests, has from time immemorial been freighted with silt and sand. Here they may have tried to cook the shellfish referred to in the tradition. From this region they doubtless made their way down to what is now Yunnan, where perhaps they found a domicile till they were pushed farther south by migrating people advancing behind them.

The name "Karen" is an imperfect transliteration of the Burmese word "Kayin," the derivation of which has puzzled students of that language. It has been thought that this word is derived from the name by which the Red Karen call themselves, *i.e.*, "Ka-Ya." The designation of the Sgaw for themselves is "Pgha K'Nyaw," which has not usually been associated with the native name of the Red Karen. In August, 1914, it was suggested to me⁶ that these tribal names, which have hitherto been thought to mean simply "men," were related to, and derived from, the name of one of the four ancient tribes of China, that is, the Ch'iang (ancient pronunciation, Giang or Gyang). This tribe, which is indicated in Chinese by the ideograph of a man combined with the character designating a sheep, conveying the meaning of shepherd, occupied

---

³ E. B. Cross, *Journal, American Oriental Soc.* (1854) Vol. IV, pp. 293, ff. and D. C. Gilmore, *Journal, Burma Research Soc.*, Vol. I, p. 191.

⁴ J. B. Vinton, D.D. and Rev. T. Than Bya, M. A., *Karen Folklore Stories.*

⁵ Dr. B. Laufer, Curator of Anthropology, Field Columbian Museum, Chicago, in a note to the writer, Jan. 6, 1920.

⁶ By the Rev. Thra Ba Te, in a letter dated August 14, 1917.

A Path through the Bamboo Jungle, Pegu Hills

The Morning Mist in the Toungoo Hills
The mists settle in the valleys, which make the mountain-tops look like islands in an inland sea.

the western part of ancient China. The first part of the name, "Ch," means "people," and the latter part, "Yang," is the distinctive tribal name. Turning now to the Karen word "Pgha K'Nyaw." "Pgha" is a general word meaning people. "K'Nyaw" is, according to my informant, composed of two elements: "K'," a prefix often found in the names of tribes in the vicinity of Burma and denoting a tribal group, as "Kachin," "Kethe," or "Karok" (as used by the Talaing of the Chinese). "Nyaw" is derived from "Yang," referred to above. The final nasal "ng" is softened in Karen to the open syllable "aw," following the analogy of many words occurring in the dialects or in Burmese and having nasal endings; and "n" and "ny" are interchangeable. Thus, if this reasoning is correct, "Pgha K'Nyaw" is derived from the ancient "Yang," and is like the source from which the Burmese "Kayin" is derived.[7] This explanation affords another link connecting the Karen with the early dwellers within the confines of the present Chinese Republic.

The language of the Karen, after being classed in various ways, has now been recognized as a Sinitic language and, according to the last Burma *Census* (1911) is set down as belonging to the "Siamese-Chinese" sub-family of the Tibeto-Chinese languages, being grouped with the Tai or Shan. I feel sure that this last grouping is subject to revision by the philologists. While at first glance the relationship of these languages appears to be remote, Major H. R. Davies makes a very pertinent statement when he says: "Doubtless owing to phonetic change and the splitting of initial double consonants, many words have been altered beyond all hope of recognition, but a systematic study of the subject would, I believe, reveal many unsuspected resemblances."[8]

When we consider that many of these languages have never been fixed by written characters and that, within the past few decades, the Karen language has so changed that the bard literature of a century ago is almost unintelligible to the present generation, we can see how complicated the problem is and that it is only capable of solution, if at all, at the hands of experts.

The Karen language, as we now have it, is a monosyllabic agglutinated speech, with no final consonants in Sgaw Karen and with nasals and finals in other dialects. These are all marks of Sinitic

---

[7] Dr. Martin in the *Lore of Cathay* gives the names of the other three of the four ancient tribes of China as the La in the North, the Yi in the East, and the Man in the South.
[8] Maj. H. R. Davies, *Yunnan, The Link between Burma and the Yangste*.

speech. Dr. D. C. Gilmore believes that the Pwo dialect branched off from the parent stem earlier than the Sgaw, but kept the original nasals and, being in closer contact with outside races, adopted more outside words.[9] The Sgaw has dropped the final nasals, because they were more difficult to pronounce, but has kept the original form of the language to a greater extent than the Pwo.

The fact that the Karen have used bronze drums for many generations has, I think, a bearing on their racial relationship. These remarkable drums have only recently been studied by Western scholars, and their full significance is still a matter for investigation. These drums were formerly thought to be of Chinese origin, but it seems that they are to be attributed to aboriginal tribes, found in what is now Tong King and Yunnan by the Chinese generals, Ma Yuon (41, A.D.) and Chu-Ko Liang (230, A.D.), who conquered these territories for the Chinese.[10]

The upper portion of Camboja is now considered to be the original home of these drums. They formed part of the possessions of the chiefs and were considered very precious, each being worth from eight to ten oxen. Chu-ko Liang is reported to have exacted sixty-three bronze drums as tribute from the barbarians and to have taken them back with him. Among the peoples of Burma the Karen seem to be the only race that has made use of these drums. They do not manufacture them, but buy them from the more industrious Shans, who do not appear to set much store by them.[11] Among the Karen, until recent times, the owner of one of these instruments was considered of more worth than a man who had seven elephants. A drum often formed the ransom of a village or the dowry of a maiden. Although so valued a possession often belongs to a chief, it may belong to any one who can purchase it.

It may have been from the Karen that the Chinese generals exacted part or all of their tribute. If so, this people was living in the mountains of Yunnan at the beginning of the Christian era.

---

[9] D. C. Gilmore, "Phonetic Changes in the Karen Languages" in *Journal, Burma Research Society*, Vol. VIII, Pt. ii, pp. 122, ff.

[10] Several pamphlets and articles in anthropological journals deal with these drums. The most extensive work on the subject, which is in German, is by Franz Heger and is entitled *Alte Metalltrommeln aus Sudost-Asien*, Leipzig 1902. An excellent short work entitled "Anciens Tambours de Bronze," is by H. Parmentier and is printed in the *Bulletin l'Ecole d' Extreme-Orient*, Hanoi, 118. See also Chapter XIII on Bronze Drums, pp. 115-126.

[11] W. W. Cochrane, in *The Shans*, mentions the Shan towns of Tagaung or Ta Kawng and Mogaung or Mong Kawg as denoting, respectively, Drum Ferry and Drum Town, and on page 62 he says: "They took also a palace drum, whose reverberations could call the people together, daunt enemies, or bring rain in time of drought." He makes no further reference to their use.

It is a belief of the Karen that their forefathers have cherished these drums from time immemorial. One drum in Toungoo district is, I have been told, supposed to be a thousand years old. Our knowledge of them is, however, too meagre to permit any dogmatic statements on the subject. Further investigation should throw more light upon it.

The religious traditions of the Karen have also been thought to possess significance in regard to their racial origin. When, in 1827, the early missionaries first discovered the Karen, they were surprised to find that these people professed having received from their forefathers monotheistic traditions in which the story of the creation was almost parallel to the Mosaic account in Genesis. (See p. 211.) The question, "Whence this story?" at once suggested itself. Was it their independent possession from the beginning of time, their only relic from a more vigorous and highly civilized past when, as they explained, they had not yet lost their book?[12] Or had it been borrowed from another people, whom they had met in the course of their wanderings from their northern birthplace to their present home? Some of the early missionaries, including Dr. Mason, thought that the Karen might be found to be the lost tribes of Israel [13] or, if not actually descended from Abraham, that they had received instruction from colonies of Jews, who were supposed to have spread to the East in ancient times.

It has also been suggested that Christian missionaries, traveling to the Orient during the early centuries of our era, transmitted this creation story to the Karen. On this point the comment of Dr. Laufer is pertinent.[14] He says: "The 'River of running sand' in the traditions of the Karen is not necessarily to be interpreted as the Desert of Gobi; at least it is not convincing. Still less is it conceivable that their legends should suggest an acquaintance with the Jewish colonies in China, or even with the Nestorian tablet at

---

[12] The tradition of the Lost Book is not peculiar to the Karen, but seems to be found also among other tribes in and about Burma, e. g., the Kaws, Was, Palaungs, and the Hkamoks of Siam: letter of Mr. Taw Sein Ko to Thra Ba Te, dated 10th Oct., 1917.

[13] In a letter to the Baptist Missionary Society, dated Oct., 1832, Dr. Mason mentions hearing of the shipwreck on the Tenasserim River some decades before of a foreign merchant who told the Karen that other white men would come and teach them about God. He adds that he thought that the traditions came from Portuguese priests who had earlier come to the East. But in a later letter, dated Oct., 1834, Dr. Mason writes that he had come to believe that the traditions were indigenous with the Karen, whom he thought to be the lost Hebrew tribes. He wrote a communication to the Government to that effect from the "Headquarters of the Tenasserim," dated Dec. 6, 1833. (See *Missionary Magazine*, Dec., 1833, p. 469, and Oct. 1834, p. 382).

[14] See *Journal, American Folklore*, Vol. XXXI, No. CXX, pp. 282, ff. for his review of Sir J. G. Scott's Indo-Chinese Mythology, in *Mythology of All Races*, Vol. XII.

Sin-gan-fu. The small number of Jewish immigrants into China, who were chiefly settled at K'ai-fong in Ho-nan, have never been able to exert the slightest influence on their surroundings, but, on the contrary, have been so completely sinsized that they are now almost extinct. Nestorianism left no trace on the thought of Chinese society. The inscription in question is written in such an exalted and highly literary style that it is quite unintelligible to the people and its technical terminology is a complete mystery to the present scholars of China. No popular influence can be attributed to such a monument." It appears that the number and antiquity of early Jewish immigrants into China have been much overestimated by many writers, so that, if present scholarship is correct, this source from which the Karen could have obtained their tradition has practically been eliminated.[15]

Though there seems to be little ground left for connecting the Karen story of the creation with either the Jewish or Nestorian colonies of China, there are one or two points that might be borne in mind in regard thereto. The story is universally known among the Karen tribes and most fully among the Red Karen, who have been least affected by outside influences in recent times. It contains no reference to the life or teachings of Christ or to any real Messianic hope, but suggests only *Old Testament material*, such as the creation, fall, flood, and tower of Babel, besides containing the Red Karen genealogy. Hence, it would seem that we can hardly attribute the story to the Portuguese missionaries, who were not in Burma until the sixteenth century or later. It would rather point to an earlier Jewish source, from which the story came back in the days when the tribes were less divided than they were later. For if Christian teachers had taught the Karen, would they not have made a deeper impression with their story of salvation than with the less significant one of creation?

Some writers have asserted that the original religion of China was a sort of monotheism, in which one god, the Emperor of Heaven, was somewhat akin to the Jehovah of the Hebrews, though not worshiped to the exclusion of all other deities. There

---

[15] See also *China and Religion* by E. G. Parker, who says (page 108) that there is no mention of any Western religion in China up to the end of the sixth century, A. D., when Christianity entered the country, except Buddhism which had come in centuries before. On page 165 he gives the date of the arrival of the Jewish colonies in China as 1163, A. D. The article on China in the latest edition of the *Encyclopedia Brittanica* also bears out this testimony.

is a bare possibility that the Karen tradition might have some relation to such an ancient belief.[16]

However, the story of the creation among these people has such a marked parallelism with the Hebrew story that, even though its origin has not been traced, we find it difficult to avoid the suspicion that it came from an Hebraic source, being carried by some wandering story-teller or unknown missionary only to become incorporated into the tribal belief of the Karen, along with their own primitive mythology.

The hilly province of Yunnan in southwestern China, with its great mixture of races, answers the description of an ancient reservoir of fugitives and migrating groups from both India and China. In the marauding expeditions and massacres taking place among the contending elements in such a "melting pot," the oriental conquerors showed mercy only to the women among the foe and made wives of them. On the assumption or theory that the Karen spent a part of their migratory period in Yunnan, they may have preserved a greater degree of racial purity by their practice of strict endogamy and their custom of retreating to mountain fastnesses.[17]

From Yunnan the route that was probably followed by the Karen was by way of the Mekong or Salween into the upper part of what is now the Shan States. Thence they spread southward over what is now Karenni and then on to Lower Burma and Tenasserim.[18]

We are unable to determine when these migrations took place, or when the Karen entered Burma. If it could be shown that the ancestors of the Karen were among those from whom the drum tribute was exacted by the Chinese generals, we should know that they were dwellers in Yunnan at the beginning of the Christian era.

Dr. Mason notes a tradition that a Karen chief went to the site of Laboung, intending to bring his people to settle there, but that when he returned with his followers the Shan had already occupied the location. The founding of Laboung has been fixed at 574 A.D. This comes the nearest to being a definite landmark in the south-

---

[16] John Ross, in *The Original Religion of China*, makes this the subject of an interesting volume. Also E. H. Parker, in *China and Religion*, gives a few hints that may show that the earliest ancestors of the Chinese held one god in much greater esteem than the other beings in their mythology.

[17] Sir J. G. Scott, Introduction to Indo-Chinese Mythology, *Mythology of all Races*, p. 258.

[18] C. C. Lowis on Burma, *Ethnological Survey of India*, (1910) p. 15.

ward migration of the Karen people. The vicinity of Laboung was probably the stopping-place on their long journey.[19]

Mr. J. O'Riley, one of the earliest English officers to travel in the Karenni, writes that he found traditions indicating that the

KAREN HILL MEN COMING DOWN TO THE PLAINS

country around Pagan was one of the early homes of the Karen and that they were driven southwest from there, while the Chinese who were with them were driven back to their own country, and the Kollahs (foreigners), northward. The Karen then appear to have gone to the Shan country, Hyoung Yuay, and thence to have been driven to the Myobyay province. Here, according to tradition, they were again attacked and, having in time greatly increased in numbers, they turned against the Shan, expelled them, and occupied the present Red Karen country.[20]

The fact that the Karen are found farther south than the Shan also argues that they migrated earlier and were perhaps pushed on by the latter, who in turn may have given way before a more powerful force at their heels. O'Riley learned of a tradition of the Red Karen which suggested that they had lived ten generations in their present home.[21] This would limit their sojourn here to a

---

[19] Lt. Col. A. R. MacMahon, *The Karens of the Golden Chersonese*, p. 114.

period of less than three hundred years. This is doubtless much too low an estimate, unless it refers to the time of their domicile in the particular district now occupied.

In so far as we may venture a conclusion, it is that the Karen migrated into Burma, coming from the ancient home of the early tribes inhabiting the country of China, with whom they are related by tribal, linguistic, and possibly religious ties, the full significance of which are yet to be determined.

NOTE. Various Theories of the Origin and Tribal Relationships of the Karen.—From the middle of the nineteenth century many theories regarding the origin and racial affinity of the Karen have been propounded by writers on Burma. J. R. Logan, writing in 1850 in the *Journal of the Indian Archipelago* (Vol. IV, p. 478) connects this people with the tribes in the highlands of the Kolan and Irrawaddy and in the lower bend of the Brahmaputra. Writing again in the same *Journal* in 1858 (New Series, Vol. II, p. 387) Logan maintains that the Karen language is a dialect of the Irrawaddo-Brahmaputran dialect, affected by Chinese influence as it came south. Professor De Lacouperie in his introduction to Colquhoun's *Amongst the Shans* (pp. xxxviii, ff.) argues that the Karen are descended from the ancient Tek or Tok tribes of central Asia. Early missionaries and other writers, including Denniker. (*Races of Man*, p. 395) believed that the Kachin and Chin formed a branch of the Karen race. *The Archaeological Survey* of Burma has linked the Karen both with the ancient Kanran, one of the three primitive tribes mentioned in Burmese annals, and with the Miao and Yao of Yunnan (*Report* of 1916). But the Kanran were driven southwestward from the region around Prome and seem to have disappeared from history. (Phayre, *History of Burma*, pp. 5-19.) The linguistic differences between the Miao, Yao, and Karen have led to the abandonment of the idea that they are closely related. In fact, all of these views have been given up, because they were based on an inadequate knowledge of the tribes concerned.

Dr. Mason, in the *Journal, Asiatic Soc. of Bengal* (Vol. XXXVII, p. 162, 1868,) says that the first historical notice of the Karen is in Marco Polo's travels in the 13th Century. He quotes Malte Brun on the basis of Marco Polo's travels, as follows: " 'This country of Caride is the southeastern point of Tibet, and perhaps the country of the nation of the Cariaines; which is spread over Ava.' This statement is confirmed by old Bghai poetry in which we find incidentally mentioned the town of Bhamo to which they formerly were in the habit of going to buy axes and bills or cleavers, as they do now at Toungoo. When this poetry was composed they lived five hundred miles north of their present locality." These geographical allusions seem so vague that it appears to be impossible to build much of a theory upon them. Perhaps the lines referring to Bhamo may refer to a trading expedition and not to a line of migration. And the statement of Malte Brun is only conjecture at the most.

In their excellent work on *The Pagan Tribes of Borneo*, Hose and Mc-

---

[20] J. O'Riley, *Journal, Indian Archipelago*, Vol. IV, N.S. (1859), p. 8.
[21] *Ibid.*

## THE ORIGIN OF THE KAREN

Dougall say that "of all the tribes of the southwestern corner of the continent, the one which seems to us most closely akin to the Kayans [of Borneo] is that which comprises the several tribes of the Karen." (Vol. II, p. 235).

The similarity in culture and physical characteristics of the Kayan and Karen with some of the tribes of the Philippine Islands, *e. g.*, the Davao and Tinguian tribes, or between the Karen and certain of the Malays, is strong. The similarity of the name "Kayan" with that by which the Karen are known to the Burmans is also striking; but it seems fairly clear that if this accidental similarity of name did not exist, the Kayans would not have been considered closer than the Dyaks in kinship to the Karen. Dr. J. H. Vinton, who has had a life-long acquaintance with the Karen, thinks that they are resembled more by the Dyaks than by the Kayans. He expressed this view after a recent tour through Borneo. These similarities suggest that most of these tribes are not far removed from one another, and that they all belong to the Indo-Chinese stock, which, in turn, resembles the South China type, due no doubt to a common ancestry in the remote past.

KAREN MEN FROM THE HILLS, THARRAWADDY DISTRICT
The second man from the left is a village chief or headman. The fourth is a plainsman, who is the teacher in Pankabin Village

## CHAPTER III

## PHYSICAL CHARACTERISTICS

The Karen are of medium height. On the plains they average about five feet, four inches, in stature, and in the hills they are about three inches shorter. The women are smaller than the men.[1] The hill people have the harder struggle for a livelihood and are also more liable to attacks of malaria. The Brecs show evident signs of stunted growth. On the plains and in the more fertile lower hills we find that the Karen are a stocky race with broad, well-built bodies, strong legs, and well-rounded calves. The legs are often short in proportion to the body. Karen players on a football team are usually noticeable for their sturdy appearance, in contrast with the slimmer Burman boys. They are capable of considerable physical exertion, but soon tire. The women are well formed and buxom. They have an erect carriage, being used to bearing heavy burdens on their heads or backs. Their teeth, like the men's, are stained with continual betel chewing. In the hills their lack of bathing and their accumulations of beads and charms detract from their appearance; but when they have taken on more cleanly ways they become not unattractive. Their youth is cut short by heavy work in the field, constant childbearing, and nursing, and soon the signs of age appear.

The color of the Karen varies all the way from a light olive complexion to a dark coffee brown. On the whole, their color could be said to range between that of the Burmans and the Chinese. Those who work indoors are, of course, lighter than those who work in the open. Many skins have a distinctly yellowish or red-

---

[1] I took a few measurements with the tape line, and found that about seventy men on the plains gave the above average. The tallest was five feet, nine inches, and the shortest was four feet, eleven inches. In the hills my measurments were confined to one village. Here the headman was the tallest, measuring five feet, six inches. The shortest man in the village was four feet and eleven inches in height. Of about twenty women measured the tallest was five feet, five inches, and the shortest, four feet, nine inches. Three were each four feet, ten inches. The average among the women was a very small fraction over five feet. Dr. Mason gives the shortest man, a Bghai chief, as being only four feet, eight inches high, while the shortest woman he measured was four feet, five inches tall. (*Jour., Asiatic Soc. of Bengal*, Vol. XXXV, p. 7.) MacMahon notes that in the Red Karen country the women are usually as tall as, if not taller than, the men. (*The Karens of the Golden Chersonese*, p. 56.)

Profile View

Karen Family With Traces of Negrito Blood—Front View

The rest of the villagers, to whom this family is related by the usual web of intermarriages, acknowledge the difference of feature, but are at a loss to account for it.

dish tinge. Infants are often almost as white as European children. Red cheeks are not infrequently found in the Toungoo hills.[2]

Though we often find considerable individuality in the facial features of the Karen, they conform more or less to type, which consists of the broad flat face of the Mongolian races with high cheek-bones and widely set eyes. The eyes have narrow palpebral openings, sometimes slanted, and the characteristic fold at the nasal end. The nose is broad and flat without much of a bridge. The plane of the nostrils is tilted upward, so that the septum and nostrils are quite noticeable. The mouth is usually well shaped, but a few individuals have thick lips and a heavy negroid mouth. The teeth are quite regular and, when not stained with betel, are white and shining.

In the Pegu Hills, in the village of Ngepe, I found a family that had decidedly negroid features. (See cuts on p. 17.) The contrast with the rest of the villagers was marked. Although I could get no hint of a different ancestry in the case of the exceptional family from that of the rest of the people, it was obvious that an admixture of Negrito blood must have taken place somewhere.

The hair of the Karen is generally black, straight, and coarse. Once in a while wavy hair is found, and in rare cases it seems to be almost as kinky as that of the African. Wavy hair is not admired, but, on the contrary, is much disliked. The Karen have an abundance of hair on the scalp. It often reaches to the waist, and I have noticed a few instances in which it reached to the ground. In the early days the custom was for both sexes to wear the hair long, but now the men usually wear theirs short.

The men have scant beards which are seldom allowed to grow, being pulled out with tweezers. The mustache is prized and is coaxed to become as luxuriant as possible. In the few cases where the beard is allowed to grow, it resembles the beards of Chinese men. However, I know a Karen teacher in Bassein who has a beard that would please any inhabitant of Russia. A mole with a few hairs growing from it is greatly treasured, the hairs being allowed to grow as long as they will. Hair on the body and chest of the

---

[2] According to Breca's plates for classifying the color of the skin I found, in examining about ninety persons, that twenty-five matched No. 30 of his series; nineteen, No. 25; fifteen, No. 44; eight, No. 26; five each, Nos. 29 and 45; three each, Nos. 24 and 31; two, No. 21, and one each, Nos. 37, 40, 47, and 53. The lightest color found was No. 24. One of the fair ones was an infant, and the other two were men, namely, a clerk and a hill boy. The darkest complexion corresponded to No. 37, of which I found but one. No. 29, which was the color of five of the subjects examined, is a much redder hue than No. 37. All determinations of color were made on unexposed parts of the body where the skin had not been tanned by sunlight.

men is rare. I can recall only one man who had a hairy chest. There is nothing unusual about the eyebrows.

The Karen seem to be susceptible to all the diseases prevalent in the country. Children are seen more often than not with distended bowels, due to worms. Enlarged spleen is the rule in the hills, where malaria is so prevalent. A number of cases in which a low vitality has caused ulcers to break out and involve the entire system have come under my notice. Epidemics of measles are much feared, due to complications induced by bathing soon after the rash has disappeared, the bathing being thought necessary. Smallpox does not cause much apprehension. The bubonic plague has never claimed many Karen victims, but the influenza was terribly fatal during the cool season of 1918-19. Tuberculosis is one of the many diseases from the West that is claiming its victims among the Karen people. Though their open-air life safeguards them somewhat, their fear of demons causes them to cover their heads at night, and they breathe only through their blankets. Those who live in the better built houses on the plains also deprive themselves of fresh air by retiring into the close inner room of their homes in order to avoid the smell of cooking, which they fear. Such superstitious practices furnish ideal breeding-places for germs. The unbalanced diet of the Karen also restricts their disease-resisting powers. One hopes that, with improved ideas on sanitation and hygiene, the people of this race will not only be relieved from the present high rate of infant mortality, but also that those surviving may attain greater longevity.

The presence of certain birth-marks on the children of Mongolian parents has been thought by some scientists to be an important criterion for distinguishing members of that race.[3] The Karen infants certainly have these blue patches on the back and buttocks. Sometimes they are so indistinct as to be hardly noticeable, and again they are clear and bright. They are irregular in shape and size. My observations confirm the accuracy of the census returns, namely, that about seven out of ten children have these marks at birth. They usually disappear by the time a child is a year old. The Karen explanation for them is that they are the stains of leaves, on which the spirits of the children sat or laid down to rest in the course of their long and wearisome journey from their former abode. These marks are thought to show that the children having

---

[3] *The Indian Imperial Census*, 1911, Burma, Pt. I, 281-286.

20 THE KAREN PEOPLE OF BURMA

Sgaw Karen Young Bloods, Ngape Eh Village, Tharrawaddy Hills (Front and Side Views)
Like most mountain people, the Karen are a stocky race.

them will be strong, and mothers are glad to see them on their offspring. Perhaps they reason that if the baby spirit was able to stand the long journey necessary to come to the birth, it will endure the longer journey of this human existence.

I have noticed a few cases of homosexuals among the Karen, though they do not seem to be as common as among the Burmese. These individuals, who assume more or less the dress and customs of the opposite sex, have been known to contract unions with others of the same sex and live as husband and wife. The cases I found have all been on the plains.

## CHAPTER IV

## MENTAL AND MORAL CHARACTERISTICS OF THE KAREN

The Karen draws the blinds over the windows of his heart and leaves one to wonder what goes on within. I once asked an educated Karen what he thought was the chief characteristic of his race, and he immediately replied that they are a people who can be afraid. Centuries of subjugation and oppression have filled them with fear. During the protracted period of their tribulations, to be caught by a Burman was to be stripped of everything, even of one's clothing, and to be beaten into the bargain. Where only a few families lived on the plains, the women with child dared not undergo confinement in their houses, lest they could not escape from a sudden attack by their oppressors. Karen cartmen still drive around a village rather than through it, although they know there is little danger of having dogs set on them, as there used to be. Not only does the Karen fear his fellow-men, but he is also terrified by the strange and weird beings, demons and ghosts, with which his imagination and credulity people the world. Should he, even by chance, offend any of these—and it is easily done he thinks—he must live in dread of their vengeance. His religion is one of fear, precaution, and propitiatory sacrifice. The trepidations of the past have been perpetuated through generations and, though education has stifled them in a measure, they still crop out on occasion even in the most advanced members of the race.

The Karen is led into all sorts of difficulties by his timidity. He is apprehensive and desirous of avoiding trouble with officers or others. When brought into court to answer questions, often this fear will lead him to deny any knowledge of the facts, instead of relating what he has seen; or he may acknowledge the opposite of what he wants to prove. Not long ago I heard of a man who had what seemed to be a good case, but on the witness-stand he swore to the opposite of what he had told previously. When asked why he did so, he replied that he was so scared that he did not know what he was saying. In thus yielding to his timidity the Karen often involves himself in serious difficulty, for his mistakes are easily detected.

Shyness, caution, and concealment are fruits of this trait of fear. I have often heard a veteran school-teacher remark that the Karen never puts his best foot foremost. In the past it was not safe for him to do so. Concealment was one of his natural means of protection. To show signs of prosperity or admit having possessions was only tempting his more powerful neighbors to come and dispossess him. I know of recent instances of persecution of one sort or another being visited upon certain Karen villages on account of their prosperous condition. In the days of the Ancient Regime the French peasantry simulated poverty, in order to protect their property from the tax-collector. The Karen has been preyed upon in various ways in earlier and later times, and in his fear and helplessness he has resorted to the method of the European peasant. Shyness and caution are marked traits of the Karen women even more than of the men. Indeed, I have seen all the inhabitants of a village run to the jungle when I came in sight. A group of girls out gathering firewood dropped their faggots and disappeared as fast as possible at the approach of my party along the path. In their attempts to hide their shyness, schoolgirls often succeed in attracting the attention they are trying to avoid.

A leading authority on Burma has said that the Karen are "absolutely devoid of humor."[1] Having had years of experience as a missionary among these people, I may be allowed to differ from the opinion just quoted. The authority referred to was a high Government official, and I am quite sure that no Karen would be so self-forgetful as to risk offending the dignity of such a personage. One who has entered into intimate association with these people, has been entertained in their houses, and has sat beside their fireplaces will testify to their love of fun and their jolly laughter. For myself I ask for no lighter-hearted companions than those with whom I have traveled over the plains and hills, and whom I have met in distant villages. They are keen enough to see the humor in some of their folklore tales, in embarrassing situations, and in the little mishaps of daily life, and to laugh heartily when these are told. They are also capable of enjoying practical jokes. This is illustrated by the instance of a young man who by mistake shot a vulture, as it flew up out of the bushes, and decided to serve the

---

[1] Sir J. G. Scott, *Burma, A Handbook*, p. 120.

KAREN BOYS

Most of the crowd that gathered to watch the foreigner have already fled. Only a few brave boys remain to face the camera.

PLAYMATES—KAREN BOYS AND THE SONS OF THE AUTHOR

Notice the unusually curly hair of one of the Karen boys, all of whom are brothers, children of a Bassein man and a Toungoo woman.

breast of the great bird, cooked with curry well spiced, to some of his chums. The flesh of the creature proved to be both tough and strong, and when one of the guests left the group to wash out his mouth, the host beat a hasty retreat. The other villagers, who promptly heard of the unpalatable feast, amused themselves by asking the guests how they enjoyed it.

The Karen are accustomed to say of themselves that "they put a thing in the heart." They mean by this that they hold their peace, but do not forget slights, grudges, disagreeable requests, and the like. If a Karen is asked to do something he does not want to do, he may reply with a grunt suggesting an assent, but does not comply with the request and fails to put in an appearance again soon. He does not refuse at the time, fearing to cause trouble. In the same way a slight or an insult is "put in the heart" without retort or demonstration of anger. He dissimulates and waits for his revenge. Before the British established orderly government in the country, many a raid was executed to pay off a grudge or an insult cherished in the heart. For the man of little or no influence in his village there was a secret method of vengeance, namely, by resorting to magic or to poison. It was the fear of this vengeful trait in the Karen that for years prevented the Burman subordinate officials from crossing Thaukgeyat Creek into the Toungoo Hills.

The repudiation of a friend is not unknown among the Karen, but such conduct is rare. In general, they are cautious in entering into friendships, but, having done so, are faithful and sincere to those whose confidence they accept in exchange for their own. Blood-brotherhood is a recognized institution among them, having been much more prevalent in the past than at present; and the bond signified by it in most of the Karen tribes was stronger than the ties of family. Westerners make friends more quickly than the Karen, but Western haste and impatience are not winsome qualities to the latter.

It has been said that the Karens are stubborn. They do not reach quick decisions in regard to matters novel to them and can not be forced to do so. But if given time to consider after a full explanation, they are pretty sure to return later and offer their reasons for not consenting to the proposition; and if allowed to talk the matter out, their objections being answered and time given for their consideration, they will most likely be persuaded. When thus convinced, their loyal coöperation may generally be depended on. I have known not a few Government officials who, by such methods, have won the confidence and earnest support of the people with whom they were dealing. It is unfortunate, however, that the number of such officers is not larger. While the Karen have not always been treated with proper consideration and have sometimes failed to understand the aims and methods of the British Government, they are deeply attached to it.

It is true that the Karen are not as quick-witted as some of the other races of the Orient. Nevertheless, they are in some respects out-distancing their more facile neighbors. They excel in the routine of their daily tasks. This is observable in the schools, where the Karen boys usually take the lead in the daily recitations, but make a poorer showing in the written and oral examinations. Several Government officers have spoken in high terms of their Karen clerks, commending their faithfulness and honesty. Not infrequently it happens that such a faithful worker finds that some astute associate has gained the credit and reward that should have been his. The Karen are not blind to disappointments of this sort, as the following fable shows: A man, about to leave home, ordered his pig and dog to prepare a plot of ground for planting as a garden. The pig was industrious and rooted until he had all but finished turning over the plot, while the dog spent his time lying under a tree. Late in the afternoon, before the master's return, the dog jumped up and scratched about here and there in the soft earth. When he heard his master coming, he ran barking down the path to meet him and told him that the pig had been working but a short time, while he had been digging all day. The faithful pig, meanwhile, was so busy rooting in the farthest corner of the lot, trying to finish before his owner's return, that he knew nothing of what was going on. The credulous man believed the dog's deceitful words, killed the pig, and only discovered his mistake when it was too late. This fable is epitomized in the proverb, "The dog scratches in the pig's place." For many a Karen this is all too true.

Early writers speak of the peaceableness, honesty, and goodness of the Karen.[2] There are, of course, in every nation those who belie any statement concerning the people as a whole. However, I have no hesitation in saying that deceit and trickery are not common among the Karen. I have been told by peddlers and others, who often have to carry valuable goods and money into the jungle, that

---

[2] Sangermano, *Description of the Burmese Empire, 1783-1808*, (Rangoon, 1885) p. 36; Maj. Snodgrass, *The Narrative of the Burmese War*, (London, 1827) Vol. I, p. 142.

they prefer to spend their nights in Karen villages and do so whenever possible. In the Karen hills the paddy-bins, in which is stored the year's supply of rice, are situated far away from the village along the jungle paths. It is almost unknown for grain to be stolen from them. Among some of the tribes east of Toungoo stealing was punished, until recently, by death. Dr. Mason says that he has never found a Karen who would not lie, if it was to his advantage to do so. This does not agree with my experience.

In various respects, certainly, Karen conduct differs from European conduct. To expect the same standards would be unreasonable. Any fair estimate of the Karen, as of any other primitive people, must take into account the fact that morality with them is group conduct. The behavior of the individual must be regarded in the light of the life and customs of the group to which he belongs. If the actions of the people, considered thus in relation to their own social status, appear capable of betterment, efforts should be put forth to lead the primitive folk to the higher level.

The Karen possess intellectual capacity commensurate with that of other races of Burma. Being subject people in the country, their ancestors were precluded from independent thought and action in essential matters. With the advent of education a sufficient number of the young men and women, though the proportion of the latter is small, has taken collegiate courses with credit to show that they are not inferior to others. The same may be said of many who have won success in practical lines of work. I could name several Karens occupying positions of responsibility that require high mental attainments, who are demonstrating that they are not lacking therein.

The old practice of village communities in exiling widows and orphans to the jungle, and the occasional abandonment of little children by their parents who were attempting to escape from raiders are, happily, things of the past. Fear, the instinct of self-preservation, and superstition serve to explain such phenomena, which must not be taken as indicating that the Karen are lacking in love for children or in humane sentiments. Nowadays orphans find a home without difficulty; widows and aged persons are cared for; parents enjoy their firesides and manifest love for their offspring, with whom they are, in fact, too indulgent, even to their hurt; and young men and women are not above giving tender care to some little niece or nephew.

A Paku School Girl, Toungoo

The Karen have been addicted to the use of liquor. Their feasts and religious observances have been occasions for drinking. It is reported that the Brecs are accustomed to store their grain in two bins, one (often the larger one) for that of which liquor is to be made, and the other for that which is to be used as food. On the plains I have not found the Karen greater drinkers than their neighbors. With the decay of the old rites and the spread of Christianity the evil seems to be on the decline. Among the members of the Baptist churches, however it may be in the other denominations, total abstinence is enjoined.

The Karen are lovers of music. In the early days they accompanied the chanting of their poems on their primitive harps and other instruments. The people of the Pegu Yomas, Tenasserim, in the delta of the Irrawaddy, have interesting tunes, which have been in use from the olden times. In other districts they have contented themselves with the rythm of chanting and moaning, melodies being conspicuous by their absence. The Maw Lay and other religious sects have had their own songs, which may be said to correspond to Christian hymns. With the introduction of Christianity came the music of the Western hymn-book, and to this the Karen have taken with their whole hearts. They love to sing and do not grow weary of it, however late the hour. Occidental music has taken such a hold on those who have become Christians that they have almost entirely given up their native music. A few hymns are sometimes sung to adaptations of their old tunes; but they prefer the Western melodies, and few of the young people know any other. They learn the new tunes readily and are able to sing glees and anthems by ear after a moderate amount of practice. Their voices are much softer than those of the Burmese and blend well in choruses. Some of the young women have very sweet voices, which seldom become harsh and rasping. While traveling in the hill country I was delighted one evening with the sweet voice of a young woman, which came floating up from the stream where she was drawing water. She was singing an old "hta" or poem, while I listened unobserved behind a clump of bamboos. No sooner did I step into the open than she ceased, and I could not persuade her to continue the song.

One discovers but few indications of a love of beauty among the Karen. They make little attempt to ornament their houses or their implements, so that the evidence of their possessing a sense of color and design is practically limited to the woven patterns of some of their garments. They have only a scant vocabulary for colors. I have seldom heard them remark on the beauty of a sunset or the glories of a sunrise. Sometimes they have called attention to a pleasing landscape, but I have wondered whether they were not doing so because they knew of my pleasure in such scenes.

The Karen is a plebeian. His manners at home are crude, although he is not without a certain personal dignity. His shyness in the presence of strangers, especially of those whom he fears, causes him embarrassment. Under such circumstances he often impresses one as being impolite. He is not servile. It has never been his custom to "shiko".[3] The greatest chief is a comrade among his men, who do not yield their self-respect in his presence. Nevertheless, the inherent timidity of the race shows itself in the avoidance of making a request in person. A request may expose the one making it to the chagrin of a refusal and the one addressed to the unpleasant necessity of giving an adverse answer. The Karen, therefore, gets a friend to act as his intermediary. Even a boy who wants to buy a book will have his classmate get it for him.

Amiability is another marked trait of the Karen, both of the educated and the uneducated, rendering them acceptable in many kinds of service. Young Karen women are in demand as nursemaids all over Burma, and not a few have gone temporarily to England and America in that capacity. They are kind, patient, and faithful in their care of the children entrusted to their care.

The remarkable chastity of the Karen is also worthy of notice. It has, however, been mentioned in several places in this work and perhaps need not be discussed further in this connection, except to say that the fear of the evil consequences of violating the laws of the elders has kept them free from many unhealthy customs that are found in many parts of the world.[4]

---

[3] "Shiko" is a Burmese word signifying the act of worship, or of showing respect to officials.

[4] See pages 139, 142, 192, 288.

## CHAPTER V
## LANGUAGE

In Chapter I I referred briefly to the relationship of the Karen dialects to the other languages of Burma and noted the bearing of that subject upon the question of the origin of the people. I adopted the grouping suggested in the last Burma *Census* (that of 1911), where those dialects are described as forming a Sinitic or Karen group of the Siamese-Chinese sub-family of the Tibeto-Chinese languages. This group comprises three principal branches, namely, the Sgaw, the Pwo (including the Taungthu), and the Bwe, which embraces several minor dialects in the Toungoo and Red Karen country. Some of these latter forms of speech have been very little studied. A few books have been published in Bwe, but at present are superseded by publications in the Sgaw. The Sgaw language was reduced to writing by Dr. Jonathan Wade in 1832, the Burmese alphabet being used in denoting most of the sounds, while certain symbols were employed for such letters as had no equivalent in Burmese. In this way a perfect phonetic alphabet was created.

It may not be out of place in this connection to point out a few of the marked characteristics of the Karen language. The order of words in the sentence is that of the English, as well as of the Chinese and Tai, namely, subject, predicate, and object. The language is monosyllabic, except in a few instances, some of which are more apparent than real. Each root may be used in any form of speech, that is, as noun, adjective, verb, or adverb, by the addition of the proper particle or in combination with other roots. Each syllable has a signification of its own and a grammatical relation to one or more of the other syllables in every compound part of speech.

Dr. Wade calls attention to the fact that the Karen often use words in pairs, verbs being paired sometimes merely for the sake of euphony, though generally to give fullness and force to the idea intended. Such pairing of words, whether nouns, verbs, or other parts of speech, invest the Karen language, Dr. Wade thinks, with "a beauty and force of expression unsurpassed perhaps in any other language in the world." These paired words, which are called by the Karen "father and mother words," may be parsed separately or together according to their position in the sentence. They may consist of two roots having similar meanings, or of a well-known root together with one which by itself has no meaning now commonly understood. Misapprehension is often avoided by the use of paired words. For example, "ni" (with the circumflex tone) means year, and the same syllable (with the long tone) means day. When this monosyllable is carelessly pronounced, one does not always catch the difference; but "ni-thaw" unmistakably denotes day, because "thaw" is another designation for this period of time; and "ni-la" clearly signifies year, the latter syllable meaning literally month. Such compound words may have compound modifiers which, when used with discrimination, give a pleasing finish to the speech.

The Sgaw dialect has six different tones and the Pwo an equal number. The other dialects have various numbers, but not so many and difficult as the tones of the Chinese language.

The Sgaw alphabet consists of twenty-five consonants and ten vowels. One character appears both as a gutteral and a consonant. There are no closed syllables in this dialect. The Pwo dialect has three nasal endings which, Dr. Gilmore thinks, are a remnant of the original speech. Evidence in support of this view is supplied by a comparison of the meanings of the single word "hpaw" in Sgaw Karen with the nasal forms expressing the same meanings in Pwo. In the former dialect "hpaw" means one of three things, namely, cook, flower, or granary, while in the latter these meanings require the use of three nasal forms as follows: "hpawn," "hpaw," and "hpan." Other roots from the two dialects show a difference of this sort, indicating that the Sgaw has dropped its original nasals.[1]

There is no proper relative pronoun in Sgaw. The particle "leu" serves in this capacity, as well as doing duty as quotation marks, a preposition, and a part of every compound preposition, this last form of speech being one of the characteristics of the language. The reflexive use of the pronoun is a notable idiom in the Sgaw. The demonstrative supplies the place of the definite article. A numerical affix or adjective is employed with every numeral. Each of these affixes is supposed to denote the leading characteristic

---

[1] *Journal, Burma Research Society,* Vol. VIII, Pt. II, pp. 122, ff.

of the noun to which it refers. Its use is similar to our saying in English "cattle, five head," or "bread, four loaves."

The verb is almost always considered transitive and, if there should be no word that could properly stand as its object, the nominal pronoun "ta" is added to supply it. The verb "to be" takes the objective case. The double negative is used with the verb after the manner of the French and Burmese idiom, "t'—ba" corresponding to the Burmese "m—bu."

The Karen numerals are based on the decimal system not only from one to ten, but also upwards by tens and hundreds to tens of millions. There is, however, a marked peculiarity in the Bwe method of counting from six to nine, six being three couples; seven, three couples-one; eight, four couples, and nine, four couples-one.

The Pwo dialect does not differ materially from the Sgaw in structure, or greatly in vocabulary, as shown by a comparison of the two by Dr. Wade, which indicates that thirteen-fourteenths of the words of the Sgaw and Pwo are from the same roots. For one familiar only with the Sgaw dialect there is difficulty in immediately understanding the Pwo, because the nasals affect the pronunciation of the latter. The Bwe and other Toungoo dialects seem to have nasals and wide variations in tones. They also possess letters that are lacking in the Sgaw, such as g, j, z, and a peculiar dj that is impossible to represent in English letters. The Mopgha have the letter f, which they pronounce highly aspirated.[2] The Sgaw have no g, j, v, or z. They have both the aspirated and unaspirated k, t, and p. Besides these consonants, they have gutterals and combined consonants to which there are no parallels in Western speech.[3]

Although in the early days the Karen had no written language, it is not to be inferred that they were without a literature. On the contrary, a large quantity of bard literature was handed down orally from generation to generation, being taught by certain elders to the youths who were arriving at maturity, in order that they might transmit it in turn without change to those coming after them. This literature comprises probably more than two hun-

---

[2] Dr. Mason in the *Journal, Asiatic Society of Bengal*, 1858, Vol. I, Pt. II, pp. 129, ff.
[3] The *Grammar* of the Karen language by Dr. Wade, now reprinted at the American Baptist Missionary Press, Rangoon, Burma, and that by Dr. Gilmore, from which the writer has largely derived his materials for this chapter, are available for those who wish to make a study of the language. *The Karen Thesaurus*, an encyclopedic dictionary of the Karen language, people, and customs, is a valuable work. Volume I of the new edition, which appeared in 1915, is especially useful, as it contains definitions in English such as are not to be found in the later volumes.

dred tales, legends, and mythical stories. A large proportion of these are in the nature of beast tales or fables, such as are found in India, Europe, and Africa. Some of the myths and legends are in the form of verse and were formerly recited at length at funerals and on other festal occasions, or were sung to the accompaniment of the harp. There are also the epics containing the "Y'wa" legends. Finally, a considerable amount of wise instruction is contained in the numerous short sayings, proverbs, and riddles that have survived. Fragments of the shorter and longer poems, chanted at funerals, have been quoted in the chapter on Funeral Customs, and some of the tales and myths have been referred to or paraphrased in other portions of this work. Further presentation and discussion of the Karen literature is reserved for a future study.

A KAREN BELLE
Though not particularly handsome, many of the Karen maidens are very attractive.

# CHAPTER VI

## DRESS AND ORNAMENTS

To describe in detail the costume of every tribe of the Karen would be like going into all the minutiae of the tartans of the Scotch and would of itself fill a volume. There are, however, certain characteristics of dress that prevail more or less widely among the whole people, and I shall endeavor to point these out. The "hse" is found in various forms among almost all the tribes. This resembles a smock in that it is a loose, unfitted garment, falling from the shoulders over the body. This "hse" is made by sewing together two narrow strips of cloth to form an oblong, inverted "meal-bag." Holes are left in the seams at the upper corners through which the arms are thrust, and another opening is left in the middle seam at the top, which serves as the neck of the garment.

For the men in the Sgaw and Pwo tribes living back in the hills this garment still serves as their entire costume. It reaches from the shoulders to the calves. In the Pegu Hills the Sgaw wear a garment that is white above, except for red selvedge lines along the seams, and has the lower third woven with red. The border between the two colors may be more or less variegated and embroidered. In the Moulmein and Papon districts and to the eastward the garment is made of alternating wide strips of white and red running its whole length.

Among the Bwe tribes the custom is to wear a shorter smock, which fits a little more closely than the one just described. It might be called a tunic. The loin-cloth (sometimes replaced by short trousers) is worn with the tunic. Various branches of the Bwe wear different arrangements of colors. The Paku wear a white tunic with a narrow red border around the bottom. In each village this border has a distinctive form. Among the other eastern hill tribes we find the Kerhker, sometimes called the Gai-hko, wearing a tunic embroidered with vertical figures like towers, from the top of which lines radiate like the rays of the rising sun. The Bwe tribes usually wear tunics of vertically striped weaves, some of them, *e.g.*, the Mopgha, with narrow red lines. In the early days they wore scant loin-cloths, but nowadays they wear longer cloths or Shan trousers, like many of the other hill tribes. The Brecs wear

A BWE KAREN MAN'S SUIT
Bwe Karen Hills, Toungoo District.

The smock is of white silk with red stripes and embroidery woven in. The loin cloth ("teh ku") is magenta and black. Both are of silk, for every man of any account feels he must have one silk suit.

short breeches belted in at the waist with a string. These trousers are at first white with narrow red stripes, but soon become a dirty yellow, growing constantly darker with wear and age. The so-called "Pant Bwes" ornament their breeches with radiating lines

## DRESS AND ORNAMENTS

at the bottom. The Red Karen, who take their name from their red garments, wear short breeches of red cotton and a short close-fitting tunic of the same color. These soon become the color of dirt from the generous accretions of that substance which adhere to them. These people use a blanket, which is red and white striped when new. They discard both the tunic and blanket in warm weather. Cotton is the most common material used, but in Toungoo silk is often used, either alone or with the cotton.

In Lower Burma, on the plains, it has become customary for the men to wear Burmese garments. The only time they put on their Karen garments, if they have them, is when they hold their "Bgha" feast. The different tribes to the east wear the Shan costume, with more or less variation, all the way to the Chinese Border.

The Karen men knot up their long hair on the top of the head or over the right or left ear, according to the custom of their par-

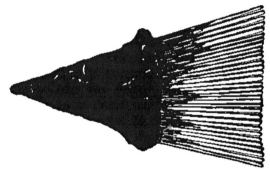

A KAREN BAMBOO COMB

ticular locality, fastening it with a small triangular bamboo comb. No other head-dress is worn, except a piece of white muslin or other light-weight cloth, which may be put over the head as a turban or around it like a fillet, unless one should include the ornamental head-bands of the Karenni youth who, before marriage, wear necklaces of stones that have been handed down from father to son for generations, and ornaments for the head, neck, and ears, consisting of mother-of-pearl buttons interspersed with the shining wings of beautiful green beetles. All these are, however, given up at marriage and become the property of the bride.

In the matter of adopting foreign dress the women are more conservative than the men. Long after every man in a village has taken on the Burmese costume, the women continue to wear their characteristic black smock over their Burmese jacket and "longyi" (skirt).

The Sgaw and Pwo women, after arriving at the age of puberty, wear a smock ("hse") and a shirt ("ni"). Little girls wear a single "hse," falling from their neck to their ankles, at least when it is new. In some villages they wear a white "hse," without any ornament or color, but in other places they wear a black garment ornamented with colored yarns at the neck and around the armholes. In some localities the maidens wear the long white "hse," reaching to the ankles, until they are married; but it is more common for them to put on the skirt and wear a shorter "hse" at about the time they arrive at maturity.

The women's dress varies from one tribe to another, and in some instances each village has its particular weave. There is considerable general similarity of the Karen designs to those in the Malay countries, in Borneo, and in the Philippines; but the particular Karen design, among the Sgaw women at least, is that supposed to be derived from the python. The story is that "Naw Mu E," one of the mythical characters of ancient times, was kidnapped by a fabulous White Python and carried off to his den. Later, her husband, hearing of her plight, came and rescued her by sacrificing himself at the mouth of the den, whereupon the woman was released and enabled to return to the upper earth again. Various versions of the story exist, one of which is that she was compelled by the python to weave patterns on its skin that still remain, but on being released showed her contempt for it by weaving skirts for herself of the same pattern, thus giving it the gravest insult she could inflict. This pattern soon became general among Karen women.

Other patterns, of which there are many, are called by various names, as seeds, little pagodas, cowries, etc. Especially beautiful is the pattern or weave worn by the Mopgha women, which consists of a variety of figures in magenta, yellow, and green on a black ground. I have been told that the weaving of the designs for these skirts has become a lost art, none of the young women of the few villages of the Mopgha tribe having learned to weave these garments. The Bwe women usually wear a black "ni" or skirt with a few horizontal stripes of white and red running through the middle.

WOMEN'S GARMENTS

(1) A "hko peu" or head-dress of a Sgaw Karen. (2) A smock ("hsě") and a skirt ("ni"), Sgaw Karen, from the Pegu Hills, Toungoo District. The smock is embroidered with colored yarns and "Job's Tears." The middle of the skirt shows the python pattern. (3) A Sgaw Karen smock and skirt from Shwegyin District. This smock is trimmed with red braid, except the lower part which is fancily woven ("u").

The women of all these tribes wear the simplest kind of a skirt; it is a straight slip which, instead of being gathered about the waist, is drawn tight across the back, folded across the front, and the fulness tucked in at the waist line, thus allowing the action of the knees. The garment remains in place remarkably well, although no belt is used. When the women bathe—those on the plains doing so with much more regularity than their sisters in the hills—they bring the top of the skirt up under the armpits and fasten it over the breasts in the same manner as about the waist.

The jackets or smocks of the women present a variety of designs. The most common is the plain black or dark blue "hse" with little or no ornament on it. Sometimes it is decorated with small rosettes or stars of colored yarns or, among the Pwo, with fern-like figures. The prettiest decorations are made with the hard white seeds of various shapes of the plant called Job's Tears *(Coix)*. The variety mostly used are those resembling barberries, called "bwe" in Sgaw Karen and found all over the hills. These are sewed on the finished garment in parallel rows, in rows forming V-shaped figures, or in the forms of stars or rosettes and edging the arm and neck holes. Red yarns or pieces of red cloth are also sewed on to add to the ornamentation. In Shwegyin we often see a "hse" that is woven with elaborate designs of red and green on a black ground, red tape being sewed in vertical lines on the body of the garment and in horizontal lines over the shoulders. The head-dress of the women is called "hko peu ki" and among the Sgaw women consists of a piece of cloth about two yards long and a foot wide. The middle part is plain white. At either end there is a fancy woven ("u") portion about twenty inches long, red in color and crossed at intervals of two inches by transverse lines. In the middle of these colored ends is a white zigzag line representing a serpent. The other lines are in pairs, those equidistant from the zigzag above and below being alike and having their special designations. These names are, however, in archaic form, and their meaning is not well known. There are long white fringes on the ends of the head-dress and shorter colored ones at the ends of the cross lines. When worn, it is twisted about the head in such a way as to form a peak over the forehead with the colored fringes hanging down about the eyes and the long white fringes down the back. In a few villages in the Pegu Hills the women wear circlets ("hko hhlaw") of bamboo or silver, around which they coil their hair. The metal circlets are made of beaten silver a scant inch in width and long enough to go once and a half around the head, being held

## DRESS AND ORNAMENTS 41

by a fancy clasp at the back, which keeps the band in place. Such silver circlets are valued at about ten rupees or more, according to the work on them.

The Karen make blankets of the same cloth that they use for their garments. They use two strips of white edged with red sel-

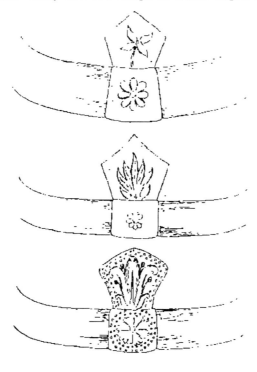

· WOMENS'· HEAD·DRESS ·
HALF SIZE

vedges, each piece being four yards long. These are sewed together lengthwise, and then one outer edge is sewed up to provide a half-open sleeping-bag. The fringes of the open end are drawn up over the head.

On the whole, the Karen are very careful about exposing their persons. The women have always worn the closed skirts and not the open "tamein," which was formerly in vogue among the Burmese. They seldom go without their jackets, though in the hills older women now and then leave them off. Little children run about more or less naked. Boy's often find their garments a bother and thrust them aside, but men usually are very careful about keeping their loins covered. When working, the men, who wear the "hse" or smock, pull the right arm inside the armhole and extend it again through the wide neckhole, so that the right arm and shoulder are entirely free for chopping or doing any other work at hand. They sometimes lower the whole garment to the waistline,

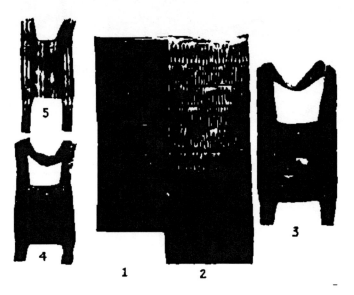

KAREN SKIRTS AND BAGS

No. 1 is a Mopgha Karen skirt, a black ground with silk embroidery in magenta, yellow, green, and red. The younger women have lost the art of weaving these garments. No. 2 is a Tavoy Sgaw Karen skirt woven in imitation of a popular Burmese pattern. The bags, Nos. 3 and 4, are Sgaw Karen, and No. 5. is Bwe.

where they knot it up in Burman fashion and thus leave the upper part of the body free. The Brecs are the poorest tribe of Karen and wear the scantiest clothing, consisting of short trousers. Often these are much the worse for wear. These people have rough small blankets, which they throw around themselves in cold weather. But more often they appear without them. The Karen on the plains bathe daily, doing so in their skirts ("longyi"), as do the Burmese. After the bath they slip the fresh garment over the wet one, which they allow to fall off as they fasten the other in place.

The wet garment is then pounded on a stone or soused up and down in the water a few times, and that is about all the laundering it gets. White jackets are washed out with soap and, in the towns, are given to the Indian washermen ("dhobies") for proper "doing up."

For protection from the rain the Karen use the wide-spreading fronds of the palm, which are nature's models for the paper umbrellas of the Chinese and Burmese. Workers in the paddy-fields make raincoats out of thatch woven on flexible bark fibre stays, which they tie across their shoulders. Three or four layers of the thatch make a protection that reaches to the knees. For a hat they tie a bit of palm leaf over the head, or wear a round umbrella-shaped hat like those made by the Shan and Burmese out of the sheathes of the cocoanut-palm or of bamboo. While transplanting rice on the plains a rain cover is made of these same sheathes or of tough large leaves covered with a network of thin bamboo splints bound with rattan. These covers are scoop-shaped and hang from the head down the back, causing a company of cultivators, bent over their work while wearing them, to look like long-legged tortoises wading in the mud.

Every Karen carries a bag ("hteu") slung over his shoulder as a part of his outfit. It is his pocket, in which he carries everything from money to the small game he has shot. The bag is woven in two parts. One, which forms the straps, consists of a strip from four to six inches wide and five or six feet long. Both ends are fringed. The other piece is from six to eight inches wide and from two to three feet in length. Each end of the long piece is folded lengthwise in the middle and sewed together, thus forming the corners of the bag. The short piece is folded crosswise in the middle and sewed to these corners or ends, thus forming the sides of the bag. The hemmed ends of the short piece form the edges of the mouth of the bag. The cloth woven for these bags is usually red with lengthwise stripes of white, yellow, or black. Different tribes have their different patterns and shades of color. The Karen do not ornament their bags so highly as do the Kachin tribes in Upper Burma. Every Karen woman and girl has some sort of a necklace. It may be a few seeds of the Job's Tears strung together, or some glass beads purchased from wandering peddlers, or silver beads made by Burmese silversmiths who visit the Karen villages during the dry season to pick up odd jobs. A common variety of beads is made by pounding out little disks of silver and rounding them into beads, according to the shape of the disk. Some of these finished beads are an inch in length and half an inch in diameter at the middle, tapering off to almost a point at the ends. When strung, they sometimes form chains so long that they encircle the neck several times and hang down over the bosom.

Bracelets of silver are, like the beads mentioned above, pounded out of coins (rupees) for the girls and young women, who not infrequently wear anklets of the same material. Even little boys sometimes wear silver bracelets and anklets.

Disks of silver, with rude figures of peacocks, elephants, and other Burmese figures, are often seen hanging from strings around the necks of children. Coins are also used in the same way. These are usually said to be simply for ornament, but I have occasionally wondered whether they might not have some magical purpose as well.

Among all the Karen tribes the most peculiar adornments are those of the Padaung women. These are rings of brass wire about a third of an inch in diameter, worn around the neck for the purpose of forcing up the chin and lengthening that member. As the process of elongation is slow, only a few rings are used at first; but as time goes on others are added, until the high metal collar thus formed consists of from twenty to twenty-five rings. The greater the length of the neck, the greater the beauty, they think. The appearance of these women is grotesque, for their heads appear abnormally small above their long necks; and their bodies, around which flap their loose garments, also seem disproportionate.[2] They can sleep only with their heads hanging over a high bamboo pillow, on which they rest their brass-armored necks. These rings are like those forming the brass corsets worn by the Iban women of Borneo, only the latter wear them lower down.

The Red Karen women wear, besides a profusion of beads around the neck, a girdle or many girdles of seeds and beads of various kinds and coils of lacquered rattans. These rattans are also worn as rings around the legs just above the calves. They often bulge out an inch or two from the leg and cause the women to walk with a stride "like a pair of compasses" and to experience some difficulty in sitting down. Indeed, it is necessary for them in sitting to stretch out the legs straight in front of them.[3] It

---

[2] *Gazetteer of Upper Burma,* Vol. I, Pt. I, p. 537.
[3] J. G. Scott, *Burma, A Handbook,* pp. 212, ff.

is not uncommon to see similar garters, if one may call them so, worn by many of the Karen, but usually they are made of a few strands of rattan interwoven in a neat band of about half an inch

A PADAUNG COUPLE—THE WIFE WITH NECK AND LEG-RINGS

A large share of Padaung wealth is lavished on feminine attire. The brass rings around their legs and necks often weigh twenty pounds. This lady is not very stylish, for her neck has not been stretched enough. The longer the neck, the more attractive the lady.

in width. Some say that they wear these simply for ornament, and others think that they find them useful in walking long distances. In fact these leg-bands perform somewhat the function of the rubber stocking of the West.

Among some of the Karen tribes to the east brass or other wire rings are worn on the legs, either from the ankles up over the calves, or from the knees up the thighs, or with only one or two rings at intervals on the legs. The arms are also more or less laden with brass circlets, as may be seen from Scott's description.[4]

Earrings are worn by both Karen men and women, but are usually in the form of plugs instead of rings. The silver ear plug of the Sgaw resembles a spool with one end flaring out more widely than the other. The larger end may be nearly two inches in diameter at the rim, tapering down to a little less than an inch

WOMEN'S EARRINGS, HALF SIZE

in diameter where it joins the cylindrical part which fits the hole in the ear-lobe. The men wear plugs that have the ends covered over with a plate of silver, while the plugs worn by the women are left open. Through these openings leaves or flowers are often inserted. Sometimes plugs made of a rolled strip of palm leaf fill the holes in the ear-lobes, these holes being rarely more than an inch in diameter. When the holes for the ear plugs are in process of being enlarged, the little rolls of palm leaf are as tightly wrapped and as large as possible when inserted. They then tend to loosen, and in so doing stretch the lobe. Sections of a stem of bamboo are sometimes worn by hill people in the lobes of their ears or, in the absence of anything else, a buttonaire of orchids or other flowers found in the jungle. More than once have I seen orchids that would bring fancy prices in a Western city fringing the dirty face of some half-naked urchin.

Karen men not uncommonly wear beads or strings about their necks, besides other ornaments on their arms and legs. But perhaps the ornament peculiar to them consists of the boar's tusk comb, such as their ancestor, "Htaw Meh Pa," made after he had killed the mythical boar. This is worn behind the ear, hanging down as a sort of earring. The comb, which is not unlike the

---

[4] J. G. Scott, *Burma, A Handbook*, pp. 121, ff.

## DRESS AND ORNAMENTS 47

ordinary Karen comb, is made of strips of the outer shell of the bamboo, each about two inches long, and held together by a sealing-wax produced from the gum of a tree. The upper or pointed end of

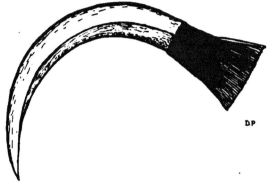

A BOAR'S TUSK COMB

the comb is made small enough to be inserted into the open end of the tusk, where it is fixed in place with wax. (See *Frontispiece*, which shows how a comb is worn.)

KAREN GIRLS IN BURMESE COSTUME
This illustrates the way in which the women secure their skirts by drawing them tightly to one side and then folding back the slack and tucking it in on the opposite side.

CHAPTER VII

MEASURES OF TIME AND SPACE. KAREN ASTRONOMY

### The Seasons and the Months

The seasons in Burma are clearly distinguished, the year being divided into two parts by the monsoon, which is the periodic wind of the Southern Asiatic tropics that for six months, between April and November, blows from the southwest off the Indian Ocean, bringing clouds and moisture which produce the never-failing rainy season, as the Karen name for it, "ta su hka," signifies. In November the monsoon shifts to the opposite quarter and the dry season or "ta yaw hka" follows, being again six months in duration. This latter period is subdivided into the cool season or "ta hkü hka," from the middle of November to the first of February, and the hot season or "ta ko hka," during which the sun is waxing hotter and hotter until the beginning of the rains in May. The rainy season has a fairly even temperature with a mean of about eighty degrees, Fahrenheit, while the dry season is marked by variations ranging from about fifty to over one hundred degrees.

The Karen term for year is "ni" and for a generation, their longest unit of time, it is "so." Eternity is designated by reduplicating the root "so," for example, "so so," or, with its couplet, "so so xa xa."

According to Karen reckoning, the year is divided into twelve lunar months, a month of twenty-nine days alternating with one of thirty. Thus, they have six months of twenty-nine days each, which total one hundred and seventy-four days, while the six intervening months of thirty days each total one hundred and eighty days. These two totals added together give but three hundred and fifty-four days. This arrangement of the calendar necessitated the addition every three years of an extra or intercalary month to make the reckoning of time correct. But the calendar was so poorly kept that confusion arose, and the people do not agree among themselves as to the proper order of the months, or the beginning of the year, or even as to the correct interpretation of the names of the months in all cases.[1] However, the names in the commonly accepted order are as follows:

1. *Th' le*, the searching month, when the villagers hunt for a new village site. It corresponds to the Burmese month, *Pyatho*, and to the moon of January.

2. *Hte kü*, the cutting month, when the Karen cut the jungle preparatory to cultivation. It is equivalent to the Burmese *Tabodwe* and to the moon of February.

3. *Thwe kaw*, the brewing month, when the women prepare the mash for brewing liquor. By some it is said to signify the month of burnings, for at this time they burn over the ground that was cut in the previous month. It is equivalent to the Burmese *Tabaung* and to the moon of March.

4. *La hkli*, the month of yams, because at this season the people were often reduced to the necessity of eating the tubers of the wild yam. It is equivalent to the Burmese *Tagu* and to the moon of April.

5. *De nya*, the lily month, when the wild lilies bloom. Equivalent to *Kasone* of the Burmese and to the moon of May.

6. *La nwi*, the seventh month, corresponds to the Burmese *Nayone* and to the moon of June.[2]

7. *La xo*, the eighth month, is equivalent to the Burmese *Waso* and to the moon of July.

8. *La hkü*, the shut-in month, when it is difficult to go about on account of the heavy rains. It corresponds to the Burmese *Wagaung* and to the moon of August.

9. *Hsi mü*, the month of a little sunshine, when after the heaviest rain there is a little fair weather. It corresponds to the Burmese *Tawthelin* and the moon of September.

---

[1] *The Karen Recorder*, a vernacular paper published by the Sgaw Karen Mission at Rangoon, printed a long discussion on the order of the months and the significance of their names, which appeared in various numbers from 1915 to 1917. The outcome of the discussion was not at all convincing.

[2] A writer in the Karen *Morning Star* in January, 1918, suggested another meaning for the name of this month, which comes at the opening of the rainy season when, as often happens, there are alternate weeks of sunshine and rain. Karens generally, probably almost without exception, understand the name of this month to refer only to its numerical position in the calendar.

10. *Hsi hsa*, the month of a little starlight, when the stars begin to show themselves occasionally. It corresponds to the Burmese *Thadingyut* and to the moon of October.

11. *La naw*, the month of the "naw," when from the seeds of this small plant is extracted an oil much like sessimum oil. It is equivalent to the Burmese *Tezaungmon* and to the moon of November.

12. *La plü*, the month of eclipses, when the moon dies and hence the month for funeral ceremonies. It corresponds to the Burmese *Nadaw* and to the moon of December.

It will be noticed that in the list as given above the seventh and eighth months are numbered 6 and 7, respectively. Two suggestions have been made to explain this incongruity. One of these is Dr. Mason's suggestion to the effect that originally the first month was *La plü* (December), which would not only correct the incongruity, but also make the Karen calendar correspond to that of Tibet, which begins with December.[3] The other explanation was given to me by a Karen teacher, who says that the month of *La hkli* (April) is the one that is repeated every three years in order to correct the calendar, and that the periodic interposition of this extra month is responsible for the names of the seventh and eighth months and the disagreement of those names with their serial numbers in the list. To me this explanation seems very dubious. One Karen writer attempts to correct the incongruity between the seventh and eighth months and their serial numbers by proposing to transfer *La hkü* (August) from its generally accepted position in the list to a place before the seventh month, but, of course, this is not a feasible change. As many Karens associate the month for funeral ceremonies *(La plü)* with the end of the year, they do not think it should be shifted into first place in the calendar.

## THE DAYS OF THE WEEK

Few of the Karen people can tell the days of the week, except according to Burmese or Christian nomenclature. Several old men have given me names for the days, which, they say, were in use a long time ago. There are seven of these, as may be seen in the following tabulation:

---

[3] *Journal, Asiatic Society of Bengal,* Vol. XXXVII, 43.

| ENGLISH | KAREN | TRANSLATION |
|---|---|---|
| Sunday | *Li naw* | The eagle's beak |
| Monday | *Htaw meh* | The long tooth |
| Tuesday | *To mü* | The slanting sun |
| Wednesday | *To kyaw* | The leaning oil tree |
| Thursday | *Thi thwa* | The big comb |
| Friday | *Mü daw hpa* | The divided sun day |
| Saturday | *Mü htaw k' hpu* | The pig's stomach day |

I have found no traditions or other information relating to these names.

The Karen divide the day into the following seven parts or subdivisions: (1) *mü hse wah taw*, dawn; (2) *mü heh htaw*, sunrise; (3) *mü heh htaw hpa htaw*, the sun is high; (4) *mü htu*, noon; (5) *mü xe law*, the sun declines; (6) *mü haw law*, evening, and (7) *mü law nü*, sunset. The night also has its divisions, such as *mü yaw ma*, meaning that the sun is deep down; *hpa hpaw mü*, midnight or literally midway between the suns, and *hsaw o*, cock crow or early morning, of which they distinguish three stages. In conversation a Karen indicates the time of day or night by pointing to the sun's position as it was at the time to which he is referring, pointing upward or downward as the occasion requires. More than once in the narration of some story I have heard the different members of a group dispute about the exact angle at which the sun stood when the incident occurred, the difference between the angles indicated being not more than a degree.

## MEASUREMENT OF SPACE

When a Karen speaks of some object, he is likely to indicate its size by comparing it with some part of his person. For example, he will describe a bamboo as being as large around as his arm, or the limb of a tree as being the size of his thigh. Applying the same principle, he has devised a system of rough units of measurement, such as the length of the forefinger, called *t' sü mü*; the distance between the end of the thumb and the end of the forefinger, *t'hpi;* the distance between the end of the thumb and the knuckle of the little finger when the fist is doubled up, *t'so;* the interval between the end of the thumb and the end of the middle finger, *t' hta;* the cubit or the distance from the elbow to the tip of the middle finger, *t' pla*, and the reach of the outstretched arm, *t' hkli*. Inasmuch as

TWO SGAW KAREN MAIDENS

One from Tharrawaddy and the other from Tavoy District. The Tavoy girl (on the right) is wearing a smock made of black velvet purchased in a bazaar and trimmed with embroidery of colored yarns. She also has on a head-band such as is worn in that district.

all of these units of measurement vary with the size and proportions of the individual, allowance is generally made for such variations. The cubit is commonly employed in all building operations, and men with long arms make the proper correction by measuring from the elbow to the first joint instead of to the tip of the middle finger. Contrariwise, small men add to their cubit the width of a finger or more to bring it to the standard length of a half-yard, which it is nowadays made to equal.

Measurements for longer or shorter distances are specified in relative terms, borrowed from one form or another of physical exertion. Such measurements are: the pace, *t'hka*; the stone's throw, *t' kwi leu*; a call (that is, as far as one can hear a shout), *t' kaw*. An indefinite distance of a mile or two, which one might walk without stopping, is a stage, *t' taw leh;* a half-day's journey, *t' mü htu leh;* a day's journey, *t' ni leh,* and so on. The Karen may on occasion speak of a month's or a year's journey to very distant places. Another method of designating distances by intervals of time during which physical effort is required is to specify the number of betel chews or quids that would be consumed during the trip. For instance, a Karen is apt to inform one that a certain village is three or four betel chews distant. As it requires from fifteen to twenty minutes to dispose of a quid of betel, the village in question may be estimated as being three or four miles away.

### THE KAREN'S KNOWLEDGE OF ASTRONOMY

It often happens that the Karen find their way through the jungle at night by means of the stars. The more brilliant constellations, called *hsa t' so,* are well known and have their particular names. Of these, the Great Bear *(Hsa k' htaw,* literally the Elephant) and the Southern Cross *(Meh la ka)* are referred to the most frequently, because they signify north and south, respectively. These two constellations were supposed, according to an old legend, to have been brothers, being thought to resemble each other in appearance; but on account of a quarrel they separated and went to the opposite ends of the heavens. Orion is known by the name of the Stealthily Shooting Stars *(Hsa kwa hka).* A legend relating to the three stars of Orion's belt, which are named *Hsa yo ma* (stars that seized wives), recounts that these stars kidnapped the daughters of the Pleiades, which are regarded as the great ones of the heavens. Later the three culprits were caught and reduced to the degraded position of servants to their parents-in-law. The Archer —Sagittarius of the ancients—is called the Bow-head Star *(Hsa hkli hko,* literally, the head of the bow where it is joined to the barrel of the crossbow). The Pleiades are named *Hsa deu mü,* a term signifying a collection of people closely related to one another; while three stars just east of the Pleiades, which look as though they had broken away from the original group, are called *Deu mü law hpa* (those separated from the company). Three stars south of the Pleiades, which form a triangle, bear the name of the Loom *(Hsa hta hko),* because the geometrical figure indicated by their positions suggests that enclosed by the floor, which forms the base; the wall, the vertical side; and the inclined warp, the hypothenuse, of the loom in the living-room of a Karen home. It ought to be added that the rising of the morning star, *Hsa tu ghaw*, marks the time for the Karen to get up in the morning; while the appearance of the evening star, *Hsa tu ha*, informs him that the end of the day's work has come and with it the time for going home.

The Karen take note of shooting stars, which they speak of sometimes as *Hsa yu* or flying stars and sometimes as *Hsa hpo tha*, youthful stars. Catching sight of them, people say that they are going to visit the maidens. They give to comets the obvious name of tailed stars, *Hsa meh htaw*, and are not different from other superstitious races in believing that their coming brings calamity. The planets have impressed them as "wandering stars," while they leave the fixed stars without names, except the Pole Star, which they call the Mouse, and a star near the moon, which they describe as the star that draws the moon, *Hsa mo la*. The Milky Way reminds the Karen of their flowering fields of paddy and receives the poetic name of the paddy flower stars, *Hsa bü hpaw*.

Like the Chinese and other Oriental peoples, the Karen attribute the eclipse of the sun or moon to some monster that devours the luminary. The Karen, however, do not discover this monster in the dragon, but believe that dogs do the devouring. According to the legend, a certain personage, who possessed the elixir of life, had four dogs. On one occasion when he was absent from home, the moon descended to earth and stole his wondrous cordial. On his return, finding the elixir had vanished, he constructed a ladder of rice-straw and mounted aloft with his dogs. But just as he was stepping upon the moon his ladder broke, causing him and one of his faithful beasts to fall to earth and lose their lives. The other three dogs were so fortunate as to find secure footing on the firmament. Now and again they become enraged at the recollection of the untimely fate of their master, attack and swallow the moon, and thereby produce the eclipse. One of these faithful dogs is black, and for some unknown reason is unable to swallow the moon entire and so causes only a partial eclipse; but the yellow one devours it completely, and it can be seen shining through his hide, which accounts for the color of the luminary during a total eclipse. On escaping through the animal's bowels, the moon regains its former brightness.[4]

---
[4] See Chapter XXVIII on Tabu, p. 289.

THE GATEWAY OF A VILLAGE STOCKADE
This is a protection not only against bad characters, but also against wild animals.

## CHAPTER VIII

## THE KAREN VILLAGE-HOUSE

The Karen on the plains live in houses of Burmese construction, which are therefore outside the scope of this work. In the Pegu Hills we find the single-structure village, which seems to have been the characteristic Karen dwelling from early times. It might be described as a bamboo apartment-house on stilts, accommodating on the average from twenty to thirty families. It is spread out on one floor, and each family occupies not one "flat" but a room, called in Karen "deu," which faces a central corridor running the length of the barrack.

Such a village, "th' waw," is usually rebuilt on a new site each year. The new location is sought by the local chief during the hot season, after conference with the elders and after the crops have been brought in. The place selected by the chief is fairly level, adjacent to the area to be cut over the coming year, and near a spring or stream that will not dry up during the hot weather. In the old days it was also necessary to choose a site that would be high and easily defended against raids. Before the decision is finally made, the chief must consult the auspices in the form of chicken bones, and if these are propitious and no laughing-bird *(Lanius)* calls "chet, chet," the men begin to cut bamboos with which to construct the village.

The bamboos selected for posts are twenty or more feet long and usually from four to six inches in diameter. They are set in the ground at intervals of four or five cubits (six to seven and a half feet). Holes are chopped through these large uprights at a height of from six to eight feet above the ground, and pins are thrust through on which bamboo girders of the same size are fastened by means of withes. At right angles to these girders and resting on them, other bamboo poles, slightly smaller in size, are tied at regular intervals of about a cubit to form the floor joists. The floor is made of large bamboos, split, flattened out, and secured to the joists by means of withes of the same material. It is six or eight feet above the ground, springy, and seamed with cracks, through which rubbish and wash water may be disposed of. As

Part of a Mountain Karen Village, Tharrawaddy District

Stockade and Gateway of the Village, Re Tho, Tharrawaddy District

the floor of the corridor is subjected to much heavier wear than that of any single room, it is made of round bamboos securely tied together.

Some six feet or less above the girders—my head has sometimes found that it was not fully six feet—another set of holes are hacked into the posts or uprights, through which pins are run to serve as supports for the "wall-plates," as the English residents of Burma call them, which run parallel with the girders below, and are secured in the same way. Other bamboos, parallel with the floor joists, are tied on the wall-plates at intervals of three or four feet. These beams give stability to the building. The tops of the posts may be only a little above the wall-plates, or they may run up several feet to the roof-plates, which are secured by pins and bamboo withes like the beams below. There may or may not be a roof-tie running across above the wall-plates. On the roof-plates rest the purlins or rafters that carry the interlocking half-sections of bamboo of which the roof is formed. This kind of roof may have supplied the model for the native round tile used so extensively in China and throughout the East. The bamboos to be used in the construction of the roof must be straight and three or four inches in diameter. They are split down the middle. The halves are laid close together with the concave sides uppermost, and the cracks between their edges are covered by a second row of halves laid with their convex sides uppermost. This overlapping of the concave by the convex halves gives a tight roof, the rain running down the troughs formed by the concave halves and off at the eaves. If one set of interlocking or overlapping bamboo "tiles" is not long enough to make the roof, a second set fits far enough under the higher set to catch the drip from above. Sometimes the roof covers the whole structure, including the corridor. In that case it has a ridge in the middle; otherwise the ridge may be over the row of posts next to that standing at the corridor. If the village-house stands in a windy location, where the rain would sometimes be driven up the roof, a small bamboo strip is tied at right angles across the upper ends of each set of "tiles." This is the more necessary because the roof is never steep, having a slope of not more than twenty degrees.

The walls of the village-house are constructed of flattened bamboo lengths nearly long enough to reach from the floor to the wall-plates. Three horizontal bamboo poles of small diameter are run through the posts, holes having been made for the purpose, and the flattened bamboo strips are woven between these. Such a wall con-

# THE KAREN VILLAGE-HOUSE 59

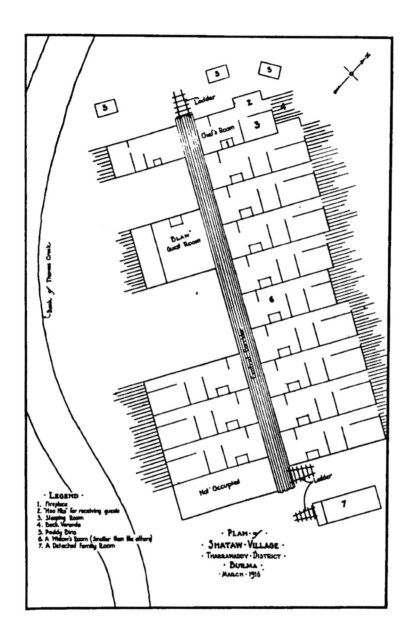

tains numerous cracks and apertures, and may be easily removed to allow a corpse to be carried out. Similar partitions divide the sleeping apartment from the rest of the family-room. (See p. 65.)

When we come upon such a village, we may find it surrounded by a stockade, as in the case of those in the Tharrawaddy district, where protection is thus obtained from tigers and other animals of the jungle and also from human prowlers. The stockade is made of bamboo poles, re-inforced by four rows of sharp pickets woven in and out of the fence. (See pp. 55, 57.) The gate of the stockade is constructed of large bamboos suspended from a cross-piece, so that they knock against one another when any one enters. Thus, the approach of a visitor is well announced. Once inside of the enclosure and past the multitude of yelping dogs which the villagers keep, the visitor comes to the ladder by which access is gained to the communal abode. The ladder, like everything else, is made of bamboo and has small loose rungs that can be easily removed. To an American it looks inverted, for it is narrow at the bottom and wide at the top. If the sun is high, heat is reflected from the burning hot bamboos. Mounting to the floor, one steps gingerly along, fearing the round flooring may turn under him. The hollow bamboos resound, as each rubs and creaks against its fellows. The whole population seems to be peering out of their doors or peeping through the cracks. The visitor enters a doorway, without its door. The first thing in the room that strikes his attention is the fireplace ("hpa k' pu"), which is only a little way from the entrance. The intervening space is largely filled with water-joints, rice baskets, and various household utensils. This is called the water-joint place ("hti pu law"). The fireplace consists of four upright bamboos fastened in the floor beams below and reaching to the cross-beams above. On the floor a rough box-like enclosure is built around the bottoms of the poles and filled in with dirt and ashes. Three round stones, or more in case the family has two pots boiling at once, give support to the cooking vessels, while the fire underneath is fed with dry bamboo fuel. About three feet above the ashes there is a shelf made of bamboo splints with their hard surfaces downward to the fire. The soot deposit on the under side of this shelf prevents the flames from doing any damage. Pots, plates, and other utensils find their convenient resting-place upon the shelf. One or two other shelves above this serve as catch-alls for herbs, baskets, tin lamps, unused food, large knives ("dahs"), and almost anything else that finds its way into the house. A hole cut in each

# THE KAREN VILLAGE-HOUSE

of the two front poles of the fireplace a little way above the floor serves as a holder for the bamboo stick kept for stirring the cooking rice or other foods.

A smaller box of ashes in the center of the room supplies a fireplace for the warming of the family when the air is chilly of nights and mornings. It is then comfortable to sit about the fire, as one visits and tells stories.

The Karen have little use for artificial light. They get up with the sun and go to bed with the chickens. Often the flaring light of the bamboo fuel in the fireplace serves for light, while they entertain visitors or do odd bits of belated work. When they need something more than this, they use a cup containing crude earth-oil (petroleum is found in large quantities in Upper Burma) with a wick sticking out, or they make torches from the resinous oil of the "xaw" *(Dipterocarpus)* tree. These enormous trees when tapped yield a good run of oil. After each run of sap they scorch the hole and get another run. The oil is mixed with bits of dry wood or punk and moulded into sticks about a cubit long and an inch in diameter by putting it into joints of small bamboo. When it has dried, it is wrapped in palm or pineapple leaves and tied up with bark fibre. When needed for use, one end is loosened and applied to the fireplace for lighting. It is then set on a rough stand fashioned out of wood, on which it rests in an oblique position and in this manner burns to the best advantage. Nowadays little tin lamps made by Burmese tinsmiths after the pattern of the old European lamps are in common use. These hold a cotton wick and give a little light and some smoke, as they have no chimneys.

A TORCH WITH ITS STAND

Usually beyond the cooking place a small partition extends out about four feet from the wall, forming a little alcove and hiding from view the family sleeping-room. The latter is a small apartment not more than eight or ten feet each way and is supplied with either a few rush mats, such as the Burmans are in the habit of sleeping on, or a single large bamboo mat, besides a quantity of old clothes, blankets, pillows, and rags scattered about or hanging from the rough ends of the walls. At either the front or back of the large outer room, whichever is toward the east—the place of honor in a Karen house—is a raised platform called the "hso hko." This is about a cubit's height from the floor and has a mat on it worn shiny with much sitting. It is the place where guests are received, especially if they are people of note. Here against the wall are a few pillows, which may be half-round bamboos of giant size, that is, from eight to ten inches in diameter, or cloth pillows filled with fibre from the cotton tree *(Bombax heterophylla)*. The guest is invited to sit on the platform and to partake of the contents of the fragrant betel-box, which is sure to be hospitably pushed in front of him. The cradle usually hangs from the crossbeams in the middle of the room, being held up by fibre ropes, although occasionally elephant chains are called into use to give full measure of security. The cradle itself may be a blanket swung up at the four corners, or it may be part of the trunk of a large hollow tree. A basket-work cradle is scarcely ever found in old Karen homes.

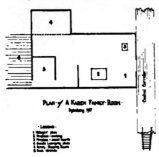

PLAN OF A KAREN FAMILY ROOM

At the back of the family apartment the bamboo joists and flooring project several feet beyond the wall, forming a primitive back veranda where clothes are hung to dry; rice (paddy), fish, fruit, and vegetables are set out in the sun, and other domestic operations are carried on in private.

In a few Karen villages a young men's club-room ("blaw") is still maintained, but not in most. Where such a room exists, it does not differ in general appearance from a family-room, except that it has no partitions. The hearth in the middle of the space serves as a social fireside on cold mornings and evenings. At the east end a raised dais extends the width of the room, being used both for reception and for sleeping purposes. Guests, unless closely related to some family in the village, usually sleep here, except when, as a mark of respect, they are invited to sleep in a room apart on the "hso hko" with the men of the house. Women guests sleep in the family sleeping-room together with the women folk and children.

The old type of Karen village-house, such as we have been describing above, is being modified by contact with the Burmese way of building, and every stage of evolution from the village-barrack to separate family houses may be observed in Karen villages to-day. (See the illustrations on pages 94, 220, and 227.)

When an epidemic breaks out in a bamboo village-house, the inhabitants are not held there by the considerations that ordinarily prevent the dwellers in durable towns and cities from taking their prompt departure. At best the Karen village-house is habitable only for a year or two, was built by the combined efforts of the men of the little community from material of which the supply is abundant, and can be replaced quickly. When, therefore, disease begins to spread among the adjacent families, they scatter to the four winds with their most necessary belongings. Soon they gather and build another village on a new site and, having removed the last of their possessions from the old infected structure, leave it to decay or set it on fire.

When a village community is removing from one site to another, the women prepare food and liquor for the journey, pack up their belongings and leave them in the jungle near the path, if they do not wish to take them to the new place at once, and, finally, prepare the offerings to be left behind. These offerings consist of four balls of cooked rice, one white, another made black by being mixed with charcoal, and the other two colored red and yellow, respectively, by the admixture of colored pigments. These balls are placed on a large winnowing-sieve that has been woven by the women for the purpose at the very last. This tray and its offerings are carried to the central part of the house, where it is visited and spat upon by every member of the village. They then repeat the following lines:

"Let all sickness and pain depart. Depart all colds.
Go eat your black rice, your red rice.
Go eat your betel and its leaves.
Go eat with your wife and your children.
Go stay in your house."

After thus addressing the spirits, the villagers take up their burdens, beat their drums and gongs, and set out for their new abode—a sight, indeed, for a motion picture camera.

On arriving at the new house, they do not enter it at once, but wait until some one has plucked from adjacent trees seven twigs growing upright, and with these has swept out the rooms. As the sweeper goes through the house he repeats the following incantation:

> "Go away, all evil spirits.
> Depart, all devils.
> We and our children are going to stay here.
> Do not remain near. Go. Go."

The members of each family then take up the various household tasks, including the building of the fireplace. If this is not completed the same night, they tie up their wrists to keep their "k'las" from wandering away and finish it the next morning. This is done among the Karen of Siam.

In the preceding pages of this chapter I have attempted to give a description of the Karen village-house. I do not say "home," for the Karen language has no word for home. The house is, however, something more than the eating and sleeping place of the village families: it is the center of their domestic life and worship and as such possesses a certain amount of sanctity. From what has been said above, it is clear that the village structure displays no attempts at artistic decoration, and is not made attractive by any of the touches that give so rich a meaning to the word "home" among Christians. The Karen bamboo house, located in a tropical climate as it is, affords a certain amount of physical comfort: the breezes blow through its airy walls, and one may lounge and gossip within during the heat of the day and not experience great oppression. At night, when the cool air begins to make itself felt, the open fire with its cheerful blaze attracts the story-teller, while out in the shadows the youthful lover strums his harp, and the children and the dogs play about in sufficient quietness not to disturb their elders.

Everywhere common dogs are kept by the Karen. These are the ordinary smooth-haired pariah hounds, which are familiar to the traveler in all parts of the peninsula. Besides these there are the hunting-dogs, mentioned in the chapter on Hunting and Fishing.[1] Only in recent days have the Karen shown any inclination to raise cats. In the early days they professed not to eat these felines; but I can testify that, whatever their former antipathies to the cat tribe may have been in this regard, they no longer hesitate to eat the wild varieties of cats that are to be caught in the jungle. They also find rats palatable.

Pigs and fowls are the most common domestic animals among the Karen. Dr. Mason speaks of the pigs as being of the "small Chinese variety."[2] They are the property of the women and know

---
[1] See p. 102.
[2] *Journal, Asiatic Society of Bengal*, XXXVII, Pt. II, 129.

their mistress's voice. When a woman dies, her pigs are killed in order that their "k' las" may accompany her into the next world. The fowls are of a variety not unlike the wild jungle-fowls found all over the country.

On the plains buffaloes have been extensively bred for use as draft animals and in cultivating the paddy-fields. As they are slow-going creatures the small native oxen, often mistakenly identified with the "sacred ox" from having a hump like the cattle supposed to have been used in ancient Israel, have largely superseded them for draft purposes. In the Toungoo Hills oxen are employed to some extent as pack-animals, especially by the Paku tribe. Both the Paku and their neighbors, the Mawnepgha, raise a few goats, while the Red Karen are breeders of ponies to some extent.

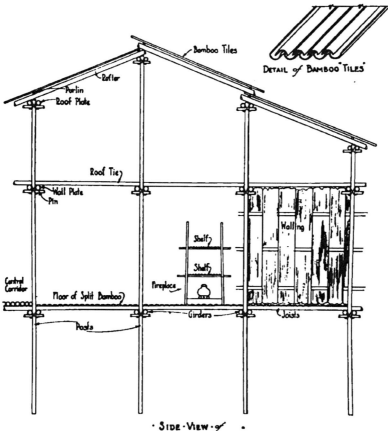

· SIDE·VIEW·of ·
· A·BAMBOO·KAREN·HOUSE ·
· KAINGDAGYI·1917 ·

# CHAPTER IX

## FOOD AND ITS PREPARATION

The dietary of the Karen includes almost everything edible in the way of vegetables that grow in their country. A great variety of fish, birds, and animals are also partaken of; but it should be said at once that three-fourths, if not seven-eighths, of the amount of food they consume is rice, of which they raise many varieties. Next to rice they resort in time of need to millet, maize, and roots, especially yams of different kinds. Besides gourds, squashes, egg-plant, roselle, sweet potatoes, and the edible fruits, the Karen eat the tender shoots of many plants and trees, including the bamboo.

All kinds of fish and eels, some varieties of crabs, snakes, locusts, and grasshoppers, snails and other mollusks, and even certain varieties of ants are comprised in the menu. Flesh of all sorts from that of the elephant to that of the rat is eaten with relish.[1] In the realm of feathered creatures the variety is equally comprehensive, ranging from the sparrow to the peacock, not even omitting the crow. Fish-paste, called in Karen "nya u"[2] but commonly given its Burmese name of "ngape," is greatly prized by the Karen, who think that it adds a very savory flavor to their food. On the plains they buy it from the Burmans from whom, it may be, they have adopted its use, but sometimes those living near streams or lakes make it for themselves.

Notwithstanding their inclusive diet, the Karen have no idea of what we call a balanced ration and, after all, are more or less undernourished. They also practice constantly the habit of betel chewing, which benumbs their sense of taste. For these reasons they crave highly seasoned foods. Chilies or red peppers are considered a necessity, while meats and powdered condiments of spices, tumeric, and chilies are used only to make the pungent curry sauce with which the cooked rice is flavored. Salt, which is obtained at the bazaars, is also used in seasoning.

---
[1] Messrs. Hose and MacDougal speak of some writer, whose name they do not give, as conveying the impression that the Karen do not eat the flesh of animals belonging to the cat tribe. I have not found this to be true. (*Vide* Hose and McDougal, *Pagan Tribes of Borneo*, Vol. II, 239).

[2] This word means literally "rotten fish."

Inasmuch as rice is the chief article of diet among the Karen, a few words should be said about its preparation. "Paddy," which is the grain before it has been cleaned for cooking, is brought home from the bins in which it has been stored and spread out on mats to dry in the sun. It is then pounded in mortars to rub off the outer husk. A second pounding removes the inner skin covering each grain and polishes the rice pure white. (See p. 68.) As cleaned rice does not keep as well as paddy, the natives pound out only enough to last a week or two. The kernels are washed in a basket with a sieve-like bottom and are then poured into a pot of boiling water. They are allowed to cook vigorously for ten minutes or less, until they swell and become soft enough to crush easily between the thumb and finger. The water is then poured off and the pot set back in the hot ashes to dry out any remaining water. When the rice is served, it remains whole, firm, and slightly hard. Soft boiled rice is most unpalatable to the Karen, who think it not so sustaining as the less cooked cereal. Nowadays the cooking is done in most places in earthen pots, which are bought from Burmese or Shan traders. These pots are of red unglazed clay, cost but a few annas, (one anna is equal to about two cents or an English penny), and last with care for some time.

Besides the rice used for ordinary meals there are many varieties of glutinous rice that are cooked or steamed on the plains for an early morning meal or for special feasts. The steamers are made like the Burmese pots, but with a number of small holes in the bottom. These are placed over vessels of boiling water, the steam of which rises through the openings and permeates the grain. I have been told that when a rare feast is desired, the rice is steamed over a vessel in which a chicken is boiling, and the rice becomes flavored with the fowl. Steamed glutinous rice is sometimes mixed with sessimum seeds and pounded in a mortar until it becomes a sticky paste. This mixture is called "to me to pi."

It is reported that long ago, before the Karen had as much dealing with the Burmese as they do now, they cooked their rice in joints of bamboo. At any rate, this is their present practice when out in the forest. The hunter or wayfarer in the jungle puts his rice into a large joint of bamboo, which he stands at the edge of a little fire until the contents are sufficiently boiled. The hard silicious sheathing of the bamboo easily withstands the heat of a single cooking. Once used, the joint is thrown away, for there are plenty more to be cut as occasion demands. Sometimes cooked rice for a journey is carried in the same joint in which it was boiled. Certain kinds of bamboo, such as the thorny variety "wa hsgu," which grows in low lands, impart a special flavor to the rice that is cooked in them. Rice deriving its taste from the thorny bamboo is thought to be one of the most delicious viands that can be obtained and is called "me taw." When certain kinds of bamboo bear fruit,

POUNDING PADDY IN A MORTAR

which is at long intervals, their seeds are often cooked and eaten in place of rice.

The larger vegetables, like pumpkins, yams, etc., are cut up and boiled until soft. Green fruits and shoots are also cooked, although many spicy kinds of shoots and ripe fruits are generally eaten raw.

There are intervals when a village community lives only on rice eaten with a little salt, fish-paste gravy, and red peppers. After a fishing or hunting expedition, however, or when some feast is held, the people gorge themselves with as many kinds of meat or fish as they can obtain. Larger fish and the flesh of animals are cut up and cleaned before cooking. No part of an animal is wasted. The intestines, when properly cleansed and prepared, are considered especially toothsome. The best-liked meats are pork and venison. Birds, pigeons, and ducks are also regarded as good eating. Small birds are often cooked without other preliminaries than a hasty

THE FIREPLACE IN A HILL KAREN HOUSE
The housewife is watching the pot boil. Signs of approaching civilization are apparent, such as the enamel plate and the kerosene oil tin.

plucking of the feathers. Meats are ordinarily cooked with the oil pressed from sesame seeds and flavored with condiments more or less in the manner of Indian curries. For this purpose a larger or smaller quantity of the following spices are used: tumeric, ginger, cloves, cardamon seeds, and cinnamon bark, besides tamarind, lime-juice, and the inevitable salt and chili. Fishermen and hunters like to roast small game, fish, or strips of meat from larger animals between splints of bamboo hung near or over a camp fire. The Polynesian way of baking such foods is often employed, the fish, flesh, or fowl being wrapped in plantain leaves and buried in a pit, which is lined with stones made hot by having had a roaring fire on them. Meat in excess of immediate needs is cut into narrow strips and dried on a rack over a fire. The strips are then covered with salt and stored away for future use. Fish are dried in the same way. Such preserved foods are eaten by the workers in the fields or help to furnish forth the repasts on a journey. In the hills, so far as I have observed, the Karen does not fry his food; but on the plains, where he has more or less taken up Burmese ways, cooking food in fat has become somewhat common. This is usually done outside the house, however, because the Karen, like the Burmese and Shan, have a superstitious fear of the smell of cooking.

While cooking is preeminently the women's work, it seems that nearly every man can cook and does on occasion prepare his own food. I have eaten many a tasty meal prepared by Karen men, who considerately took pains to have clean utensils and to use only such condiments as they knew white men were likely to relish.

The serving of food among the Karen is a simple matter. The rice is emptied into a tray, the meats or vegetables are put in little bowls, and all are set on a mat on the floor. The members of the household squat around this "family board" and eat with the hand. They pour gravy from the meat, fish, or other side-dishes on the rice, work it in with the fingers, and convey the food in compact lumps to their mouths. Among the more primitive large plantain leaves often serve as trays and plates. The Karen on the plains use separate dishes of china or enamel-ware, which are readily obtained in the bazaar. These are set on a low table, standing no more than six inches above the floor. This manner of serving is in vogue among the Burmese. There is not much sociability about a Karen meal. Each person attends to his eating until he has finished, when he rises, rinses off his hands, quenches his thirst with a drink of water, and withdraws to sit down, or leaves the house without formality. The members of a family generally eat together; but if guests are present, the women usually wait until the men are served. Large quantities of food are prepared for wedding and funeral-feasts, which, as a rule, the men and women partake of separately without particular order or arrangement:

The safety-match is nowadays the common means employed by Karens in producing fire; but formerly the flint and steel were used, as they were all over the world in the early days of the nineteenth century and before. A simpler, and probably indigenous, method was by the friction of two dry pieces of bamboo. One piece was sawn back and forth through a groove cut crosswise on the crest of another, the latter being a half-section of large bamboo laid over a quantity of shavings or punk. The heat thus generated in a minute or two produced smoke and a flame, and the tinder caught the blaze. A generation or two ago Karens carried fire pistons, when on a journey, to light their pipes. The description of this simple mechanism, which has been given to me, is that it was a bone or metal cylinder with a small hole at one end into which a tight-fitting piston was driven by a sharp blow and then quickly withdrawn. The air within was thus sufficiently compressed and heated to ignite a bit of tinder at the bottom of the cylinder.[3]

Milk does not form a part of the diet of the Karen people any more than it does of some other Oriental races. There is little with which to feed babies whose mothers can not nurse them. However, it is a comparatively rare thing for a mother not to be able to nurse her child. The first solid food given to babies is rice that has first been masticated by the mother. The kind of food eaten by the parents is given to their children as soon as they cry for it. This, I think, is one of the most fruitful sources of the high death rate among Karen infants.

The people in the hills eat three meals a day, one soon after rising, one at mid-day, and the third in the evening after the work is done. On the plains an early "chota hazri" of glutinous rice is sometimes, but not always, taken.[4] The regular morning meal comes somewhere between eight and ten o'clock and the afternoon repast between three and five. Tea is coming to be much used among the Karen, either the native pickled tea which is imported by the Burmese from the Shan states, or the Chinese and India teas which are now sold all over the country. The Karen drink their tea without milk and often put in a little salt in place of sugar. Coffee is used to some extent in the Karen hills and is drunk without milk, unless some one has brought home a can of condensed milk from town, this preparation being considered a most delicious sweetmeat.

Alcoholic beverages are brewed or distilled among the Karen. A kind of rice beer is made by allowing boiled rice to stand in jars of water and ferment. Old fermented rice is left in a jar, and fresh rice water is poured upon it. After standing several days, it ac-

---

[3] The fire piston is used by the Ibans in Borneo. It is also found throughout the Malay Peninsula and in Sumatra: Hose and MacDougall, *Pagan Tribes of Borneo*.

[4] "Chota hazri" is the Hindustani word used throughout India for the little breakfast of toast and tea or coffee that Europeans take immediately on rising.

quires the desired strength or percentage of alcohol. Distilled liquor is obtained by boiling the fermented beverage in a closed vessel, from the top of which issues a bamboo pipe that leads to another vessel in which the steam condenses. A more concentrated solution of alcohol is thus secured. On the plains the glutinous rice, which is raised there, is much more commonly used in making liquor than the ordinary grain, because it contains a higher percentage of sugar. The plains possess another source of intoxicant in the "toddy-palms." (See pp. 105 and 220.) The juice of these palms, which exudes from the cut stems of the fronds, is collected and allowed to ferment, thus producing a liquor that is responsible for much of the crime committed by the rural people of all races.

In former days, in the more backward Karen districts and in Siam, the preparation of drink constituted a considerable part of the work of the women. It was used with every meal and was regarded as a necessary part of the native diet. Large quantities of liquor were provided for every festival. But its use is lessening among the more progressive natives and is rapidly disappearing among the Christian Karens.

The use of betel and tobacco is prevalent among the Karen people. Indeed, one might say that it is almost universal among them. The betel-box is always carried on a journey and is ever at hand where work is being done. When the guest arrives, the first act of hospitality is to push the box, replenished with its masticatories, in front of him. Betel, in the estimation of the Karen, forms a part of his food. Small bits of the areca-nut are laid on a fresh green leaf of the piper betel vine; lime is also smeared on the leaf, and perhaps a few cloves or shreds of tobacco leaf are added; the betel leaf is then folded into a wad and put into the mouth. In the process of chewing this "quid" the saliva is turned to a bright red, being secreted in such quantity that frequent expectoration is necessary. Wherever this spittle falls it leaves a red stain. The interior walls of the houses, especially in the corners, and the floors near the cracks are much stained with red. It is not safe to stop under a window or beneath a house, unless one is sure that nobody is within. An early missionary, who traveled with a white pony, was surprised one morning to find his animal wonderfully streaked with red, which yielded only to a vigorous washing. Betel chewing stains the teeth black, though it does not materially injure them, except that the hard usage wears them down or causes them to break off prematurely. Karens often speak of a short space of time as being about a betel-chew which, strictly speaking, would mean fifteen or twenty minutes. The women in the hills, instead of chewing the quid, allow it to remain on the tongue and mull it for hours at a time, much to the annoyance of any one trying to follow them in their conversation, which they keep up meantime.

The areca-nut is cut up with a kind of scissors or a sickle. Some use a section of deer's horn about six inches long in breaking

KAREN TOBACCO PIPES AND A PISTON FOR BREAKING BETEL-NUT
Nos. 1 and 2 are sections of bamboo decorated with etched designs; Nos. 3 and 4 have monkey-bone stems, and No. 5 is a bamboo root decorated with silver bead-work.

up these nuts. The horn is perforated by a hole large enough at one end to admit a whole nut, but considerably smaller at the other end. In being driven through this orifice the nut is broken into bits, which issue from the smaller opening. This nut-breaker is not used as much now as formerly. The areca-nuts and other supplies for betel chewing are kept in the ever present betel-box, which in the hills may be nothing more than an end of bamboo or, among those having due regard for the social amenities connected with the practice, is likely to be a round laquer receptacle or, in rare instances, even a brass box. These more pretentious containers are fitted with one or two trays, on which the supplies are conveniently disposed.

The habit of tobacco smoking is almost as prevalent among the Karen as that of betel chewing. It is indulged in by both sexes and all ages. The dried leaf is rolled into a rude cigar and smoked without further preparation. Pipes of various kinds are also used. The Karen analogue of the American corn-cob pipe is the simplest form, consisting of a short section of a small bamboo with a stem of the same inserted in the side. An approach to our brier-root pipe is made of a curved root of bamboo, nicely smoothed off and fitted with a stem of monkey-bone or silver. The bowl of this latter kind of pipe is sometimes supplied with a silver lining and has a silver wire wrapped around it by way of ornamentation. The ordinary straight pipe may be etched with geometric figures in fine lines and with borders of saw-tooth and star designs. Designs incised on bamboo are found throughout the Malay countries, Borneo, and the Philippine Islands.[5]

OFFERINGS AND TRAPS ON THE EDGE OF A FIELD
The bamboo platform and basket contain the offerings of the "ta maw a hku" ceremony. Two kinds of rat traps are seen at the left. On the right is a "wa hkaw" or spear trap, the point of which is under the offerings at the opening there.

[5] Skeat and Blagdon, *Pagan Tribes of the Malay Peninsula*, Vol. I, pp. 395, ff.; Cole, *Wild Tribes of the Davao District*, 71; Hose and MacDougall, *Pagan Tribes of Borneo*, Vol. I, 228-230.

## CHAPTER X

## AGRICULTURAL PURSUITS AND OTHER OCCUPATIONS

### IN THE HILLS

The Karen's chief occupation is the cultivation of the most important article of his diet, namely, rice. Throughout the Orient this grain is called "paddy" during all the stages of its growth and curing, until it is husked and polished ready for cooking. The method of cultivation in the hills is widely different from that on the plains. We shall consider the former first, as it is more primitive and, until recently, was practiced by far the larger number of the people. In Burma this more primitive method is often spoken of as the "ya" cultivation, from the Burmese word designating it. It is characteristic of this cultivation that a new hill field, called "hku" in Karen, has to be selected, cleared, and burned off each year. The planting of the grain must follow immediately after all seeds and small roots have been destroyed by fire, or no crop can be raised with the primitive implements in use, on account of the rapid resuscitation of the jungle. The ashes from the consumed vegetation act as a fertilizer, without which the crop would scarcely be worth the reaping. At the present time the Government so limits the areas open to the Karen for cultivation in some districts that a sufficient interval does not elapse between plantings to allow the growth of enough timber for the production of the ashes necessary to fertilize the soil properly. Hence, crop production is declining in these districts. At least seven years should intervene before a plot is cleared and planted a second time, and even this period is too short for the production of the best crops.[1]

---

[1] The "ya" cultivation, it is obvious, is most destructive of the forests. Unsuccessful efforts have been put forth to induce the Karen in the hills to give it up. It has been suggested that the people keep gardens and raise produce for sale. This proposal overlooks the lack of adequate roads for transporting the crops to market. The Karen are backward about engaging in new undertakings. They raise their food and obtain what else they need by barter. Until recently this mode of living has sufficed for them. They have not been accustomed to handling money or making it last long.

With the introduction of new ideas and the increase of mining concessions and forest restrictions, changes are inevitable and should be planned for, especially as the granting of new mining concessions will increase the number of outsiders. It has seemed to the present writer that "ya" cultivation might be limited to a term of years, during which a number of British

When a crop has been harvested, the village chief and elders choose the ground to be cut over the following year. Each village has its well-recognized farming areas, beyond which are the lands of the neighboring village. Each member of the communtiy then picks out his particular plot for cultivating, takes home a lump of the earth, puts it under his pillow, and sleeps on it. If he has an auspicious dream, he consults the chicken bones for a confirmation of the good omen. Securing this confirmation, he regards his choice as fixed. Otherwise, he selects another plot and repeats the ceremonies. Once his selection is approved by the auspices, the spot is called a "du la," and he clears a little space on the land, after which he addresses the spirits as follows:

> "Depart all you evil spirits ('ta we ta na').
> We are going to work here for our food,
> To get sustenance for our wife and children.
> Let no sickness come upon us.
> We are going to work until it is finished."

Next he places a lump of soil on the clearing and, having wrapped the chicken bones in the leaf of a creeper ("ki ku"), he touches the lump with them, raises them towards the sky, and again touches or strikes the clod with the mystic bones. He now breaks these apart and scrapes them until he can insert splints of bamboo into the holes of the bones. If this act of divination is also successful, he is ready for work.

In the early days, when much of the primeval forest was still standing, the Karen would clear out the brush and bamboos from among the giant trees on the hillside they were preparing to cultivate. Then they raised platforms at the foot of the trees from which they could cut them above the broad-spreading buttresses at their base, leaving enough of the trunk intact to keep them from falling. When the whole hillside tract had been cut over in this manner, they felled the uppermost tree so as to crash down on those just below, and these in turn would bring down others until

---

officers, who should become familiar with the Karen people and language, should develop a plan in accordance with which these tribes might be given reservations of land in exchange for the valuable areas now under their control. These reservations might be either in the hills or on the plains, but the Karens should be taught to cultivate them according to approved methods, in order to gain an ample livelihood. Old racial animosities and the temptation for one people to exploit another militate against entrusting such a policy to Burman officials. It ought to be placed only in the hands of earnest, straightforward Government officials, who have gained the confidence of the Karen and are able to deal with them sympathetically but firmly. This general program would doubtless involve some outlay in supplying cattle, not to speak of competent instruction in modern agricultural methods, animal husbandry, etc.

## AGRICULTURAL PURSUITS AND OTHER OCCUPATIONS 77

A Hillside Plot Cut Ready for Burning

A Paddy-bin for Storing Grain in the Field
The bamboo clappers in the foreground are for scaring away the birds.

the whole mountain side seemed to be swept by a mighty avalanche, which resounded far and wide across the valleys, drowning the shouts of the people who were wild with excitement at seeing the culmination of the labor of weeks. The fallen timber and heaps of brush had still to lie for a fortnight or more in the hot sun until dry enough to burn.

The burning-off process, which is always a necessary part of clearing the land as mentioned above, is preceded by its appropriate ritual, in order to prevent any wandering shades or "k'las" from being consumed. As a means of warding off evil, the ritualist ties up his wrists and, as he does so, invokes the "k'las" as follows:

> "Pru-u-u k'la, come back. Remain not in the forest,
> Nor in the places where the jungle is newly cut.
> Do not stay with evil demons.
> We are about to burn our cutting.
> Come back and stay in the house. Come back."

In lighting the blaze, they do so with fire from bundles of twigs that have first been sprinkled with the blood of a fowl. The burning is carefully watched, so that the fire may be kept from spreading to the surrounding forests. When bamboos are burned, the air in the hollow joints expands and bursts the stems with sharp reports. A burning field sounds like the fusillade of a battery of machine guns and affords as much delight to the Karen as a packet of firecrackers to a small boy.

When the rains have begun, the villagers begin their planting. With a sharp stick or the point of a long knife ("dah") they make tiny holes in the soft ground about a foot apart and drop into each two or three seeds of paddy. The field is now called a "hku." About this time also each family builds the little hut in its plot of ground that is to serve both as a shelter and home until the harvest shall have been gathered. It is a rude affair made of a few bamboos, either saved when the field was cleared or newly brought from the jungle, and consists of a platform, roof, and loosely fitted sides.

When the paddy has sprouted and tinged the hillside with green, another ceremony ("theh a khü") must be performed. Offerings of liquor and a fowl, which has been cooked at home, are placed upon an altar with a platform and roof, built upon six posts. The platform consists of two parts, the upper, enclosed like a miniature hut and the lower, open like a porch. Sometimes a second altar is erected upon four posts and is called "ta th' mo." Close by the first altar a flaring basket ("ta theh") is set up, which is made of splints woven through the split end of a bamboo, the other end of which is planted in the ground, and a similar "ta theh" is placed in front of the altar. A cup containing some rice mixed with chaff, from which projects a little bambo branch, is put upon the altar. The little branch is a "hto bo" or pole. Water is now poured over the offerings, and the cup of liquor brought from the house is placed at the foot of the altar posts. Along the path leading to the altar sharp bamboo spikes are set, following a custom said to have been handed down from earlier times, to prevent wild elephants from disturbing the offerings. When all these preparations have been completed, the spikes and the altar are smeared with the blood of a fowl, and the spirits are again addressed:

"Let this cool you and please you, O Lord of the hills, O Lord of the land, Lord of fire, Lord of heat and cold. I am making you cool and comfortable. Therefore, moderate the heat of the soil and make the paddy good. Make the rice good. Do this until the field is full."

If there is a second altar, its posts are smeared with the blood of another fowl, while the suppliant prays:

"I am offering you that which is good, that which is comforting. Therefore make the rice and paddy good, and cause it to fill the whole field."

An offering of a live chicken, with its legs tied together, is laid in the basket near the larger altar, while the following words are uttered:

"I have prepared this for you. I am doing you good. I am making it comfortable for you. When the eagle flies, the crow is afraid. When the laughing-bird laughs and the barking-deer barks, let us not fear their bad omens."

The suppliant now burns the feathers off of the dead fowls; lays down five yam leaves; cuts bits of the tip of the bill from each, treating the nails and extremities of the wings in the same way; carefully distributes the different clippings from each fowl on each of the leaves, together with a morsel of rice and, finally, disposes one of the leaves upon each of the three offering-places mentioned above, besides one upon the roof of the hut and one upon a stump in the field. Then he dips a cup of liquor and, holding it aloft, pours out a libation, saying as he does so:

"Come partake of your liquor and your rice. Make the rice and paddy better. May we work and eat in comfort and pleasure. Let

OFF FOR THE FIELDS WITH BASKETS AND BAGS
The Karen always travel single-file. This picture shows four patterns of smocks trimmed with white seeds.

us not be overtaken by illness. May we work until the task is finished and eat to the end."

After examining the bones of the sacrificial fowls to learn their omens, the suppliant and his family cook and eat the chickens. He then weaves a basket with large meshes and on a leaf laid in the bottom places a black pepper and sprinkles some salt. He takes a small branch from an upright-growing plant and, moving about in the growing grain, strikes both the grain and the basket, which he is carrying, and recites this prayer:

"O Guardian Bird of the field, do not let anything eat the paddy in the plot where you watch. Do not let men come in or go out. Do not permit any one who may get in to redeem himself with money, but cause him to expiate his transgression by increasing the yield of grain."

Then, cutting off the head of another fowl, he smears its blood on the basket, which he sets down in the path near the edge of the field, and returns to his house.

In many places these rites are not now so carefully observed as the above account implies. Sometimes the larger altar is dispensed with altogether, and the offerings are placed upon the little altar and in the flaring baskets. Where the elaborate ceremonial is dying out, a single fowl may be used in place of several as an oblation sufficient to please the spirits and secure a plentiful harvest. In the illustration on page 74, from a photograph taken in the Pegu Yomas, are shown the various offerings, including the live chicken that has been left on a post to die. The flaring baskets with the other offerings are also shown. The bamboo reaching above the other things was set up to mark the height which, it was hoped, the paddy might attain.

Having sought the favor of the unseen powers that preside over the growing crop, the cultivator has soon to turn his attention to the numerous enemies that prey upon his field from the neighboring jungle. Elephants, wild pigs, and a number of small animals, including rats, eat the tender plants and later feed on the ripening grain. Birds and wild fowl of various kinds are also destructive from the time the grain is in the milk. Supplication to the Guardian Bird of the field does not relieve the rice-grower from the need of fencing his plot with reeds and bamboos, setting traps and snares, and erecting scarecrows and clappers to keep devouring creatures from his grain. Little hoeing is done, but the Karen and his whole family occupy themselves in watching the growing paddy, operating the clappers, and clearing the traps. When wild elephants appear in the field, those on guard are unable to do more than produce affrighting noises from a safe distance, in the hope that the great animals will be scared away before they have destroyed the entire crop.

As soon as the rains are over in October the hill rice ripens very quickly, and the harvest-time is near. Among some of the people it is the custom for the eldest member of the family to reap a little of the grain as the first fruit, as it were, of the season's produce. After this has been done, the whole family take part in the reaping. (See page 89.) The implement used is a sickle ("xeh"), the long handle of which bends backward from the grip, the tool as a whole having the shape of the letter S. The outer end of the sickle extends under the arm of the reaper, enabling him to cut with greater ease than if he depended only on his wrist muscles. The grain is cut about half-way down the stalks and is tied in small sheaves no larger than can be easily grasped with one hand. Even though all the paddy in the plot could be cut in one day, a fraction is left for reaping until the next morning, in order to have the crop good and make it last longer. The sheaves are thrown into piles, and then collected near the hut, where they are beaten out. In some places the sheaves are beaten over the edge of a trough improvised from half of a hollow log, and in others they are beaten over a horizontal pole tied by withes to two bamboo posts, the pole being about three feet above the ground. A large bamboo mat is spread down under the pole or the trough, as the case may be, to catch the grain. Those who engage in the beating are careful to tie up their wrists and call in the "k'las" or wandering shades. They also deem it necessary to complete the threshing before they leave the place. Both men and women or either alone serve as threshers. When the paddy has all been beaten out, it is winnowed by holding it aloft in a tray or basket and letting it fall, while the wind carries the chaff to one side and the grain falls on the mat. (See page 91.) The grain is now ready to be stored in a bin built in the field or along the path leading to the village. In the districts inhabited only by Karens these bins are to be found along the jungle trails a mile or more from any village or house. Stealing is very uncommon in these regions and is severely punished if detected.[2] In the Pegu Hills near the Burmese the same security does not exist, and the paddy is stored within the village stockade.

---
[2] See pages 27, 149.

Plowing a Paddy-field in Lower Burma

Women Transplanting Paddy
They simply push the plants into the soft mud, and they grow without further attention.

The grain is carried in baskets on the backs of the beaters (see p. 94) and is poured slowly into the bin so as not to settle compactly. Should a basket slip and fall into the bin or its contents be dashed in, a fowl must be killed and an offering made. The storing of grain must be finished as speedily as possible; but if it can not be done in one day, the workers may rest over night.

The task of storing finished, they bring an offering for "Hpi Bi Yaw,"[3] consisting of a clod of earth, a morsel of rice, and a small cup of liquor. These are placed on the paddy in the bin, and a prayer of thanksgiving is said to her. After these ceremonies the cultivator feels at liberty to take grain from his store and carry it home for food.

A small supply of paddy is always put aside in a special basket for seed, each family preserving its own, which is supposed to date back to a time when its forbears had an unusually good crop in some favorable year. Only in the last extremity will a Karen eat his seed-grain. There are many varieties of rice having their special names, each cherished by particular localities and families. Hill rice is greatly prized as being more delicious than plains rice.

The Karen raise different kinds of vegetables in their rice-fields, such as certain varieties of gourds, beans, yams, a kind of sweet potato, and peppers of various sorts, especially the red chili so generally used for condiment. Cotton is also grown in the fields along with the rice, standing until long after the paddy has been reaped. The cotton is usually considered to be the women's crop. They tend it, gather the bolls, and carry them home. The other products of the field seem to belong to all members of a family alike. The tips of various plants are used for greens. These must be plucked with the fingers and not cut off with a sharp instrument, inasmuch as the spirits dislike their being dissevered with a knife. A few plants of cockscomb are grown in the field, the red variety ("hpaw ghaw") being preferred to the yellow, because they are supposed to dazzle the eyes of the demons and prevent their harming the crop. In the lower hills sesame is often raised for its seeds, which are threshed out and sold to the Burmese, who press the oil out of them. This is serviceable in cooking and lighting. It is said to be not unlike linseed oil in certain respects, but supplies a large amount of the fats required in curries.

In the Toungoo and Shwegyin Hills great quantities of betel-nuts are grown. These regions furnish, I believe, the greater part

---

[3] The divinity who presides over the cultivation of the paddy: see page 226.

of the supply of these nuts for all Burma. The trees bearing them are tall slender palms *(Areca Catechu)*, which flourish in moist mountain valleys where they are shaded by larger trees. The nuts grow in clusters just below the crown of leaves. A tree may produce as many as four hundred nuts a year, which are sold in baskets at three or four rupees a basket. There are several gardens that number these palms by the thousands and many others by the hundreds.

Plantain gardens are cultivated on the bottom-lands near the rivers, where there are rich alluvial deposits. Plantains or bananas, of which many varieties exist, are comprised in the genus *Musa*. The stem grows from four to fifteen feet in height and produces sprouts, which are set out at the end of the rainy season and begin to bear by the next year. The new plants send out sprouts in their turn, these growing from the sides of the herb and continuing its life indefinitely. Some varieties of the plantain in the hill-country bear very delicious fruit, which I have almost never seen on the plains. As far as I know it is raised for home consumption, although it may be sold in a few cases to Burman and Shan traders for a small price.

In the Toungoo and Moulmein districts oranges are extensively grown. The groves are along the well-watered valleys, and the fruit is ripe in late September and in October. Nothing has been done, so far as I am aware, to improve the varieties, but a ready market is open to the fruit produced. The Karens bring the supply down to Toungoo in dugouts, and sell it to traders on the river bank at prices varying from one to three or four rupees per hundred, according to the size and quality of the fruit.

A few years ago coffee was widely planted in the Toungoo district; but a blight ruined the greater part of the groves, and the industry ceased to develop. A little is still raised here and there, but it is of an inferior grade.

Tobacco is grown along the sandy banks of the rivers, not in large quantities but sufficient for home consumption and petty trading. It is cured in the most primitive way and consumed in many forms.

I have been informed that in the early days the Karen trained the vines of the betel leaf creeper *(Piper Betel)* to run up a certain kind of rough-barked tree, which a few vines would completely cover with their glossy green foliage, supplying a large crop of leaves and thereby a considerable income for the possessor of such a vine-clad tree, which was called "pu la." Wanderers of other nationalities, happening to discover such trees, dispoiled them of their treasure by cutting the vines. Thus, but very few "pu la" remain.

Dr. Mason tells us that "Karen boys and maidens engaged in harvesting these leaves with great zest and it was not uncommon for young men, in seeking companions to inquire who were the most agile climbers of 'pu la' or betel leaf trees." [4]

The Karen in Toungoo have always raised more or less silk and woven the material for their best garments from it. The silkworms are of a native variety and spin a thread far inferior to that of improved species. Not many years ago the attempt was made to introduce a worm of larger size, but it met with ill success, because the creature made a peculiar creaking sound in chewing the leaves of the mulberry tree. The superstitious people thought the new worms were possessed of some strange demon and killed them, in order to ward off an unknown danger.

Many of the inhabitants of Karenni gather stick-lac, which is the deposit of an insect on certain trees found in the jungle. They also increase the supply by attaching the insects to other trees. The deposit is used extensively in making red dyes [5] and is marketed in Toungoo on the twigs to which it is attached.

The Karen is skilled in all jungle-craft. He knows the woods and what may be found there. He has learned, among other things, that bees establish their hives high up in the branches of the oil-tree *(Dipterocarpus lociis)*. When he finds a new hive he marks the tree by putting a tuft of grass at its foot. Others will recognize the mark and respect his claim. To climb the fifty or seventy-five feet to the lower branches of these giant trees is no easy task. However, it is accomplished by means of pegs driven into the trunk and a rope encircling it. Often a honey-gatherer makes his ascent at night, lest he grow dizzy in looking down from such a height. Once at the hive, he smokes the bees out with a smudge and collects the honey into joints of large bamboo. The Karen villagers in the vicinity of Thandaung used to be called "Wild Bees" by the Burmans of Toungoo, on account of the supplies of honey which they brought in from their hills.

Besides the pursuits already mentioned, the Karen of the hills sometimes engage in other occupations, such as transporting pro-

---
[4] *British Burma, Its People and Productions,* p. 495.
[5] See page 110.

duce and luggage from the town into the hill-country or to trading centers. They cover long distances, and before the recent war they received about eight annas (about twenty-four cents) a day for such work. In a few villages they raise oxen, which they train as pack-animals to carry grain and other produce of the hills to Toungoo or other markets. With two baskets slung on either side of a rough pack-saddle, these oxen can carry not more than one hundred and fifty or two hundred pounds each.

Karen men are experts at catching and training elephants and often become most excellent drivers for these intelligent beasts. Several travelers testify that Karen drivers seemed to be more gentle with, and careful of, their elephants than Burman drivers and acknowledge the pleasure which they derived from seeing the Karens handle their charges. Owners of elephants are usually employed by the Government Forest Department to draw logs out of the jungle to the streams, by the current of which they are floated down during the rainy season. This is a lucrative business, but the risk involved is large, because the elephants often sicken and need attention to restore them to working condition.

In some localities forest officers have employed Karens living in the hills to tend the adjacent forest reserves. But the Karen has a distaste for steady work under supervision, especially if the immediate overseer is a Burman. The latter usually does not hesitate to exhibit his feeling of superiority and to appropriate an undue share of the rewards. Only in a few instances have I known satisfactory results to be obtained through such an arrangement; but the few officers who did secure satisfactory results had a good word to speak for the Karen.

## On the Plains

The Karen on the plains in Burma practice methods of cultivation like those of the Burmese, which have often been described. When the rainy season is about to begin in May the cultivator, if his land is at a distance from the village, carries thither a few bamboos and some thatch and builds a hut in his field. Here he lives during the cultivating season. The rains having softened the hard clay soil, he may resort to the very primitive practice of driving a few cattle or buffaloes around over a muddy place until they cut the ground with their sharp hoofs and thus prepare it, after a fashion, to receive the seedlings. Or he may use the method of scratching the ground with a primitive wooden plow, called a "hteh." During recent years, however, iron points have been imported which make these implements more effective. If there is considerable water, he has still a third alternative, namely, to use a kind of rough harrow, named a "hto tu." (See page 83.)

Previously, and as early as possible, the cultivator has prepared a small plot in which he has sown his paddy seed. When the plants have reached about a cubit's height, they are pulled up, tied in sheaves, and carried to the water-soaked field to be set out. This work is done either by the members of the family or by women hired for the purpose. It requires about five persons to transplant an acre in a day, their compensation being approximately eight annas a day each. The process of transplanting consists merely in sticking the plants into the mud, usually by hand but sometimes with a forked stick. (See illustration on page 83.)

After this has been completed, little remains but to regulate the quantity of water on the fields by opening or closing the small dikes enclosing the plots. Later, when the grain is in the milk, birds are often rapacious, and I have seen Karens scaring them off their fields with a kind of slingshot. With this device they throw mud balls ("naw blü tha") from which a stalk of grass trails, fluttering and whirring as it flies, to the confusion of a flock of sparrows or weaver-birds. Larger balls, moulded and dried beforehand, have a hole through the middle. The air whistles through this when the ball is in swift motion, and big flocks of birds are badly scared by it. The slingshot, with which these two sorts of missiles are cast, consists of a bamboo of four or five feet in length with a rope attached, the missile being hurled from the end of the rope. It flies with amazing swiftness and to a great distance.

In October the rainy season is at an end, the ground begins to dry, the paddy turns a golden yellow or, as the Karen say, "becomes red," and by the first of December is about ready to be reaped. If it is not already leaning over, a man walks through it with a long heavy bamboo and pushes the stalks all in one direction to an angle of about forty-five degrees, so that it will be easier to cut. (See p. 89.) With sickles like those used in the hills, the members of the family reap in the direction in which the stalks are bent and bind the grain in sheaves about a foot in diameter. The average reaper will cut one hundred and fifty sheaves a day, but the best workers have a record of two hundred and fifty. Nowadays the sheaves are usually collected on the same day they are cut, and

REAPING PADDY WITH SICKLES

A THRESHING-FLOOR ON THE PLAINS
Oxen and buffaloes treading out the grain

carried to the threshing-floor, which is near the hut or, in the case of the fields lying near the village, is just outside the village gate. If they should be left in the field, they might not be there next morning. The pile of sheaves is always guarded, some of the men spending the night on it. They also take the precaution to hang up a gourd with a hole in it which, with a breeze blowing, emits sounds like mumbled voices.

The threshing-floor is a plot of ground perhaps a hundred feet square, or larger in proportion to the quantity of grain to be trodden out, which has been packed hard and flat by leading cattle around on it, or by using a cart or a drag for the purpose. (See p. 89.) A smoother surface is secured, not unlike that of a dirt tennis-court, by covering the floor with a coating of cow-dung. The name applied to the threshing-floor is "t'law," which is a corruption of the Burmese word "talin." The paddy sheaves are piled up in tiers around the "t'law" so as to shed water, should untimely showers fall before they are trodden out. For the threshing, however, the sheaves are distributed evenly over the floor to a depth of two feet with the heads of the grain on top. Banks of sheaves support the sides of the layers. The process of separating the grain from the heads is a tedious one. From two to a dozen cattle are tied together, and a boy or girl or, if neither of these is at hand, a woman takes the nose rope of the animal nearest him and stands in the center of the floor. The threshing often begins soon after midnight and continues until sunrise, the cattle being constantly prodded on their apparently endless round. At the conclusion of the tiresome task the other members of the family appear, remove the bulk of the straw, sweep up the smaller fragments, and begin to winnow the grain. This is accomplished either by holding it aloft in a basket and letting the wind blow off the chaff as it falls, or by pouring the grain and chaff from a platform four or five feet into a loosely-woven tray swung from a tripod of bamboos. To insure that all the chaff and dust are driven off, men and women fan the grain with closely-woven trays as it falls upon the pile. (See p. 91.) The winnowing process being finished, an offering for "Hpi Bi Yaw"[6] (the Karen Ceres) is placed on the apex of the pile. Lest any one should try to help himself to the grain, little tufts of charred straw are put at close intervals around the pile, after which those who have been doing all this dusty work unwrap their heads, repair to the village well or tank and indulge in a refreshing bath.

---
[6] See pp. 84, 93, 226

# AGRICULTURAL PURSUITS AND OTHER OCCUPATIONS

**WINNOWING PADDY**
The grain is poured through a sieve in order to scatter it as it falls, so the wind can blow off the chaff more easily.

**FANNING THE PADDY**
The man on the top of the pile throws a trayful of sweepings from the threshing floor into the air and those below fan it as it falls and thus drive away all the chaff.

In these days it is the usual practice to sell the grain to the traders directly from the threshing-floor. Sometimes it is stored for a few months in the hope of an advance in price, but most of the smaller cultivators are compelled by their poverty to sell at once. The buyers may be Burmans, but in these later years are more often Chinese. A few Karens have done some trading in paddy, although they are generally not so successful as the traders of the other nationalities.

The grain kept for family use is stored in bins of bamboo made in the shape of great baskets or "weh." These "weh" vary in size from those having double the diameter of a bushel-basket up to the huge ones of ten or twelve feet in diameter and of equal height. They are set upon platforms several feet above the ground and adjoining or close to the house. The planks forming the bottom are firmly secured together and coated with cow-dung. After a bin has been filled, the top is covered with a layer of straw, well packed in, and a thick coating of cow-dung is spread over it to seal the grain.

It is not my purpose in this work to enter into a detailed economic study of Karen agriculture. Here I have but a few observations to offer. Under the conditions obtaining just before the World War, the economic outlook for the Karen cultivator was none too good. The Karen people are no more provident than the Burmese. At the beginning of the season they borrow money, for which they must pay one hundred baskets of paddy for fifty rupees of money.[7] If they have no oxen of buffaloes of their own they must hire them, paying from fifty to sixty rupees a yoke for the former and ten rupees additional each for the latter. To hire a man to work in the rainy season and to plow costs about the same as paying for the use of a team of oxen. If he is employed until the threshing is finished, he costs another fifty rupees. The yield per acre varies all the way from twenty-five to seventy baskets, according to the quality of the land and whether a little manure has been used or not. For many years the price of paddy remained close to one hundred rupees for one hundred baskets, being sometimes a little below and at others a few rupees above that price. Before the war competition and speculation had forced the price up gradually, until it reached a maximum of one hundred and thirty-five rupees.

---

[7] The size of baskets varies in different districts, ranging in capacity from forty to sixty pounds. Those having a capacity of forty-six pounds are now considered to be of standard size. As the price varies inversely with the size, the result is about the same.

No one can presume to predict the outcome of the present unsettled conditions. We can only hope that better days are in store for the cultivators, whether Burman or Karen.

If, before the war, a man owned his field and cattle without encumberance or other debts, he could till some twenty acres and make a comfortable living for himself and family. If, however, he was under the necessity of borrowing money and hiring men and cattle, he could hardly keep his head above water.

There are some Karens who own large fields. They may have acquired them by careful management, by purchase, or by foreclosing loans. Many of these proprietors make a business of hiring out their fields to men who cultivate them at a rental of from ten to fifteen baskets of paddy per acre, the cultivator supplying his own materials and help. In case the owner has oxen, he rents them at the usual price. In addition, he usually makes a loan of cash to his tenant, on which he gets a big return, namely, a hundred baskets of paddy for the sum of fifty rupees for six months. If the tenant borrows from a money-lender, he has to pay anywhere from fifteen to fifty percent a year for it.

On the plains the cultivator is almost entirely dependent on his single crop of paddy. If high water has washed out his first settings, there is not time enough left to raise other produce after the water has disappeared. Under these circumstances they sometimes plant sesame, but it requires only a little less time to mature than paddy. The lack of water in the dry season renders cultivation impossible without extensive irrigation.

Along the river-bottoms may be found a few plantain groves, patches of tobacco, sugar-cane, or vegetables; but these are unusual sights. They may add a little to the cultivator's income. But very few persons derive their chief support from such gardens.

The Karen on the plains do not observe the old religious customs of the hill people. Many times they resort to Burmese soothsayers to prognosticate the proper times for planting, reaping, and other tasks. Not a few, however, follow the old ceremonies in greater or less part. A ceremonial similar to "theh a hkü" in the hills [8] is observed on the plains where it is designated "mo a si." It is performed when the paddy is set out. Offerings are seldom seen along the paths in this region, but when the paddy has been winnowed an offering is made to "Hpi Bi Yaw" by transferring the rim of earth around a crab's burrow to the summit of the pile of

---
[8] See *ante*, pp. 78, 79.

SGAW KAREN WOMEN CARRYING GRAIN IN LARGE BASKETS
Tharrawaddy Hills

KAREN HOUSES ON THE PLAINS

paddy. A few paddy heads or even a few leaves of the ginger plant may be inserted in the burrow as a talisman to make the supply of paddy last the year out. The oblation on the threshing-floor or a similar one is then put on top of the paddy in the bin.

The Karen who is untouched by outside influence does not like to take up any other occupation than that of raising paddy. He regards his other pursuits as occasional and accessory, including the gathering of forest products, such as stick-lac and wild honey and the sale of fruit from the few mango trees he may possess. He has not been found satisfactory as a day-laborer or coolie for any continued work; he avoids hiring out as a cartman and does not succeed as a petty trader. In more extensive business he has achieved success in only a few instances. With the advantages of education, however, a few have prospered in commercial life and other callings. Many have entered Government service and risen to positions of trust. A large percentage of those who have passed through the schools are clerks and teachers. One of the largest department stores in Rangoon employs Karen clerks with satisfaction, besides Europeans. Educated Karen girls take employment as teachers and nurse-maids, and recently a few have been engaging in clerical work.

TURNING THE BUFFALOES OUT TO GRAZE
These heavy animals are easily managed by Karen children, but are easily frightened by the presence of strangers.

## CHAPTER XI

## HUNTING AND FISHING

There is nothing in which a Karen delights so much as to hunt, unless it be the gastronomic pleasures that follow a successful chase. Schoolboys spend their Saturdays in the jungle with their slingshots and blowpipes. Teachers and clerks spend their holidays in the same way. The villager may go by himself to stalk deer or shoot birds and other game along the runways; but the sport that he enjoys most is the drive for game, which is abundant in the hills of Burma, participated in by all the men of the village armed with their weapons and nets. A promising place is chosen, such as the open end of a ravine, where some of the hunters stretch and make fast their nets and retire into an ambush near at hand. The others of the party go to the far end of the area included in the drive and begin to beat the bushes with their spears and knives, while shouting and making a great noise generally. The game is thus driven from cover to the nets, where it usually gets entangled and is soon dispatched by the spears and crossbows of the men waiting there. Nearly all kinds of game are caught in this manner, from rabbits to tigers and elephants. Pigs and deer are, however, most commonly hunted in this way. This is men's sport, and the women never take part in it, so far as I know. The game is divided among the hunters, each sharing more or less equally. If any parts of a carcass are supposed to possess medicinal value, they are appropriated by the one who killed the animal and distributed by him as he thinks best.

Besides the ordinary weapons used in warfare and described in the chapter dealing with that subject, the Karen employ in the chase the blow-gun, the crossbow, the bow, and the spear. The blow-gun is similar to that used in Malaysia, Borneo, and the Philippine Islands, but is not decorated as are those of the Malay tribes. The implement consists of a ten or twelve-foot length of a slim variety of bamboo, the tube or bore of which is the size of a small pencil. The length is first straightened by being hung from a tree with a weight of stones or logs to the bottom end. The transverse membranes at the joints are then drilled out with a sharp stick of hard wood, and small arrows are shaped and smoothed to fit accurately the bore of the blow-gun, the rear end of each arrow being tufted with a circle of feathers. A quick expulsion of the breath against one of these missiles inserted in the long tube drives it with sufficient force to kill small birds and game at a distance of a few yards. To use the implement effectively one must be able to stalk the game noiselessly and to bring the weapon to bear on it unawares. This gun may have been copied from Burman guns, for I do not find it in the hills.[1] The Karen hunters do not seem to be as skilful in its use as are the tribesmen of the Philippines, Borneo, and the Malay States.

The crossbow ("hkli") is one of the favorite implements for hunting among the Karen, but never seems to have found favor with them as a fighting weapon.[2]

The stock is made of some firm wood and has a small handle, like that of a cheek-gun.[3] Its entire length is not more than three feet. The bow is shaped out of cutch wood ("nya"), which is very tough and resilient. It varies in length, but is usually about four feet. The string is twisted fibre, generally that of the roselle plant *(Hibiscus sabdariffa)*. The bow is so strong that sometimes it takes two men to bend it, the string being held back by a rough trigger. The arrows consist of straight pieces of bamboo sharpened and slightly charred in the fire at one end to harden them, while they are tufted with feathers or fitted with a slip of dry palm or plantain leaf at the other end, which is bound around with string. Sometimes the arrow tips are barbed or supplied with flat iron points, and sometimes they are smeared with a thick gum taken from the Upas tree *(Antiaris ovalfloria)*, which is indigenous to Burma. This species of tree is similar to that from which the Malay and Borneo tribes obtain poison for their arrows. The milky juice exudes from incisions made in the bark of the tree and drys into a dark viscous gum, which is very bitter. This poison is supposed to be more virulent if gathered at certain times of the year. After being smeared with the poisonous substance, the arrow-tip is al-

---

[1] For a discussion of the blow-gun, see Skeat and Blagden, *Pagan Races of the Malay Peninsula*, Vol. I, 254-257.

[2] The crossbow is found all over Yunnan among the Lisu and the Lolo. It is used in China, having been evidently adopted from the Lolo, as its name there indicates. It is not seen in Tibet, or is it used by the Burmese or by the Malay tribes, except as a toy by the children in Borneo: Hose and MacDougall, *The Pagan Races of Borneo*, Vol. I, 46. The crossbow does not seem to be found in the Philippine Islands.

[3] See p. 158.

lowed to dry for a short time; but if kept too long it loses its noxious quality.

The crossbow will send an arrow thirty or forty yards with considerable accuracy. Those skilled in the use of the weapon can shoot to a greater range. The arrow will pierce the body of a man or a tiger and sometimes protrude on the other side. When wounded by a poisoned dart the Bwe may bind up the wound with the juice from young bamboo shoots, but he immediately tries to obtain what he considers a good antidote, namely, the hog-plum (*Spondius mangifera*), which he eats either dry or green. Failing to find this remedy, he resorts to alum. The Paku tribesmen eat a little of the poisonous gum itself, thus producing vomiting, which seems to counteract the effect of the poison in the wound. They sometimes apply alum to the injured part and bind it up. The Burmese, who greatly fear the consequences of being infected with the poison, poultice the wound with white sweet potato, which they chew into a paste for the purpose.[4]

The Karen have a kind of bow that resembles in general the long bow used in the English Army back in the fourteenth century. It is called "hki p' ti" and is fashioned of bamboo with elastic ends, being fitted with two parallel strings held an inch apart by little struts of bamboo. A tiny mat is plaited between the strings at the center to hold the pebbles or mud balls that are used instead of arrows. A block of hard wood, some four inches long and an inch and a half wide, is lashed to the middle of the bow. This serves as a handle by which a twisting motion is imparted to the bow when it is sprung, thus enabling the ball or pebble to pass to one side of the bow-shaft. This weapon is much used by children in shooting birds and small animals.

The trap is one of several automatic contrivances which the Karen fashion and leave in places frequented by birds or animals for their capture. Besides the spring trap, there are the box trap and the pitfall. As the name of the last contrivance suggests, the pitfall is a large hole that has been dug deep enough to prevent an animal from jumping out, once it has fallen in. All traces of the digging are obliterated, and the top is covered with branches and

---

[4] *Cf.* Mason, *British Burma*, 489. For an account of the poison made in Borneo from the Ipoh (*Antiaris toxicaria*) see Hose and MacDougall, *Pagan Tribes of Borneo*, Vol. I, 218. Skeat and Blagdon, in *Pagan Tribes of the Malay Peninsula*, Vol. I, Chap. VI, pp. 242, ff., give an account of the preparation of poisons employed by the various tribes of that country. But a map of the area in which the poisons are used does not include Burma, probably because their use among the Karen was unknown to the writers.

twigs and then disguised with leaves. The unsuspecting animal, going in search of water, steps on the insecure footing and falls through. As its efforts to escape are unavailing, it is soon found and dispatched by the spears and arrows of the hunters.

The box trap is a rude box-like structure varying in size from those built to catch rats to one, which I saw, designed to put an end to the prowlings of a tiger. They are laid up like a miniature log cabin, with an opening either at one end or on top. A dog or some other live bait is tied inside of the larger traps, and when the wild animal jumps in to seize the decoy, he must needs touch the string attached to the trigger that supports a trap-door weighted with stones or logs. The door is thus released, falls, and closes the opening. Oftener the door of such a trap is made from a tree with thorny bark, and the game only wounds itself by struggling to get out. There is usually little chance to escape for an animal caught in one of these traps.[5] (See lower illustration on page 100.)

The spring trap, commonly called in Karen "wa hkaw,"[6] is built across an opening in a game-run or in a fence around a paddy-field. It is fitted with a single spear. The name "meu" is applied to a larger trap of this kind, which has a row of bamboo spears. A description of the former will suffice to show the plan and operation of the trap, which, we will assume, is built across a game-run. At some spot in the jungle, where the runway can be narrowed to a mere opening by driving a few bamboos into the ground on either side, the spring trap is set up. It consists of a bamboo spear some five feet long projecting horizontally through a hole in a bamboo post, its point but a few inches from the opening through which the animal must pass. The shaft of the spear reaches back several feet to the end of a stiff bamboo pole, also in horizontal position and nearly at right angles to the spear. The function of this pole, which is rigidly fastened to a tree or heavy post at its butt end, is to thrust the spear forward at the right moment. The free end of the pole moves along a horizontal rack or bar and, when pulled back, is held by a catch. A stout string fastened to this catch is stretched across the opening in such a way that the animal

---

[5] The similarity of these traps to those of Malaysia and Borneo is striking: see Hose and MacDougall, *The Pagan Tribes of Borneo*, Vol. I, 145, ff; Skeat and Blagdon, *Pagan Races of the Malay Peninsula*, Vol. I, 206, ff.

[6] The name "wa hkaw" is taken from the spear that forms an essential feature of this kind of trap. The head of the spear is of bamboo, being cut from the side of a large piece. The hard silicious skin of the bamboo is left on to form the cutting edges of the spear. The Karen have different names for different sizes of these traps, which are set for smaller or larger game from wildcats to tigers.

SETTING A SPRING TRAP ("WA HKAW"), PEGU HILLS
This trap was set to catch a barking-deer.

A BOX TRAP FOR CATCHING BIRDS
The watcher hides in the pile of straw seen at the right and pulls the string to drop the lid. One hundred and seventy-six parroquets were caught at one drop in this trap. A trough used for beating out grain stands nearby.

emerging will run into the string, lift the catch, and thereby receive the thrust of the spear in its body. (See page 100.)

Small animals, such as squirrels and rats, are killed by means of a heavy pole, one end of which is propped up from the ground just inside a tight fence enclosing or partly enclosing a field. Lengths of large bamboo lead the rodents through holes in the fence, and as they emerge on the inside they have to push by a string which releases the little prop under the log. Such traps are called "tu."

A small trap for catching rats consists of a joint of large bamboo fitted with a trigger like that on English steel traps, the trigger being connected with a bow of bamboo that fits over the open end of the section. The bow is opened, bait is placed inside, and the trigger is set. The rat enters, touches the food, the bow springs down over the open end, and he is imprisoned inside.

Birds are caught in a box trap similar to the one described on page 99, but of lighter construction and larger dimensions. In the specimen shown in the illustration (page 100) one hundred and twenty-seven pigeons were taken at one fall, I was told. It was set near the paddy threshing-mat, and a line of grain led the birds into it. The man who was watching the trap lay concealed in a pile of straw a few yards away and, when he saw the box well filled, pulled the string attached to the support upon which the end of the cover rested. The captured pigeons were killed by spear-thrusts through the cracks of their cage.

Pigeons are also taken by means of bamboo cages divided into two compartments. A young bird, caught before it can fly, is placed in one of the compartments as a decoy; and the cage, covered with green leaves, is hung near a tree in fruit to which the birds resort for food, or it is set near a field that is known to be a favorite feeding-ground of the pigeons. The calls of the decoy attract usually an aggressive male into the open compartment, the trigger snaps, and the door flies shut. Birdlime, made from the sap of certain varieties of the banyan, is smeared on twigs to catch small birds.

Besides birdlime, cages, and box traps, various kinds of snares are utilized in capturing birds. A noose, made of tough fibre or hair, is hung over a path in the thick grass just high enough to catch the head of a pheasant or jungle-fowl as it walks along. Sometimes a series of standing snares or loops are used. A chain of twenty or thirty bamboo splints, each fitted with its own slip-noose, is staked on the ground by means of a spike of horn or bamboo attached to one end of the chain. The nooses form a succession of wickets encircling perhaps a clump of grass or an open space in the jungle. Two or three such chains may be connected to describe a larger circle. In either case the circle is left open in the direction from which the birds are expected to approach. Grain may be scattered along the path and into the circle, or a decoy cock may be tethered there. If a decoy is not used, a boy hides near at hand until the birds are within the ring and then starts them to running by coming into the open. Otherwise, they wander and pick about until startled by the decoy or something else. In trying to scurry away at least some of the flock thrust their heads through the open loops and pull them tighter and tighter by their struggles to escape. It only remains for the hunter to come and carry off his catches.

In the Toungoo Hills the Karen hunt with dogs, which they know under the name of "htwi maw seh" and train for use in the chase. These dogs are small, smooth-haired, and allied to the terrier, and follow game with great tenacity. They are highly valued by the Karen, the price of a good one equaling that of an ordinary pony or buffalo. Deer are said to be so afraid of them that they lose strength when pursued by one of these curs and thus become an easy prey for the hunter. While in pursuit the dogs yelp continually. The hunter has only to follow them to be sure of his game in the end. They do not hesitate to trail a species of large snake, which is considered palatable eating by the Karen, but will not attack it. They will pull down a deer and set upon a bear or boar, but stand in fear of tigers and leopards. Indeed, they turn back from the track of a tiger, if they come upon it.

Elephant hunting, to which the Karen were much given in the old days, has been revived to a considerable extent in recent years among the Karen of Tavoy and the Tenasserim division. Their practice is to build a large V-shaped stockade and drive the animals into it. At the apex of the stockade they erect a high-fenced enclosure into which tame elephants are sent to mingle with the wild ones. Hunting elephants merely as game is no longer allowed by the Government; but when that practice was tolerated, beaters drove the animals along an elephant-run, while hunters, who were adepts at spear-throwing, stood in wait behind trees and speared

## HUNTING AND FISHING

A LARGE FISH-TRAP

This trap is used by Burmese and Karen in large streams. The bait is fastened to a string which, when pulled, drops the door. A smaller "beu" or Karen trap is seen at the right.

CLIMBING THE TODDY-PALM

The trees that are tapped have a bamboo ladder attached, so that the climber can more easily obtain the sap for making liquor.

the great creatures as they rushed past. The effort of the spearmen was either to thrust the elephants through the heart or to hamstring and disable them with their long knives, in order that they might be put to death later.

The Karen hunts primarily in order to obtain food, although he certainly enjoys the excitement of the chase as well. But he is not a sportsman, in the proper sense of that term. He does not discriminate in his slaughter of wild creatures. He does not look far enough ahead to appreciate the necessity of sparing the females among the game animals, even those that are with young. He is apt in imitating the calls of many animals and birds. Almost every Karen can entice the barking-deer within short range by imitating the cry of its fawn. He does this by putting a green leaf between his lips and blowing through it. The sound thus emitted often brings the doe bounding through the jungle, only to be shot down.

## Fishing

The rivers and smaller streams of Burma are full of fish of many kinds and sizes. The Karen is fond of fish for his daily fare, and on the plains the fermented fish-paste of wide repute is a part of his regular diet. Fishing is not confined to the men. Indeed, I have sometimes thought that the women do more of it than the men; but this, if true, is explicable by the fact that many times, while their men folk are at work, the women go to catch a supply for the next meal.

The Karen on the plains use much the same methods in fishing as the Burmese, which they have probably copied from the latter. In this chapter, however, I shall confine myself to an account of the practices that have come under my observation along the hill streams. Nets, large and small, baskets, traps, jars, weirs, the hook and line, and spears are the more common kinds of implements employed by the highland folk in obtaining their aquatic food.

In shallow water many fish are taken by means of the "thwe," which is an oval hoop a foot or more in its longest diameter, on which a net of cotton strands is woven. The fisherman wades through the water with his net in hand, plunges it down over the fish within his reach, and scoops it up and out toward him. In the shallow water of submerged fields what may be called a push-net of closely woven material ("hti hsaw") is used in catching minnows. It has two handles that cross and form the sides of the spreading scoop, and is pushed ahead by the one handling it. A longer scoop of similar construction is called a "paw," a name probably derived from the Burmese designation, "pauk."

The "pu" is a basket shaped like an Egyptian vase and has a hole near the bottom fitted with a trap-door. It is baited and set in the water. (See page 103.) The fish entering this contrivance are prevented from getting out not only by the trap-door, but also by

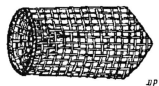

CYLINDRICAL FISH-TRAPS

a circle of sharp points converging inwards around the door. There are many forms of basket and cage traps, all built on the principle of the lobster-pot or "pu" just described, either with trap-doors or inward converging bamboo splints through which the fish enter to nibble at the tempting bait. Considerable ingenuity is shown in the construction of some of the basket traps. One type has the shape

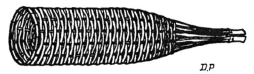

BOTTLE-SHAPED FISH-TRAP

of a long-necked wine bottle, but considerably larger. A trap of this shape is made from a joint of bamboo, which is about two inches in diameter. At one end the joint is split into six or eight segments about two-thirds of its length. These are spread far enough open to form the body of the "bottle," being kept in that shape by the interlacing of transverse strips in circles that get smaller toward the neck of the trap. The bottom or open end of this bottle-shaped basket consists of bamboo strips that converge inwards, and as the basket is staked down on its side in a narrow and shallow place in the stream, the fish gain their entrance through the elastic funnel provided for them. The fisherman extracts his catch by spreading open the segments forming the neck of the basket. Another type of the basket trap is cylindrical in shape, three and a half or four feet long, and some four inches in diameter. It, too, has the inward-converging strips of bamboo at one end. Once inside the long and narrow tube, the fish is unable to turn around or, indeed, to do anything except move forward to the front end of the cage in which it finds itself. Sometimes a jar is set low in the shallow narrows of a stream through which the fish are running and, in jumping for the deeper water above or because the watching fisherman purposely frightens them, they fall into the jar ("t' leu"), from the narrow mouth of which they are unable to leap to freedom.

Jars, basket and cage traps, scoops, and small hand-nets are familiar to the Karen fishermen, as we have seen. The hook and line are also in common use, for fish-hooks are a commodity readily obtainable in the bazaars, and earthworms are to be had for the digging. Men and women, to say nothing of children, are, therefore, much given to angling and always seem able to draw fish from any little pool that may be near. Eels are much prized, and double-pointed iron spears afford the readiest means of their capture. On occasion nowadays the rods of an old umbrella are turned into these implements. Seins have been used extensively among the Burmese and by the Karen on the plains, but not much in the hills.

The large catches resulting from seining are obtained by more primitive methods among the Karen. For example, a number of men, provided with baskets ("hsaw") wide and open at the bottom, form a line across a shallow stream and work the bottom foot by foot up the course. The fish either move ahead of the line of advance, or are caught in the baskets. In the latter case the fishermen remove their catches by hand through the round opening in the top of each basket. Sometimes nearly the whole population of a village, old and young, male and female, take part in a fishing expedition in the dry season. As the stream is low, it is barely more than a succession of pools connected by tiny rivulets. Accordingly, they build a dam and throw into the water above it sheaves of a poisonous plant, which they call "xaw hter." This benumbs the fish, without rendering them inedible or impregnating the water to the detriment of the waders. Various members of the crowd, especially the boys and little girls who strip for the purpose, busy themselves in stirring up the water and mud to bring the fish to the surface, where some are already floating apparently lifeless. The older people occupy themselves with hand-nets, scoops, etc., in dipping out their helpless victims. As the water in these mountain streams is often cold and the villagers soon become dripping wet, a fire is built on shore by which they may dry and warm themselves. Many of the persons in the water wear at the waist a small-necked basket in which to drop the fish picked up or, lacking this convenience, toss them to their neighbors, who collect them into ordinary baskets on the bank. When the place has been thoroughly "combed," the supply is distributed among the villagers, every family getting its share.

I have been informed that there are several kinds of plants that may be used to poison fish; but as certain ones are dangerous to man and beast, the people in the Pegu Hills prefer the "xaw hter." Surely, this method of taking quantities of fish by means of poison would not commend itself to the sportsman and is comparable to the dynamiting of fish, a thing that has been done in rare instances in parts of the United States, although it is not countenanced by public opinion or the law.

When the fish are beginning to spawn in the creeks, bunches of straw are sunk in the creek pools for their spawning beds. Later the young fish are taken from their hiding-places in the straw, or the bunches are carefully removed from the water and shaken over a cloth spread on the bank.

On the plains when the streams are overflowing the fields and the fish are running up to spawn, the people build weirs of rushes across the shallows of the water courses and insert long trumpet-shaped tubes ("hk'ya") of basket-work in them at intervals. These tubes are perhaps three feet long and only a few inches in diameter, the broad end being pointed down-stream and left open, while the small end is plugged with grass or twigs. The fish seek to pass beyond the obstructing weirs through these tubes, only to find themselves unable either to back out or turn around. The plains people make their fishing expeditions to shallow lakes or, better, to pools left standing after the subsidence of the rains, or to the creeks that traverse the alluvial soil of Lower Burma. In part they use nets like those in vogue among their brethren of the hills, but they also have a cast-net of circular form and a square dip-net. The former is about five yards in diameter, with weighted edges that sink on all sides, thus covering and enclosing the fish nearer the center, where the rope is attached by which it is slowly drawn out.

CHAPTER XII

SPINNING, DYEING, AND WEAVING. MAT-MAKING AND BASKETRY

I. SPINNING

In the chapter on agriculture (Chapter VIII) I have already referred to the fact that the cotton plants are tended by the women, who also pick the bolls, pack them in their deep baskets, and carry them home on their backs. The seeds are removed by a machine like a small mangle or clothes-wringer, with two closely fitting rollers of hard wood. The fibers pass through between the rollers, leaving the seeds behind divested of every filament. This Karen cotton-gin is like that of the Burmese, the people of Borneo, and the Filipinos.[1] (See upper illustration, p. 109.)

After ginning the next process is whipping the fibers into a workable mass, much like cotton batting. This is done with a bow whose handle is straight and heavy, while the thin tip is bent in a sharp curve when the bow-string is drawn tight. The women and girls engaged in whipping the cotton, which corresponds to carding in a cotton-mill, move the bow with the left hand in small circles just above the cotton and keep snapping the string with the right thumb, which is protected by a cloth wrapping, until a layer of fibers encircles the string in a more or less parallel and compact order. When the space between the string and the belly of the bow has become filled, the aggregation of fibers is removed and flattened out on a mat. The twanging of a room full of oscillating bows sounds like a battery of unmuffled motors, at the same time filling the air with flying bits of cotton as though one were in a snow-storm. (See lower illustration, p. 109.)

The layers of cotton-fibers are next divided into narrow strips, and rolled on the mat or the thigh into small rolls of about a cubit's length and of the thickness of one's thumb. From these rolls the yarn is spun by means of the spinning-wheel, which is like those

---

[1] See Hose and MacDougall's *The Pagan Tribes of Borneo*, Vol. I, 221, for description of the processes of cotton-ginning in the region of which they treat. The methods they describe are remarkably like those used by the Karen.

## SPINNING, DYEING, AND WEAVING

GINNING COTTON IN THE PEGU HILLS

BATTING COTTON INTO SMOOTH LAYERS WITH A BOW
This Burman woman, who lives in the village of Ngape Eh, was more ready to pose for this photo than her Karen sisters.

found all over Burma. This contrivance is of the simplest form, consisting of a driving-wheel about two feet in diameter with spokes and rim of bamboo, the axle of which is fitted in an ornamental flat post rising from one corner of a thick bottom board, which is three and a half feet long and a foot or more wide. Near the middle of the other end of this board a shorter post rises, to the base of which is affixed a little wheel, with a grooved rim, in line with the driving-wheel, the two wheels being connected by a slender belt. There is a handle on the large wheel and a horizontal iron spindle fastened in the center of the little one. The spinner sits on the floor, with her machine drawn up to her knees in front of her, the driving-wheel at her left hand and the point of the spindle at her right. She attaches some fibers of a roll to a spun thread tied to the spindle, and sets this to rotating rapidly by turning the large wheel with her left hand, meantime continuing to pay out the fibers from the roll with her right hand. After the spindle has twisted the loose filaments into a tight yarn, the spinner feeds the newly spun yarn on to the spindle and repeats the process with another roll of fibers, until the spindle is full.

## II. Dyeing and Weaving

The next stage in the work is that of dyeing. The colors imparted to the skeins of cotton yarn are shades of blue to black, red, and yellow. In producing the blue shades the skeins are soaked in a solution of the bark or leaves of the wild indigo plant, called "naw xaw" in Karen, the depth of the color depending on the duration and repetition of the soaking, until a blue black has been obtained. The red dyes are derived from the stick-lac so commonly found in the Toungoo Hills. During the years just preceding the World War a good deal of foreign dyestuff was introduced among the Karen people, and yellow came to be used in addition to the other colors.[2]

The weaving of the yarn into cloth comes next in order. The threads that are to form the warp of the cloth must first be got ready for the hand-loom ("hta"). This is done by unwinding the skeins and stringing the thread around a few pegs driven into a leveled and cleaned space of ground, until enough has been laid down to fill the loom. If there is no convenient place out-of-doors for this purpose, the long threads are strung on pegs around the

---

[2] For an account of dyes and methods of dyeing in Burma, see *The Upper Burma Gazetteer*, Vol. II, Pt. I, 337-399.

family living-room or along one side of the corridor of the village-house. The Karen loom is a primitive affair much like those to be seen among the hill tribes in Burma, the Kachin, for example, or to be found in Malaysia and the adjacent regions. The Karen loom has no frame, differing in this respect from the Burmese loom. It consists of little more than a bamboo pole five and a half or six feet long, over which the warp-threads are passed, this pole being held in place four feet or so above the floor against the back partition of a living-room, two of whose large bamboo uprights have holes in them for inserting the pole. From this support the warp extends at an incline some ten or twelve feet to the lap of the weaver, who holds it taut by means of a strap around her waist, while she sits flat on the floor with her feet braced against a section of large bamboo. The threads of the two layers are kept in place by being passed through heddles consisting of small loops attached to bamboo bars, alternate threads being thus strung on one or the other of one or more pairs of bars. On a shuttle of bamboo the filling or woof-thread is wound. It is passed by hand from side to side between the separated layers of the warp, is pulled taut, and then forced tight against the last of the interwoven threads by a piece of Burmese ebony wood, shaped like the enlarged blade of a pocket-knife. As the work progresses, the finished cloth is rolled away on the rod in the weaver's lap, only a yard or two being the product of an ordinary day's work. On the plains the younger generation of Karen women use the Burmese loom and can accomplish more with it. (See illustrations, pp. 112, 114.)

Variations in color are obtained by introducing different colors of thread. When a colored pattern is woven for a skirt or the border of a blanket, this process is called "u," meaning primarily "inserting the fingers" in reference to picking up certain threads under which the filling threads must be passed in order to produce the desired pattern.

After its removal from the loom the cloth is plunged into water and spread out to dry. Knots are tucked in and straggling ends removed, but no other finishing is thought necessary. Such cloth is very firm and almost indestructible. The width of a strip as it comes from the loom is from eighteen to twenty inches. Between three and four yards are required for a skirt. This length is cut in half. By sewing the two resulting pieces together side by side the proper dimensions for a skirt are secured. The ends of this

A KAREN GIRL AT A BURMESE LOOM
This loom, which has a frame and is more easily operated than the Karen loom, is in common use among the Karen women on the plains.

THE KAREN LOOM
This loom is simplicity itself. The airy construction of the Karen family-room is shown in this picture.

larger strip, which is nearly two yards long and about forty inches wide, are sewed together, and the skirt is finished. The cloth for a man's garment is cut and sewed in much the same way.

### III. MAT-MAKING AND BASKETRY

The making of mats and baskets is almost wholly confined to men, who prepare the materials out of rattan and bamboo and spend their leisure hours weaving them. Common mats ("klau"), such as are used as floor coverings in their houses and to sleep on, and the large ones that serve as winnowing and threshing-floors in the hills,[3] are woven of bamboo strips about half an inch wide in checker-board pattern. The strips do not run parallel with the edges of the mat, but diagonally at an angle of forty-five degrees. The better and stronger mats are made of strips with the silicious outer surface intact, giving them a smooth and glossy appearance. The softer rush mats of Burmese manufacture are often found in Karen houses, but are not made by any of the occupants, except such as have learned the art from their neighbors.

The people distinguish between several different kinds of baskets, for which they have particular names and special uses. The large baskets ("kü") for carrying paddy and other produce from the fields to their houses are shaped like an elongated egg with a truncated smaller end and are slung on the back with a bark-fiber strap which passes over the forehead and attaches to loops on either side a little above the middle of the basket. When thus carried, the receptacle reaches below the waist and a third of its own length above the shoulders. If the bearer is heavily laden, he or she partly relieves the weight on the strap by hooks of horn or bamboo root, hung from the shoulders and supporting the bottom of the basket. These large receptacles are woven in diagonal pattern with small strands of rattan, those of the upper half being less than a quarter of an inch in width while those of the lower half are a little wider. The bottom of such baskets are square and flat, and its edges are bound with round rattans. From the corners rattan stays are run vertically to the large oval mouth of the basket, which is finished off with a large rattan around the edge. A midrib down each side from top to bottom adds strength and durability.

Cotton and vegetables are carried in loosely woven and large-meshed baskets, called "seh," meaning rough or flimsy. A man will

---
[3] See *ante*, p. 82.

cut a green bamboo, divide it into strips, and weave one of these in a few minutes, and then discard it after he has reached home.

Inasmuch as the people of the Toungoo country have higher hills to climb and longer distances to travel than those dwelling lower down in the Pegu ranges, they carry their produce in smaller baskets than do the latter. These Toungoo baskets have the shape of an inverted pyramid with the apex blunted. Sometimes they are woven of rattan and nicely finished, sometimes loosely made of bamboo splints. In the houses of the Toungoo Hills I have seen enormous spreading baskets for the storage of grain and other things.

The hill people make small, closely woven receptacles for carrying ordinary articles and also for keeping things dry during the rainy season. They render these baskets water-tight by coating them with gum and afterwards with "thitse" (Burmese lacquer). Probably the Karen have copied this type of basket from the Burmese or the Shan, who make extensive use of them. On the plains the small round basket, holding about three pecks, is in constant service. It is Burmese in origin, as is one of its names, "taw" (from the Burmese word, "taung"). Its other name is "na."

A KAREN MATRON WEAVING UNDER HER HOUSE

## CHAPTER XIII

## BRONZE DRUMS

Early travelers noticed the presence of large bronze drums in the Karen houses in Karenni and in the Toungoo Hills; but it is only recently that these drums have been made the subject of careful study. In the latter part of the nineteenth century Europeans first began to examine similar objects that were brought from China. It has been discovered that these objects are scattered through a vast area extending from Mongolia on the north to the Celebes Islands on the south, but that their place of origin was probably in the old Cambodian kingdom of the Indo-Chinese peninsula. Four or five classes of such drums are distinguished, of which the Karen drums form one group.[1]

The Karen drums are characterized by a nearly straight cylinder or body, which has a slightly narrowed waist. The cylinder is encircled by bands of conventionalized designs between sets of straight lines forming the borders of the bands. In some cases there is a line of molded figures of elephants and snails down one side of the cylinder. The flat circular metal head extends a little beyond the body, forming a rim. In the center of the head is a large star enclosed by concentric circles between which are narrower or wider zones filled with figures of different patterns. Distributed at equal intervals around the outer edge of the head are four or six frogs in relief. Sometimes these frogs are in sets of two, one on top of the other; sometimes in sets of three, superimposed one upon another. The two pairs of small handles are situated on opposite sides of the body of the drum well toward the top, and present the appearance of neatly braided straps. These bronze drums vary in size from about eighteen inches across the head to about thirty inches.

---

[1] In addition to the authorities mentioned at the foot of page 9, Chapter II, the article by W. Foy, entitled "Über Alte Bronzetrommeln aus Sudost Asien" in the *Mitteilungen der Anthropologischen Gesellschaft in Wein*, Vol. XXXIII, (1903) is a valuable contribution to the general subject of bronze drums. Herr Foy, however, differs somewhat in classification from Franz Heger, who is followed by M. Parmentier. Origin, shape, and ornamentation form the basis for the differentiation into classes. Heger puts the Karen drums in Type III, while Foy distinguishes them as Type V.

Concerning their origin much that is legendary has been written. In the *Karen Thesaurus* we are told in substance that these drums ("klo oh tra oh") are very expensive and are owned in Lower Burma by a few very wealthy persons, who make offerings of food and liquor to them annually, fearing an early death if they fail to do this. The drums are said by some to have been brought from the "K' wa" country and by others from the "Swa" tribe.[2] Those who went to buy these objects paid according to the number of frogs on them, the price of one with two frogs being twenty rupees. The buyer put down the price and took away the drum, after which the owner came and got his money. If the buyer did not leave the money, he risked losing his way and being overtaken and eaten by the owner. The drums are used in making a noise like that of a gong.[3]

Dr. Francis Mason, writing at Toungoo in 1868, speaks of these drums under the name of "kyee-zees," and is better informed than the writer in the *Thesaurus* in saying that they are obtained from the Shan. He also states that the Karen distinguish ten different kinds of drums according to sound and have a different name for each kind. Dr. Mason tells us that the best-sounding drums are worth a thousand rupees apiece, while the poorest bring only one hundred each. Dr. Mason continues: "The possession of Kyee-zees is what constitutes a rich Karen. No one is considered rich without one, whatever may be his other possessions. Everyone who has money endeavors to turn it into Kyee-zees, and a village that has many of them is the envy of the other villages and it is often the cause of wars to obtain possession of them."[4]

Some of the Karens have told me that in the beginning these drums were obtained from the "Yu" people, who seem to have been the Jung or Yung who occupied Yunnan in ancient times.[5] Indeed, various indications point to the probability that the drums existed or were in use in Yunnan when the ancestors of the Karen passed through there from their home in western China into Burma,

---

[2] The Swa are mentioned in some of the old Karen tales and appear to have been wild cannibals, of whom but little was known. Their location seems uncertain. Some of the tales place them beyond the great waters, while others suggest that they live to the north. Probably the references are to the Waer, who are one of the head-hunting tribes still living in the northern Shan States, on the Chinese frontier.

[3] *The Karen Thesaurus*, 1847, Vol. I, pp. 327, ff.

[4] *Journal, Asiatic Society of Bengal*, 1868, Vol. XXXVII, Pt. II, pp. 128, ff.

[5] Mr. Taw Sein Ko, in *Annual Archaeological Report*, Burma, 1917, pp. 22, 23. Mr. Po Lin Te writes in the *Rangoon Gazette*, Sept. 27, 1919, that the Yu were the oldest of five families who emigrated from the Sandy River and were, therefore, entitled to use the drums.

where they settled.⁶ This is the view of the origin of the drums held by Heger and others.

Certain Karen traditions associate the drums with "Pü Maw Taw," one of the mythical characters of ancient times. This man was at work in his field and, seeing a flock of monkeys emerge from the forest, feigned death. Thereupon, the monkeys sent several of their number back to bring their drums for the proper performance of the funeral rites. Of the three brought, one was silver, one, gold, and the third, white in appearance. The last one fell into a pool of water and was lost. "Pü Maw Taw" suddenly interrupted the funeral ceremonies and the monkeys ran away, leaving the other two drums in the field. The old man took them home and they at once became the most sacred possession of the people, being consecrated every year with very great ceremony, until at last the Pwo Karen grew tired of making their annual journey for this purpose and carried them off. They were named "Gaw Kwa Htu" and "Gaw Kwa Se" ⁷ and are still believed to have been deposited in a cave near Donyan in Thaton district. Each drum had two sticks and a striker, all made of bronze. The smaller stick, which produced a rolling sound, was in the form of a centipede. The striker had a quilted surface, in appearance like the scales of a cobra. Unfortunately these drum implements had been left behind with the Sgaw, of Loo Thaw Ko village in the Papun district. Almost every year the Sgaw came down and demanded that the drums be given back to them, but without success. Gaw Le Bay and Gaw Ser Paw were the two Pwo Karens who committed the sacrilege of stealing away the drums, being punished for it with sore eyes, from which their descendants in Donyin suffer even unto this day.

All the elders believe that the bronze drums connect the Karen people with a remote past. But few of these objects that are still in existence can be traced back more than a century or two. Nevertheless, I have heard of some that are reputed to be much older, especially one in a Mopgha village, near Toungoo, which is said to date back "nearly a thousand years." This drum has a name, and innumerable offerings have been made to it year after year.

It was formerly thought that the Red Karen were the only tribe who possessed drums, but it now appears that these instruments were known among all the tribes. In many places, however, they are no longer used. It is in the remoter hill regions, where

---
⁶ See Chapter I, pp. 9, 12.
⁷ "Gaw" is the prefix used for drums, as "saw" is for men.

the Karen are less affected by outside influences, that the use of the drums has been the most prolonged.

There is considerable difference of opinion among the people of the various sections of the country about the classification of the drums. A writer in the *Rangoon Gazette* divides them into two general groups, the older and the later. He regards the older, more melodious, and more highly prized group as comprising those which have four single frogs, snails, or elephants on their heads. He subdivides this group into three divisions, namely, (1) "Klo ka paw," (2) "Klo ma ti," and (3) "Klo gaw ple." The drums in the first of these subdivisions are the oldest and best-sounding. The second general group, comprising the later and poorer drums, may be subdivided, according to this writer, into five classes, which he names as follows: (1) "Raw tear," (2) "Raw la," (3) "Raw ser," (4) "Raw saw," and (5) "Raw boo." These have four sets of double or triple frogs or elephants on their heads. Each class has its characteristic design, for example, ears of paddy supplying the decorative figure on the "Raw boo" and Karen hand-bags that on the "Raw tear."[8]

In the Pegu Hills the drums with the single frogs on the head and no figures down the side are known as the "hot" drums, that is, those which are beaten on occasions of death or disaster. The others, with the superimposed frogs and with elephants and snails down the side, are called "cool" drums, these being used on festive occasions. In Toungoo, however, the people do not appear to make the distinction just mentioned, but use both kinds of drums indiscriminately for festive and sad occasions, such as weddings and funerals, respectively.

That the drums are regarded as sacred objects can not be doubted. In the back districts, where the old customs are still perpetuated, offerings are everywhere made to them. I was informed that during the month of March, 1918, a feast was to be held in honor of certain drums in the village of Pyindaing, Tharrawaddy district, and that offerings were to be made to them, the customary period of seven years having elapsed since the last feast and offerings. I held myself in readiness to attend the celebration, but was finally told that the ceremony had been postponed indefinitely. The account in the *Karen Thesaurus* speaks of the offerings as having

---

[8] Mr. Po Lin Te in the *Rangoon Gazette* of Sept. 27, 1919. I regret that this writer's article appeared after I had left Burma on my furlough. I have not been able, therefore, to identify the designs mentioned by him on any picture or sketch of the few I have with me or that are accessible to me.

been presented annually. Other sources of information indicate that they might be made at any time, especially on occasions of ca-

KAREN BRONZE DRUM, NABAAIN VILLAGE, THARRAWADDY DISTRICT
A drum of almost black metal, used for weddings and other festal occasions.

A "RUBBING" SHOWING THE PATTERN OF THE HEAD OF THE NABAAIN DRUM

lamity or epidemic. As far as I am able to ascertain, these offerings usually consist of food and liquor. In the early times, at least, to withhold such oblations from a drum was to invite the descent of illness and misfortune upon the owner.

Of the various drums which I have had an opportunity to inspect, I wish to describe two with some fullness, one of these being a "hot" drum and the other a "cool" one. The latter is shown on page 119, and was obtained in 1918 from the Nabaain village tract by Thra Shwe Thee. It is a fine specimen of its class and was used on festive occasions. Its head is twenty-one inches in diameter; its bottom or mouth, sixteen and one-half inches in diameter; its cylinder, fifteen and one-half inches long. The surface of the metal, which is black, is much worn. It has four sets of frogs on the head, each group being composed of three of the creatures, one above another. The frogs are flat and conventional in form. In the center of the head is a large twelve-pointed star, the angles close in between the rays being connected by several arcs, from the outermost of which radiating lines diverge. The points of the star are encircled by nineteen zones, which fill the space to the edge of the rim. These zones are not separated from one another by equal spaces, but fall into five groups. Counting from the center outward, the first three of these groups comprise four zones each, each group being separated from the next one by four concentric circles, while each individual zone is separated from its fellow by three circles in close proximity to one another. The fourth and fifth groups consist of three zones each, four circles separating the two groups and three circles, each zone from its neighbor. The rim zone, on which the sets of frogs stand, is broader than the others, and the edge of the rim is finished with a braided beading.

The ornamental designs contained in the several zones, group by group, are indicated in the following table:

ORNAMENTAL DESIGNS IN THE ZONES ON THE HEAD OF THE NABAAIN DRUM

| Group I | Group II | Group III | Group IV | Group V |
|---|---|---|---|---|
| Hatching | Hatching | Hatching | Hatching | Hatching |
| Circles | Circles | Circles | Plaiting | Plaiting |
| Plaiting | Plaiting | Hatching | Birds' heads | Diamonds |
| Birds' heads | Six diamonds, circles, three birds | Six diamonds, circles, three birds | | |

Little comment is necessary in regard to these zone decorations. In the fourth zone of Group I and the third of Group IV the birds' heads follow in close succession. In the fourth zone of both Group II and Group III three birds are followed by six diamonds or lozenges, each lozenge being separated from its fellow by two circles, while the series is terminated by three circles. The combination of decorative figures is repeated over and over around the zone. The birds are represented side view, standing with their heads extended horizontally as if looking for food. The outer zone, on which the frogs stand, has less ornamentation than the other zones. At intervals groups of six circles, arranged like the sides of a pyramid, appear in this zone, the rest of the space being left vacant.

The cylinder of the Nabaain drum is encircled by numerous engraved bands, arranged in three groups. The smallest group, consisting of four bands with indistinct patterns, is at the bottom or open end of the cylinder, the individual bands being separated by close parallel lines which number three in two instances and four in the other. Around the waist of the cylinder run two sets of five bands, a space wider than any of the bands separating the two sets. Parallel lines separate the individual bands from one another. Three bands of the lower set are ornamented with lozenge-shaped figures. The two outer bands of the upper set are filled with hatching and the other three, with the lozenge patterns. Three or four parallel lines separate these bands from each other.

The "hot" or "sad" drum, which I shall next describe, was obtained from the village of Kondagyi at the head of Thonze Creek in the Tharrawaddy district. It has a bronze color and is reputed to contain gold and silver in the alloy. As drums of the class to which this one belongs were used only on occasions of calamity or death in the owner's family, they were kept hidden away in the jungle and were brought out only when necessary. The patterns on the Kondagyi drum are much worn, and part of one side of it is broken off. It was also once somewhat injured at a funeral feast, where a dispute arose about the tonal qualities of this and other drums whose owners were present. Many of the guests regarded the tones of the Kondagyi drum as more melodious than those of the other drums. The partisans of the latter resented this adverse opinion of their favorite instrument with such vigor that they left three knife-cuts on the edge of the sweet-sounding drum before it was rescued by its owner and his friends. The Kondagyi drum

122 THE KAREN PEOPLE OF BURMA

Bronze Drum from Kondagyi, at Head of Thonze Creek, Tharrawaddy District. Used at Funerals

Head of the Kondagyi Drum

is said to have come into possession of the family from whom I purchased it in 1917, back in 1757, at the time when the Burmese overthrew the Talain kingdom of Pegu. It was supposed to have come originally from "the Eastern country," that is, probably Papun or some locality near the Shan States. A few years ago, when the funeral customs were beginning to fall into disuse, the owner refused three hundred rupees for this drum. Later, realizing that the old usages were gone, he hobbled over the hills to the house of his son, who knew the place of concealment of the drum in the jungle, ordered him to bring it forth from its hiding-place, and sold it for fifty rupees, although still fearing that he might be dishonoring his ancestors. (See illustrations, p. 122.)

The ornamentation of this drum is not so well marked as that on the Nabaain instrument. On the head (lower figure, p. 122) the star in the center has six slightly rounded points, which do not extend more than about three-fourths of the distance from the center to the inner circle of the first zone. The total number of zones is fourteen, arranged in four groups of four, three, two, and four zones, respectively. The two inner groups are separated by a single circle and the others, by two closely drawn circles. The patterns in the zones are given in the following table:

ORNAMENTATION IN THE ZONES ON THE HEAD OF THE KONDAGYI DRUM

| *Group I* | *Group II* | *Group III* | *Group IV* |
|---|---|---|---|
| Hatching | Indistinct pattern | Alternating groups of two fishes and three birds | Two rows of oval dots |
| Hatching | Indistinct pattern | Same as above | Hatching |
| Hatching | (Both zones are wider than those in Group I) | (Each of these zones are twice the width of those in Group II) | Indistinct |
| Two rows of oval dots | | | Two rows of oval dots |

Two concentric circles enclose the last zone, and beyond these to the edge of the rim is an open space. The four well-molded single frogs are in the last zone and face to the left, as do the flat patterns also.

The cylinder of this drum is worn and weather-beaten, and the bands in low relief are some of them indistinct. Near the bottom or mouth, which is rounded off with a molding a little thicker than the rest of the metal, there are two indistinct bands, the upper one having been apparently ornamented with hatching. A second group of seven bands encircles the waist of the cylinder. Four of these are below the seam that runs around the drum at its smallest diameter. The lowest of the four seems to have been filled with hatching and the other three, with the lozenge pattern. Of the three bands above the seam two are indistinct, and the third is filled with hatching. Between the bulging shoulder and the rim are four bands with patterns hardly discernible. There is no line of elephants and snails running down the side. Double flat handles of bronze project from opposite sides. These are narrow in the middle and wider at the ends, where they are joined to the cylinder.

Besides the two drums above described, I have seen several others that conform in general to one or the other of the two types to which these belong. I have no data at hand, however, from which to give accurate descriptions of them. On none of them have I seen the figures of men, houses, or boats with which the ancient drums of Cambodia are decorated, but all of them display the characteristics usually attributed to Karen drums, namely, narrow circular zones on the head, containing geometric designs and conventionalized figures of fishes and birds, and the straight cylinder with a slightly narrowed waist.

Drums are still being made for the Karen by the Shan people at the village of Nwedaung, near Loikaw in Karenni. I have never witnessed the process, but Mr. Franz Heger quotes the following account of it from a letter written in 1884 by Dr. Anderson, of the Calcutta Museum, who acknowledges his indebtedness for his information to a Mr. Lilly, of Rangoon. This information agrees with descriptions given by others who have visited the place: "A clay core is first made of the size of the inside of the gong and on this wax is placed and correctly modeled to the exact shape and covered with appropriate ornamentation. When the wax model is finished, fire-clay and water are dashed on the face of the wax with a

# BRONZE DRUMS 125

A BRONZE DRUM OWNED BY REV. A. V. B. CRUMB, OF TOUNGOO

HEAD OF MR. CRUMB'S DRUM

brush. The clay and water, being thrown with great force, penetrate into the small hollows and angles of the wax. When a sufficient thickness of clay has been added in this way, a coarse clay is laid on outside to give strength. The wax is then melted out and the mould made nearly red-hot. The metal is then poured in." [9]

Whether the Karen ever cast their own drums is a question not yet settled, and one that will be very difficult to determine. Certain it is that their other possessions are generally rude and lacking in decoration. If they were once able to produce articles of such artistic merit as these drums, they must have been more advanced than we now find them and have lost accomplishments which their ancestors possessed in a more vigorous northern clime, before they migrated to their present abode and became dependent upon their more thrifty neighbors for their present supply.

If a more careful study of these drums and their uses, both among the Karen and the other tribes of Indo-China, can be made, it may yet be possible to throw new light on the relation of these peoples and to supply historical data that has been long sought.

---

[9] Heger, *Alte Metalltrommeln aus Sudost-Asien*, 227, ff. The quotation goes on to say that "the frogs on the top of the drums are cast in one piece which, considering the thinness of the metal, is a good example of Karen art." I think the author of this account is mistaken in ascribing the manufacture of these drums to the Karen. It has always been said in recent times that the Shan are the makers of them.

# CHAPTER XIV

# SOCIAL CONDITIONS

### Political Arrangements

The Karen race does not possess what may be termed social solidarity. It is broken up into many tribes, some of which differ considerably from others, as, for instance, the Brecs of Karenni and the Sgaw Karen of Lower Burma. There is, however, enough similarity of dialects and traditions, as well as of religion and customs, to make it certain that they really belong together and are descended from a common ancestry. Even the individual tribes do not consist of compact groups of clans. To be sure, there is more cohesion among the members of one tribe than among those of different tribes; but the village rather than the tribe has the greater claim upon their adherence. In the days before the British conquest and annexation of Burma [1]—when the country received a stable government that put an end to feuds and petty warfare—the village was the political unit. In the village the houses were ranged side by side, or else, as in the Pegu Hills, all the families of the little community lived within what may be called the village-house, each family having its living-room opening off of the common corridor. Everybody was thrown into intimate contact with everybody else in the village. Politically and socially the village was the center of their common life. The family group, the natural unit of kinship, although not always confined to the village, was economically and politically subordinate to it.

In the village the elders ("phga tha phga," literally, the old men) were looked up to as connecting the village life with the past,

---

[1] The British conquest of Burma was accomplished in three wars, each of which was brought on by the arrogance and stupidity of the Burmese kings and their high-handed dealings with British subjects. The First Burmese War (1824-26) resulted in the ceding of the provinces of Tenasserim and Arakan to the British, in the former of which there was a considerable Karen population. The Second Burmese War (1852-53) ended with the annexation of the country of Pegu or Lower Burma, in which dwell the great body of the Karen people in Burma: and the remainder of the territory ruled by the despotic Burmese kings came to enjoy the privileges of the Indian Empire after a single short campaign of only two months' duration in 1885, known as the Third Burmese War. Soon after this an orderly government was established throughout what is now known as the province of Burma: Sir J. G. Scott, *Burma, A Handbook*, 190-206.

in which all wisdom and culture were supposed to have been revealed. The older the man, provided he had not begun to show too evident signs of decay, the wiser and more worthy of reverence he was thought to be. These old men repeated to the younger generation the "sayings of the elders" that had descended to them from former

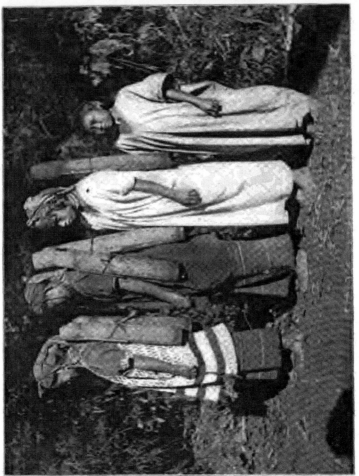

Bringing Water for the Visitor, Nabaain Village, Tharrawaddy District

generations. They were consulted on all occasions, and their advice was usually followed.

Above the elders was the village chief ("th'kaw" or "s'kaw"). He was actually the chief man in the village. His position was usually heriditary, but he might have no son or nephew to succeed him. In that case the elders chose one of their own number as his successor. In so far as the villagers obeyed any authority at all, they obeyed him. They generally observed his commands, although he possessed no well-defined jurisdiction. Ordinary quarrels, disputes relating to land, questions concerning the ownership of animals, etc., were referred to him for settlement. In most instances his court was a free and informal meeting of villagers and elders; and his decision, incorporating the opinion of the latter, would have the sanction of the group and be accepted by the parties concerned. He was the patriarch of the village, and often its high priest as well. A foray would not be undertaken without his consent. He was accorded the place of honor in the family living-room, which was usually the mat on the side facing eastward. If his rule became extremely displeasing to the villagers, they quietly went to a different site from that chosen by him at the time of the annual migration of the village. Thus, he would be left with only those who remained loyal to him, usually his relatives. The other families were now free to select a new chief or headman.

The chief levied no taxes. He tilled his field like his fellow villagers. He often received gifts of choice game, fruit, or grain; but these were largely a tribute to his personal popularity. If the village was about to engage in a raid, he might assess the people for the purpose of fitting out the expedition; but this would bring him no direct personal benefit, unless he was the organizer of it himself. The Karen had no caste of chiefs, no royal family, or even a privileged social class. Every member of the community shared alike in the ordinary tasks and the privations or prosperity of the seasons.

## Community Life

Wealth formed the only basis of social distinctions in the village life. But this made little difference in outward conditions. The land was free and belonged to the community. Every man was at liberty to take for his own use as many acres of hillside as he could fell. On this score there was little chance for inequality. However, the accumulation of money, which in the early days was represented by silver ingots, later by rupees, enabled one to purchase buffaloes or cattle or even an elephant, although the last was more often caught than bought. The ownership of a bronze drum brought more distinction to a family than that of seven elephants.

But these forms of wealth brought with them only more or less prestige within the single stratum comprising the entire community.

There was little occasion for individual initiative among the Karen, on account of the important part played by communal activity amongst them. One could claim no particular credit for his deeds of blood on a raid. That belonged rather to the organizer and leader of the foray. One never set out on a journey or attempted any special work alone. In some sections it was the custom for the chief to beat a gong or blow a horn as the signal to go to the fields. Every one went at the signal. None would go without it. If a supply of fish was wanted, instead of an individual taking his or her rod and going alone to catch them, the whole village, or as many of its members as were free to do so, would join in a fishing expedition, first gathering the herbs to poison the water if the fish were to be taken in that way, or carrying along their funnel-shaped baskets with which to work the bottom of a shallow stream, or going prepared to resort to whatever other method they thought suitable to the time and place. Likewise hunting was commonly conducted as a drive for game in which all might participate, at least all the men; and a motley variety of implements was brought out for the purpose, including nets, crossbows, spears, knives, and perhaps an old rusty gun. Thus they hunted and fished together, as they often do still. Even those who failed to go were not left out in the division of the spoils, if they managed to be present at the proper time, and they usually did.

This communal sharing was so much the order of the day that personal rights were more or less disregarded. If a man got a few seeds and planted a garden near his house, he was fortunate, as is sometimes still the case in the hills, if he gathered half the crop he had planted. His neighbors, asking no leave, helped themselves generously without hesitation and perhaps without intending to steal.

While one's personal rights were thus disregarded, they were not entirely ignored. A man's field or "hkü" and his betel gardens were his own; and his paddy-bins, which may have been built in the jungle a mile from the village, were respected. If he marked with a bunch of grass a tree in which he had discovered a hive of wild bees, no one would attempt to rob it of its honey. Many of the Karen people are like children in their regard for the rights of other persons: they understand and abide by the law of established usage, but they are somewhat puzzled by new situations and in such cases are apt to give themselves the benefit of the doubt. Stealing, such as appropriating paddy from a bin or leading off another's ox or taking somebody's money, is severely dealt with among the Karen. But carrying away a small trinket that takes the eye, either with or without the owner's permission, is not considered important enough to be noticed.

## THE WOMEN

Among races less advanced than the Karen the attention of the men is almost entirely taken up with warfare and hunting, while the work about the house and village is left to the women. The Karen have not progressed far enough beyond primitive conditions for the men to assume all the burdens of the home life that properly fall to the stronger sex. The men still feel their superiority and remain idle, while the women do work too heavy for them. Even apart from the care of the children, the women bear the heavy end of the burden. They are, to be sure, accepted as necessary and useful members of the family, but, none the less, the men consider themselves dishonored if brought into close contact with a woman's garment or compelled to appear in any way subordinate to a female. They will not, or would not in the olden days, go under a house, lest they should have to pass under a woman. In this respect they entertain feelings similar to those of Burmese men.

As housekeeper the Karen woman's work is by no means confined within the irregular partitions of her living-room or house. She draws the water, which means in the hills that she must descend to the stream and carry up the family supply in bamboo joints hung by strings across her head. She has been trained to do this from the time she was so small that she could only struggle up the hillside with one undersized bamboo at her side. Usually she has her little girls' help in this daily task. (See p. 140.) She must pound and winnow the paddy, polish it in a mortar, wash it, and prepare the meals. Either she brings in fagots of wood and splits it, or the young women fetch bundles of dry bamboo upon their heads and stack them near the ladder of the house. (See p. 132.) She is as skilled in the use of the "dah" (long knife) as her husband. When the meal is cooked she sets it out, if she follows the old custom, on a wide wooden tray or, if she has adopted new ways,

Young Women Bringing in Bamboo Fuel, Tharrawaddy Hills

Plains Women Bathing in the Irrawaddy, in the Lee of the High-sterned Burmese Boat

on a low table. The pile of rice on the tray looks like a heap of snow. The curries or condiments are placed beside the tray in small cups. The members of the family usually eat together. If there are guests the women often wait, either to serve in case the supply needs replenishing, or because they are shy about eating with strangers.

In addition to attending to their domestic cares, the women take their place beside the men in the fields. It should not be forgotten, however, that the latter can cook and perform the work usually assigned to women more readily than men in the West can. In the field the women and girls assist in the sowing, planting, and transplanting of rice on the plains, as well as in the reaping, threshing, etc., doing their full share along with the men. They tend the cotton and vegetables and carry the greater part of the paddy to the storage-bins and from these to their homes. The only work I have seen men doing that I have never observed being done by women is plowing.

The women mingle in the village gatherings and take part in the wedding and funeral festivities, their share in the latter being specially prominent.[2] Their position in their own families depends largely on their personal character. If they possess strong personalities, they gain considerable prestige and exercise influence accordingly. The older they grow the more conservative they become, and not infrequently the opinions of a grandmother will keep a whole family from bettering its condition by engaging in some new occupation. The Karen grandmother holds the first place in the family at the "Bgha" feast, when all of the members are gathered together. She is then the "Bgha a' hko." This peculiar position of hers has been discussed in the chapter on Feasts to the "Bgha."[3] Its religious significance is remarkable and may be a relic of matriarchal government, which is still found in Tibet. But it does not appear to have any effect on the social position of the sex, except in so far as it prevents the younger members of the family, both men and women, from breaking with the religious and social traditions of their forefathers.

In the olden days three classes of people were condemned "to live without the camp." These were cohabiting couples who had not complied with the marriage rites, widows, and orphans. A couple whose union had been formed without the performance and

---
[2] See Chapter XX, p. 202.
[3] See Chapter XXIV, pp. 248, 249.

sanction of the recognized marriage ceremonies were ostracized to the extent of having to live outside of the village stockade or, if they belonged to a community living in a single village-house, they were required to occupy a room detached from the main building. The two other classes of ostracized persons, namely, widows and orphans, were supposed to have incurred the displeasure of their "Bgha," and it was feared that their misfortune would become contagious if they were allowed to remain in the village. That is, the "Bgha" of other families would imitate the "Bgha" of the widows' and orphans' families in eating the "k'las" of other husbands and parents, thus depriving the village of more of its members. It was believed that this danger could be avoided by driving the bereft ones into the jungle to shift for themselves. The added risk of the future marriage of these baneful persons was taken into account. This was perhaps negligible in the case of the widows, but the orphans should not be allowed to grow up with other children to become in time eligible for marriage with them. Left to range through the jungle, such orphans, if they survived, generally developed a daring and resourcefulness that inspired the ordinary folk of the village with wonder. Their deeds came to be thought of as due to a supernatural power. In short, they were believed to be magicians.[4]

## Family Relationships

In the chapter on Marriage Customs mention is made of the general chastity of the Karen and of their monogamous marriages within the tribe. The rule is for a man to have one wife; but now and then a secondary wife or concubine, known as a "ma po tha," is supported. It may be that on account of the childlessness of the first wife the new connection has been entered into for the sake of offspring, or that the man has simply followed his own inclinations in the matter. Such unions are effected without the formality of marriage ceremonies and are not recognized by Karen society, being entirely irregular.

Westerners, accustomed as they are to doing their own courting, sometimes wonder how happy marriages can be effected in the case of young men and women who are strangers and have never met perhaps till they come together in the marriage chamber. We must remember, however, that with a people like the Karen the physical relationship is more significant than the spiritual. Senti-

---
[4] See Chapter XXVI, pp. 269-270.

ment cuts little or no figure in the arrangement. The parties to a marriage expect to live together and take the affair as a matter of course. At the beginning they have no affection for each other, but through parenthood they become united in mutual love and, as the years pass while their family grows up about them, they are bound together as securely as if they had married in the Occidental and more romantic way.

In a Karen family children are desired and expected. To grow old and remain childless is regarded as a great misfortune. Boys are much preferred, but girls are not disliked as much as in China and some other parts of the world where they are abandoned. The child early accompanies its mother to the field or wherever she may go. In infancy it is slung in a blanket on her back, but later rides on her hip until long after it is able to walk. (See page 172.)

Family relationships are not neglected among the Karen people, although they do not seem to keep genealogical records or to remember ancestors back of their grandparents. However, they are particular in taking account of, and displaying regard for, their contemporary relatives. The grandfather and grandmother, both paternal and maternal, are called "hpü" and "hpi," respectively. Great uncles and great aunts receive the same designations. The father and mother are, respectively, "pa" and "mo." Children are called "hpo," the root of this word meaning "little." Sons are "hpo hkwa" and daughters, "hpo mü." Contrary to the Occidental custom of grouping brothers and sisters according to sex, a Karen ordinarily groups them according to whether they are younger or older than himself. Older brothers and sisters are "weh" and younger "hpü." If he desires to specify whether they are male or female, he employs the usual masculine and feminine designations, commonly adding one or the other of the words given above for son and daughter. Thus, for elder sister he says "weh hpo mü" and for younger brother "hpü hpo hkwa." While there are definite words for cousin, uncle, and aunt, namely, "t'khwa," "hpa hti," and "mügha," respectively, these are often loosely used. Any man or woman older than one's self may be called uncle or aunt as, for example, among the negroes in the United States. The word "weh," signifying older brothers and sisters, as also the correlative word "hpü," designating younger brothers and sisters, are often used of cousins and more distant relatives. For instance, a cousin, called "weh," is usually one whose father or mother was an older brother or sister to one of the speaker's parents. "Hpü" would similarly apply to the son or daughter of a younger brother or sister of one of the speaker's parents. Grandchildren are "li," a word that is also used of grandnephews and nieces. In conversations with individual Karens I have almost never heard them speak of relatives back of their immediate grandparents, although they use an equivalent compound for our designation, great grandfather. They likewise have more or less frequent need of, and a term for, great grandchild, namely, "lo."

Relationship by marriage is much esteemed among the Karen. It is designated by the general term "do," which is sometimes combined with the word "daw." Thus, a "daw do" is a person related to one by marriage. This relationship is often talked of and is remembered to the second and third generation. It is not an uncommon thing for the usual terms for brothers, sisters, and cousins to be adopted for those standing in the "daw do" relationship to a family.

### Blood-Brotherhood

In the early days the Karen cultivated three or perhaps only two relationships in blood-brotherhood, that is, brotherhood by the mingling of blood. These three relationships were called "do," "tho," and "mwi," respectively. I should say at once that personally I have found only the two latter, and I note that in Dr. J. Wade's *Karen Dictionary*[5] no mention is made of the "do" relation. Hence, the query has arisen in my mind as to whether or not there has not been a confusion of "tho" used in a different tribe with "do," in somewhat the same way as "th" and "d" are interchangeable consonants in the Burmese language. I offer this explanation merely for what it is worth and proceed on the assumption, until conclusive evidence is adduced, that three is the correct number of relationships in blood-brotherhood.

Writing back in 1868, Dr. Mason describes the "do" relation substantially as follows:[6] "The first and strongest and most sacred of these relationships is that of 'do,' which is entered into in the following way. Of the two persons desiring to enter into relationship the one at home takes a hog or a chicken, cuts off the snout or bill, rubs the flowing blood on the legs of the other and, in case a fowl was used, attaches some of its feathers or down to the drying

---

[5] Dr. J. Wade, D.D., *A Dictionary of the Sgaw Karen Language.*
[6] *Journal, Asiatic Society of Bengal,* Vol. XXXVII, 159.

blood. They then consult the chicken's thigh-bones to see whether or not the auspices are favorable. If they are favorable, they say:

" 'We will grow old together;
We will visit each other's houses;
We will go up each other's steps.'

"The visitor then kills a hog or a fowl and performs the same rites on the other. On consulting the chicken bones, if the fowl's bones are unfavorable, he says:

" 'We will die separately;
We will go separately;
We will work separately;
We will not visit each other's houses;
We will not go up each other's steps;
We will not see each other but for a short time.' "

If the auspices are favorable, the two agree that they have entered into this relation of "do." They regard themselves pledged to each other as friends and bound to help each other in any manner necessary as long as they shall live. They call each other only by the name "do." In seasons of famine one aids the other to the extent of his ability. In case evil is spoken of one, the other defends him, saying: "That man is my 'do.' Do not speak evil of him. To do so is to speak evil of me. I do not wish to hear it."

Formerly it was the custom for many to multiply their "dos" in numerous villages, so that they might receive hospitality wherever they went and, in case of the planning of forays against some village, the "dos" might learn of it from their adopted brethren in other such communities. It is said that "dos" rarely quarreled, but remained faithful to each other. The institution seemed to exert a favorable influence on wild Karen society. Finally, Dr. Mason adds: "It may be compared to Masonry with its secrets."

The relationship named "tho" is formed by two men wishing to become brothers, by each drawing a little blood from his forearm, mingling it in the same cup, and drinking therefrom. Formerly the chicken bones were inspected in connection with this ceremonial, although nowadays they are not always used. This is a lifelong relationship and binds each to defend the other. From the time of the mutual adoption each calls the other "tho," and each speaks of the other by the same name.

The third relationship, "mwi," is one that may be mutually assumed by two young men, two young women, or a young man and a young woman. If the relationship is formed by the latter, they probably have met at a funeral celebration and become interested in each other. The ceremonial requires each of the pair to twist seven strands of cotton into a cord to serve as a necklace. The youth first puts his cord over the young woman's head, taking great care not to touch her head-dress or person. In similar fashion the young woman slips her cord over the young man's head. Probably a formula was originally repeated in confirmation of this dual action. If so, it has vanished together with any consultation of the chicken bones that may have taken place. The cords must be worn seven days without being broken or removed, lest the agreement be made void. Thereafter they address each other only as "mwi." The relation thus established does not allow one to take any liberties with the other, but rather tends to the safeguarding of each as if they were brother and sister. The relationship is supposed to be for life, but does not, of course, prevent the separation of the two by a greater or less distance. In such an event, when one goes into the neighborhood of the other, a present is taken along for one's "mwi." Often mementoes or gifts are exchanged when the compact is first made. It is current usage for school friends to call one another "mwi" without any ceremony, but simply in token of kindly regard.

### The Guest-chamber and Club-room

In the earlier days among the Karen of the hills the "blaw" was an important feature of village life.[7] It is still retained, although it seems to have lost some of its former significance. It is the guest and club-room reserved in the central part of the village-house. Strangers coming in for a visit or passing by on their journey are entertained here. Such a convenience was quite necessary in the days when the tabu of the "Bgha" feast was strictly observed, and no outsider was allowed to enter the family-rooms. My party and I have been entertained in the "blaw" of villages in the Pegu Hills on the Tharrawaddy side, while on tour. In one village, which had adopted some Buddhist practices, along one side of the guest-room extended a high shelf upon which stood a small image of Gautama Buddha, with the usual offerings of paper flags and wilted leaves and flowers. At the back of the room was the raised dais on which I spread my bed, but I was pre-

---
[7] In Sir J. G. Scott's *Burma, A Handbook*, p. 123, this institution is referred to under the name of "haw." See also *Upper Burma Gazetteer*, Vol. I, Pt. I, 539, ff.

vented from enjoying a good night's rest by the number of other occupants. My cook prepared my meals at the little fireplace in the middle of the room. The villagers sat about and visited with us. When meal-time came the women and girls brought in their generous supplies of food, consisting of two large trays piled high with snow-white steaming rice, besides smaller trays and bowls filled with several kinds of curry, "ngape" water, and vegetables. The visitors were expected to eat something from every dish. While the meal was in progress the hosts withdrew, except one or two elders, the women returning afterwards to clear away the dishes and uneaten food with the polite remark that their guests had eaten very little. Many shared in receiving us; and we were spared the embarrassment, not to say the danger according to our belief, of violating the tabu that prevented our being entertained at the time by a family in their own quarters.

Besides serving as a guest-chamber, the "blaw" has another important use, namely, as the gathering-place for the young men of the village. When a boy becomes a youth ("hpo tha hkwa taw"), he is expected to spend his leisure time in his parents' room, working and eating with them, as seems to be the custom. When evening comes, he repairs to the "blaw" to be with his fellows and to sleep there. This is a custom that is common among the Kachins of Burma and many other tribes of the Orient. Among the Kachins the "blaw" is a place of license. The Brecs also allow a great deal of liberty to their young people, and evidently advantage of it is taken by them. But among the Sgaw Karens, at any rate, the girls remain with their mothers. There is no common room for the girls, or any place where both youths and maidens may meet for restrained intercourse. No doubt among the Karen the use of the "blaw" as a club-room is for the purpose of keeping the young men together and separating them from the young women, thus preventing offence of the "by na," which would bring a curse upon the soil and damage to the crops.

It has never been possible for parents to prevent all social intercourse between young people of the opposite sexes. In fact, it has hardly ever been attempted. As is shown elsewhere in this volume, there are occasions among the Karen when the sexes mingle, for example, on fishing expeditions and at marriages, funerals, etc. If, however, a youth desires to visit a maiden, etiquette prescribes the way: he must take his harp ("t'na"), appear before her house, and serenade her. Sitting down, he sings to the accom-

CARRYING WATER IN BAMBOO JOINTS
Pegu Hills, Tharrawaddy District.

When the village is on the high bank of a creek, it is no easy work to labor up with six or eight of these bamboos full of water. The strings holding the joints are of bark fibre. Both these girls are wearing Burmese jackets under their Karen "hses."

paniment of his instrument. If she replies to his request to be permitted to visit with her, she does so on the jew's-harp ("t'xe"), answering him in verse. He than mounts the ladder and they visit together, either singing over "htas" already familiar to them or, if skilled in improvising, putting their own thoughts into rhyme. If too long an interval should elapse without the sound of either instrument, the elders would very likely put in an appearance to find out the reason.

## SLAVERY

Slavery no longer exists among the Karen; but when it did, it was incidental to war. The British acquisition of Lower Burma during the thirty years before 1886 brought with it the cessation of village raids and tribal conflicts in which the captives taken might, and frequently did, become slaves. Such captives were treated according to the changing whims of their masters. When first brought in they might be harangued by the leader of the victorious war-band, in case he chose to denounce them for starting the war and to recount all the alleged or real wrongs they and their people had inflicted upon him and his village. The proof of their guilt lay in their capture. While being kept in captivity they were subject to rough treatment, such as beating and wounds, which might be preliminary to their being killed. If they were spared and not redeemed within a short time, they were either kept as slaves or sold to traders, who might be other Karens or Shans. Old people were not marketable, and it was difficult to find buyers for them at any price. Men and women in the prime of life, that is, between the ages of thirty and forty years, brought about one hundred rupees each; young men and maidens, approximately three hundred rupees each, and boys and girls from twelve to fifteen years, who were considered the most valuable, sold for four hundred rupees each. Such prices did not always prevail, for Mr. Mason in 1868 reported that once, when he was in Karenni, he saw two Shan women brought in and sold at fourteen rupees apiece.

While slavery was a recognized institution among the Karen, it does not seem to have become a rigid system.[8] When the captives were redeemed, they returned to their previous status of

---
[8] This mild form of slavery, which we find previously existing among the Karen, seems rather general among some of the other peoples in the neighboring regions, as in Borneo: see Hose and MacDougal, *Pagan Tribes of Borneo*, Vol. I, 71, ff. and Cole, *Wild Tribes of the Davao District of the Philippine Islands*, 96, 182.

tribesmen. When they were not redeemed, they appear to have lived on under the control of their masters, but, as time went on, became more and more accepted as members of their masters' families, while the children of the slaves became ordinary villagers. In other words, the form of slavery that existed among the Karen did not lead to the permanent establishment of a slave class in the tribal organization.

## CHAPTER XV

## LAWS AND PRECEPTS

The Burmese were accustomed to telling early travelers in their country that the Karen had no laws or government. But this statement was wrong. The investigations of Dr. Mason some sixty years ago brought to light a considerable body of unwritten regulations that were preserved in memory and handed down by word of mouth. The Karen have no knowledge of an early lawgiver among their people, unless their traditions of "Y'wa" might be regarded as pointing to him as having exercised such a function. These regulations, which are cherished as the sayings of the elders, consist of definite precepts that deal with various social relations and obligations, the cultivation of certain traits of character and the suppression of their opposites, the prevention of crime, the punishment of evil-doers, etc. I have already remarked in the chapter on Social Conditions that the unit of political and social life among the Karen is the village.[1] In consequence, the village chief is the highest civil authority in his little community. In the early days a chief of strong personality, such as Saw Lapaw of Bawlake or East Karenni, would extend his control over several villages and perhaps weld them into a kind of state; but, unless this son and heir possessed an equally dominating nature, the fabric would fall apart as soon as the controlling hand was removed. The organization of the village was patriarchal, but the government was really democratic. The elders of the village comprised an informal council, which heard all communal business and talked matters over with the chief, who usually expressed their opinion in rendering his decision. As a rule there was at least one man in every village who was especially versed in the ancient lore, laws, and customs, civil and religious, and who repeated them, together with illustrative stories, to some one of the younger generation who was interested in learning them. A village without such a legal authority was more than likely to be a concrete example of the proverb: "Where there is no smith, the axes are soft. Where there is no cock, the rooms are still." The

---

[1] See *ante,* p. 127. What follows in this chapter is largely condensed from Dr. Mason's article: *Journal, Asiatic Society of Bengal,* Vol. XXXVII. Pt. II, 130-150.

inhabitants of such a community were without proper guidance in the conduct of their affairs. They were left unaided by the experience of the past. The elders in the properly instructed villages were the custodians of the ancient laws, which they were not supposed to change but were expected to transmit exactly as they had received them.

The form in which these laws have been handed down is illustrated by the following saying on love:

"Children and grandchildren, love one another. Do not quarrel; do not find fault with each other. When we are in the village we are separate persons, but when we go to clear the fields we are brethren; and if one is taken sick on the road or in the jungle, we must take care of him. We must look after each other. When we cut the fields we are brethren. If one is sick, all are sick. If one dies, all die; and we must carry his body back to his house and lay it in the hall, that his brethren may see and his wife and his children may see that he is dead."

Other sayings of the elders are expressed in language similar to that just quoted and deal with such subjects as industry, indolence, helping the poor, widows and orphans, evil-doers, duty to parents, humility, swearing, covetousness, partiality, backbiting, hatred, quarreling, falsehood, oppression, theft, exacting fines, killing, famines, etc. Each saying or precept is in the verbose style of the one given above, telling the younger generations what they should or should not do. Dr. Mason has recounted these various sayings at length, as they were reported to him by a member of the Bwe group of Karen tribes. The sayings thus recorded are found to be similar to those handed down among the Sgaw and other tribes. It is worthy of remark that few of the elders on the plains can repeat them at the present time. Dr. Mason's record covers some twenty pages in the *Journal of the Asiatic Society of Bengal*, but I shall content myself with calling attention to a few salient points in the precepts.

The one on famines has but little of direct import to say about that specific subject. It reminds the "children" that the elder has seen much of life and its vicissitudes, including fires, floods, plagues of rats, and massacres by Burmans and Talaigns. He has seen one man invite another to a meal, in order to accuse him of stealing his food and thus have an excuse for selling him into slavery. He has seen a bronze drum exchanged for a sheaf of paddy and a basket of grain sold for a basket of money. He has seen the people dig unhealthy yams and suffer from eating them. In the last three statements the elder is clearly showing the effects of a great scarcity of grain, both on the price one had to pay for food and on the people who were reduced to the necessity of eating bad food. His reference to fires, floods, plagues, and massacres seem intended to suggest the causes of some of the famines that have come under his observation. Notwithstanding the importance of the subject he is dealing with, the elder addresses no exhortation to his hearers, except by implication.

The precept on indolence is full of moralizing. It condemns laziness and enjoins hard work in order to obtain paddy. It teaches the people to do their work with cheerfulness and gladness, as also thoroughly and well. "We love happiness," says the precept, "and our greatest happiness is to clear our fields and build our houses. Everything is in the earth. Work hard with the hoe to dig it out, and one can buy drums and silver and other things. It is better to work for wealth than to obtain it by raids and forays." This saying overlooks neither the spiritual nor material rewards of labor.

The precept on helping the poor, as well as those on fornication and adultery, contain references to famine, indicating that periods of extreme dearth of food must have been of frequent occurrence among the Karen. Fornication and adultery are dreadful sins because, among other reasons, they produce bad crops and scarcity of game. In times of famine the rich should help the poor, but the obligation of the former to the latter seems to stop there, so far as the sayings of the elders go. The admonition to help the poor is as follows:

"Children and grandchildren, work, every one of you, and be prepared for a time of famine. Then, when a time of scarcity or famine comes, let not the rich and those who have all the rice and paddy reject the poor who have nothing, that you may not lose your honor and be abused, but may be honored and respected. When hard times come and there is famine amongst you, let the wealthy help those who have nothing with which to buy and who can not borrow."

In a similar vein the people are urged to care for widows and orphans lest other countries, hearing of their mistreatment of their helpless ones, shall abuse them and call them poverty-stricken. Even if there are rich men among them, others will not believe it. This precept does not appear to have been well observed in practice.[2].

Love of peace is enjoined, because it conduces to happiness, long life, and prosperity. The daughters of one who loves peace,

DIPPING WATER FROM A SHALLOW STREAM
These little girls are all wearing the single white "hse," but the men have their loins girded up after the Burmese fashion.

the people are assured, will conduct themselves with propriety, and his sons will live happily. Evil-doers are doomed to ruin and disaster. Their "drums will become the property of others, their daughters will become slaves, and their sons, servants. Their lands will be destroyed, and their country will come to destruction. Evil-doers do not live to grow old."

The section relating to duties to parents recounts the many cares of parents and enlarges on the expenditure of strength and sympathy by the mother in behalf of her children. The deduction set forth is that children should care for their parents when they grow old and provide them with food and drink. Those who fail in the performance of such filial duties will suffer for their sin, and

---
[2] See pp. 134, 288.

their work will not bring success. They will become sickly, weak, and helpless.

The virtue of humility is extolled at length, as one who knows the Karen people might expect. The people are told that he who does not humble himself but exalts himself, who regards his relatives with disdain, makes forays, is extortionate, beats others for nothing, and, in general, does as he pleases, will die young. Such a man will be punished by the Lord of heaven, losing his drums and money, being left wretched and childless, unable to work, without means to purchase anything, and to die without apparent cause.

Cursing is condemned, and its retributive consequences are shown in the story of a man who was the father of ten children and cursed one of his brethren without a reason. The curse did not harm the one on whom it was pronounced, but reacted upon the other, causing the death of every one of his children. Among the other evils denounced and forbidden are covetousness, partiality, backbiting, hatred, quarreling, falsehood, and exacting fines for the infringement of arbitrary rules or for trespass on one's property. The condemnation of such vices, as well as the encouragement of mutual helpfulness, filial piety, generosity to the needy and helpless, and fear of punishment by the Lord of heaven, show that the Karen had no mean standards of personal conduct. Whether these ideals were lived up to or not is another question. In fact, cursing a person by whom one had been injured was a recognized form of retaliation and punishment. It was necessary to go to his house, stand in front of his door, and recite certain verses imprecating him. The person venting his wrath must do this three evenings in succession, taking with him on the third evening an expiring fagot, an addled egg, and the scrapings from the dish out of which the pigs are fed. On this occasion he closes his imprecation with the words: "May his life go out like this dying fagot. May he be without posterity like this egg. May his end be like the refuse of the dishes."

Theoretically, the principle of the old Mosaic law of a tooth for a tooth and an eye for an eye was valid among the Karen, but it was tempered in the sayings of the elders as follows: "In order not to subject ourselves to fines and punishment, we must allow others to treat us as they choose. If we are struck, we must not strike again. If one strikes your head, strike the floor. If some one blinds you, do not blind him in return. The long is before; the short is behind [that is, the future is long; the past is short]. Love of peace gives a wide space; love of evil gives a narrow space. If we want evil, it is present even before all the water has run out of a vessel that has been upset."

The people were warned not to commit fornication or adultery. When they married they were to do so openly. They were told that if they were guilty of fornication, their sons and their daughters would die and the country would be defiled and destroyed on their account. The begetting of illegitimate children was declared to be displeasing to "Thi Hko Mü Xa," the Lord of heaven and earth, and to be the cause of irregularity of the rains, bad crops, failure of seeds and vegetables to germinate, disappointment in the hunt, poverty, and slavery. On the discovery of illicit relations between two of the villagers they were brought before the elders, who required the guilty persons to buy and kill a hog and each of them to dig a furrow in the ground with a leg of the animal. They were then to fill the furrows with the blood of the hog, after which they were to scratch the soil into little holes and mounds while repeating the following prayer: "Lord of heaven and earth, God of the mountains and hills. I have destroyed the productiveness of the country. Do not be angry with me, do not hate me; but have mercy on me and pity me. I now repair the mountains. I heal the hills and the streams with my hands. May there be no failure of crops, no unsuccessful labor, or unfortunate efforts in my country. Let them be dissipated on the distant horizon. Make the paddy fruitful and the rice abundant. Cause the vegetables to flourish. If we cultivate but little, may we obtain but little." When each of the guilty pair had completed this ceremonial, they said that they had made reparation and returned to their houses. In Shwegyin, however, such culprits were driven from the village and required to live outside.[3]

Among the Bwes it was customary to fine adulterers, unless they were single or widowed; but if a wife was involved, her paramour was compelled to pay a fine to the injured husband and take the woman as his wife, the former husband being considered divorced and free to marry again with the money he had received. In case a husband was found guilty of adultery, the woman concerned must pay a fine to the injured wife, who became free to contract another marriage.

If the crops were poor, the villagers suspected that it was due to secret sins of this sort and felt the need of making offerings to

---

[3] See pp. 192, 287.

appease the Lord of heaven and earth and to find out the guilty persons.

On the subject of stealing the exhortation of the elders was not to steal, destroy, defraud, or act dishonestly. Such deeds are by no means secret. Even though unconfessed, they become manifest in the ordeal by water and in that of ascending a tree. The God of heaven sees. The Lord of the mountains and hills, "Thi Hko Mü Xa," sees. If one is hungry, one should work, should bend the back. If one wants fish, one should use the hand-net. If one desires game, let one repair to the jungle for it. Families are to be fed in this way, not by stealing or by running into debt.

A person who had been caught stealing might be let off, if it was his first offense and he restored the stolen property and promised to reform. If, however, he became a confirmed thief, he was sold into slavery. In some parts of the Toungoo district it was not uncommon for one guilty of stealing to pay the penalty with his life. If positive proof was lacking and there was doubt as to his guilt, the ordeal by water was resorted to.

Murder was, of course, utterly condemned in the sayings of the elders, for "man is not like the beasts. He has a Lord and Master. We are the children of Thi Hko, of Y'wa who created us. Therefore, do not kill one another." The murderer will be surrendered to the Lord of the lands and will be put to death. He can not escape. His body will be left naked in the fields, and the vultures will devour it. "These things," the elders declare, "have we seen with our own eyes, and we know them, and they have often happened among us." However, the circumstances under which a murder was committed were taken into account. A homicide at a drunken feast was considered an accident, for it was thought that the one guilty of the crime would not have committed it had he been sober. No cause for an action existed in such a case.

Men killed while taking part in a foray were to be redeemed, that is, a fine was to be paid for them, unless the leader had been excused from such payment in advance.[4] Likewise, the accidental death of a man during a trading, hunting, or other trip undertaken at the request of another, was chargeable to the latter, because otherwise it would not have occurred.

The recognized way of bringing to justice an offender who was accused of causing the death of another, was for the near relatives

---
[4] See p. 157.

of the latter to take active measures to avenge themselves. A dying father, whose condition was due to the assault of an enemy or who had suffered other injury, would charge his sons to avenge his wrong. The chief and the elders, recognizing the justice of the cause, would further it and join in to punish the guilty inhabitant of another village. As a precaution against a fatal accident or a secret murder, persons were not allowed to have in their possession dangerous poisons gathered from the jungle. Any one guilty of doing so was acting unlawfully and was condemned by the elders to be bound out in the hot sun for three days. He had also to destroy his store of poisonous herbs and to promise never to commit the offense again. After this he might be received again into the village, or he might be sold into slavery. If he was believed guilty of murder, his life was taken.

There appears to have been no law against suicide, and perhaps for this reason, as well as others, the practice was once common among the people. Nevertheless, voluntary self-destruction is regarded as an act of cowardice and, though not spoken of as displeasing to the spiritual powers, it prevented an honorable burial from being given to the one guilty of it. Hanging has been the usual method of committing the act among the Karens, while taking poison has been the common means of suicide among the Burmese. Incurable diseases, great disappointment, jealousy, and forcing a young woman to marry some one she dislikes, have been the usual causes of self-murder. Dr. Mason mentions a young man who was able to recall the occurrence of twenty-five suicides in a group of villages within a period of fifteen years. At the present time, probably on account of outside influences, such instances are rare indeed.

Inheritance regulations and customs are not definite or uniform among the Karen; but usually property is divided among the children, the eldest being given a little more than the others and the youngest receiving a slightly smaller share. The widow has no legal right to anything, although she generally succeeds in retaining the use of more or less of the property during her lifetime. Should she marry again, even this quasi-right terminates. The second husband can not appropriate the property of the first, nor can his children share it.

It seems hardly necessary to comment on the worthy ideals and fundamental principles of human conduct embodied in the precepts of the elders, which we have been discussing in this chapter. They constituted a code which, if it had been observed, would have produced a highly developed society, in so far as the virtues are concerned. But, as in the case of many primitive peoples, the Karen have fallen far short of their traditional ideals, a fact manifest, I think, from the record presented in the pages of this volume. It may be said with little fear of contradiction, however, that the Karen have more nearly lived up to the commonly accepted standards of human conduct than some of the other peoples dwelling in their vicinity.

BUFFALOES AT THEIR DAILY BATH
Nothing seems to delight them more than to wallow in the mud or swim in a stream.

# CHAPTER XVI

# WARFARE AND WEAPONS

### Private Forays

Two or three generations have elapsed since the Karen in Lower Burma indulged in their old-time warfare, which consisted of forays secretly organized and carefully executed against their enemies. In the Toungoo Hills and in Karenni these raids have been suppressed only in recent years, as the regions named have been brought more fully under British rule. The people used to call such expeditions "ta hseh hsu ma beu," which means a strong and concealed thrust. A foray was undertaken by an individual to avenge a personal wrong committed by an inhabitant of another village. It was a recognized method of settling a grievance, like the sheriff's execution of the judgment obtained in a suit at law in a more civilized community. The conflict was not one between village and village, but between personal enemies. The man who inaugurated the foray set up his spear in the open space of his village and marked a white line half-way up on the spear shaft. Those who were ready to go on the expedition and renounce the right of their families to an indemnity in case they were killed, placed their marks above the half-way line, while those willing to join without making this renunciation added their marks below it. Of course, the chicken bones had to be consulted both as to the feasibility of the raid and a favorable time for it.

When this time had arrived, the organizer of the foray killed a hog or a fowl; took a bit of the heart, liver, and entrails; minced them together; added a little salt, and wrapped the mixture in a leaf. This talisman was then entrusted to two spies, who were to carry it to the village where the foe dwelt. They were admonished to note whether or not any spikes were planted along the paths leading to the place, the best means of access thereto, and the precise location and general arrangement of the village. Finally, they were to visit with the inhabitants there and find an opportunity of dropping the contents of their leaf into the food of their hosts. If they succeeded in this last stratagem, they were supposed to have swathed the heads of their foes. That is, their hosts by partaking of the talisman would become so confused as to fail to seize their weapons when needed for defense and would be overwhelmed by the enemy. Unlike the spies of Israel these Karen spies, on their return, usually gave a favorable report and displayed great eagerness for the combat.

The instigator of the foray now sent out for his men, who came not only from his own village, but also from neighboring ones where he had friends and blood-brothers. He might gather in as many as two hundred warriors. These he feasted, but before passing around the liquor he poured some on the ground as a kind of libation, while praying:

"Lord of the seven heavens and the seven earths. Lord of the rivers and streams, the mountains and hills. We give thee liquor to drink and rice to eat. Help us, we entreat thee. We will go forth now and attack yon village. We have swathed the heads of the inhabitants. Assist us. Render their minds oblivious and cause them to forget themselves, that they may sleep heavily and their slumber may be unbroken. Let not a dog bark at us, nor a hog grunt at us. Grant that the villagers may not seize a bow, sword, or spear. May the Lord help my children and grandchildren who go to attack yon village, and may he deliver them from all harm. May they subdue their enemies and not be lost. May they be delivered from the bow, the sword, and the spear."

After this prayer the elders drank in turn of the liquor, and it was then circulated freely among the assembled warriors. The instigator of the foray now killed a fowl, preparatory to inspecting its bones for a favorable omen as to the success of the undertaking, but before the inspection he offered up the following petition:

"Fowl, possessor of superhuman powers, fore-endowed with divine intelligence, thou scratchest with thy feet and peckest with thy bill. Thou goest to Hku Te (the king of death). Thou goest to The Na (monarch of death). Thou goest to Shi U, the brother of God. Thou goest into the presence of God. Thou seest unto the verge of heaven and unto the edge of the horizon. I now purpose to go and attack yon village. Shall we be hit? Shall we be obstructed? If we go, shall we suffer? Shall we die by the bow? Shall we be pierced by the spear? Shall we grow weary or exhaust ourselves? If so, reveal thyself unfavorably." [1]

---
[1] This prayer, in which superhuman powers are attributed to the fowl, is similar to prayers of the Kenyas of Borneo, who ascribe like powers to the pig.

If the reading of the chicken bones proved unfavorable, another fowl was slain, and a third, if necessary. On obtaining a favorable omen, the organizer of the raid harangued his men, telling them that they would surely prove victorious, that he would indemnify the families of any who might be killed, and that he would replace all weapons that might be lost or broken. He assured them that he expected all to return, and declared that no disaster could befall them. Thereupon he called for two volunteers to lead in ascending the ladder to the village-house and making the attack on the arrival of the war-band at its destination. Addressing the volunteer leaders, he promised them drums and buffaloes as rewards for the deeds of valor they were soon to perform. They were to be the hunting dogs, the wild boars, full of cunning and courage. If they should be slain, their families would receive the rewards. If, however, they failed, the disaster of the expedition would be their fault.

At length, the war-band set forth, chanting verses, as follows:

"I go to war. I am sent.
I go to fight. I am sent.
Clothe me with an iron breastplate.
Give to me the iron shield.
I am not strong. May I take on strength.
I am weak. May I attain vigor."

"I go with a host of men.
We will reach the steps of the house
And fire muskets and shout aloud.
The men will come with wives and children.
Raise the spear and draw the sword.
Smite the neck and pierce the side.
The blood is gushing purple."

"The great hawk flies above the house.
It pounces on the chief's red cock.
It grasps its prey near the lowest step.
It seizes then the chief's white cock,
And the great hawk flies away,
Leaving the chief behind in tears."

Whatever one may think of the poetic quality of these three stanzas, they depict vividly the successive stages in their adventure, as the chanting braves conceived it. In the first stanza they

KAREN OF THREE GENERATIONS ON THE PLAINS
Only the old grandmother retains any part of the Karen dress, and that is the skirt

KAREN GIRLS OF THE PLAINS CARRYING WATER IN EARTHEN POTS OF BURMESE MANUFACTURE

don their armor and muster up their wavering courage. In the second they go into action with their lust for blood fully aroused. In the third they compare themselves to the great hawk carrying off its prey before the eyes of the chief, whose village they have invaded. The mission of the war-band was to accomplish some such program as this.

The warriors so timed their march as to reach the vicinity of the foe's village after dark, distributed their force around the unsuspecting inhabitants before dawn, and sallied forth with a great shout as soon as it was light. The charge against the village-house was led by the two volunteers, and all the inmates who jumped to the ground were cut down or pierced with spears by the armed men in waiting. No quarter was shown, even the women and children being either slain or taken captive, according to the orders of the instigator of the raid. Their main object was evidently plunder, for they lopped off the heads, hands, and feet of their victims, in order to obtain the necklaces, bracelets, and anklets more easily. They also slew the small children, perhaps because they would otherwise be doomed to a lingering death.

From an old man I learned of one of these forays, in which his father had participated while still a young man. The father professed to have had but little interest in the expedition, being forced to join it by circumstances. Lagging behind the other members of the attacking party, he saw two girls who had escaped from the house and hidden in the forest. When they saw him they started to run, thus disclosing themselves to others who gave chase, struck them down with their swords, cut off their hands to get their bracelets, and left them to die. A man and his wife and baby were also in a fair way to escape, but were hard pressed by pursuers, whereupon the husband compelled his wife to throw away the infant, who impeded her progress; and as they rounded the crest of a hill they looked back only to see their child being cut to pieces.

If the villagers made too stout a resistance to the first onset, the raiders set fire to the inflammable bamboo structure, thereby bringing the conflict to a quick conclusion, though at the same time reducing the amount of available loot. They frequently mutilated the bodies of their victims, carrying off their jaw-bones as trophies of their ghastly work. It is not clear from any extant records that the Karen were once head-hunters, but this may have been the case. In token of the utter destruction of a village, vegetable seeds were sometimes planted on its desolate site.

The organizer of the foray did not go in person with his men, lest he be killed and thus rendered unable to dispense the spoils, but remained at home to receive and reward the valiant fighters on their return with the booty. As they approached, they announced their victory by the notes of their horns. After being welcomed with a feast, they were sent to their homes. Any claims for indemnity on the part of the families of slain warriors were now settled, some of the booty being evidently used for this purpose, the rest of the plunder and such captives as were brought back becoming the property of the duly avenged and victorious one. The captives remained slaves, unless they were redeemed by their relatives. If they were not redeemed, they were often sold in exchange for oxen or buffaloes, one of which might be presented to each of the villages represented in the war-band. No indignities of any sort were visited upon women captives, prisoners of both sexes being kept for awhile either in rude stocks or within the house.

### Redemption of Captives

It sometimes happened that a number of captured villagers would escape from their captors. In such a case they would immediately try to effect the redemption of any of their relatives still remaining in captivity. For this purpose they would engage an elder of a neighboring village and send him to negotiate the terms. If the victor was inclined to listen to the proposals of this agent, he gave evidence of accepting his good offices by killing a pig, cutting off its snout, and smearing some of the flowing blood on the legs of the messenger. This betokened the early return of peace and brotherhood between the belligerents, together with the redemption of the captives. In further proof of his successful mission the negotiator brought back the head and legs of the slain pig. There was still danger of a quarrel over the redemption price that might be demanded by the victor.

With the conclusion of the negotiations and the establishment of peace, the peace-making water must be drunk. This was concocted by putting chippings or filings from a spear, sword, musket-barrel, and stone into a cup with a little blood from a dog, a pig, and a fowl, and filling the remainder of the cup with water. The dog's skull was then split open, and the participants in this solemn ceremony, namely, the victor and the leader of the peace delegation, each hung a part of the skull around his neck and took hold of the cup, while they mutually promised to terminate their feud, to intermarry their children, not to destroy each other's property, and to live amicably together unto the third generation. In pledge of these promises each of the twain drank of the cup. Imprecations were then called down upon the head of any one who should renew the feud, and the visiting delegation was dismissed. A shower of arrows was sent after the departing guests, and a salute of muskets was fired in token of the power of the raiders. Sometimes the peace-making water was drunk and the pledges were made under a hardy and well-known tree, on which a notch was cut in testimony of the compact. Dr. Mason in his account of these forays and peace pacts states that the Karen had no monuments other than these notched trees.[2]

As already remarked above, the treaty of peace was ratified between the organizer of the victorious raid and the vanquished villagers. The former and his descendants were bound by the compact not to renew the attack; but that did not prevent another foray if a new occasion arose for seeking redress, just as a man in a more advanced community might win a suit against another and be compelled to go to law with him again to settle a fresh dispute. Moreover, the pact did not remove the possibility of another foray being organized by some other inhabitant of the village where the first one originated, for the purpose of revenge on his own account. Thus, it would appear that these treaties were not mere "scraps of paper," and yet they did not suffice to prevent frequent raids. It was not until numbers of the Karen removed to the plains and thus came more closely into contact with a common enemy, the Burmese people, against whom they had to defend themselves, that they seem to have largely given up the killing of one another. I have not been able to find any evidence to show that the Burmese Government exercised its power in suppressing the forays among the Karen, and I think that such private wars decreased in number for the reason just given.

## Weapons

The weapons used by the Karen in their fighting were spears, javelins, swords, and flint-lock and match-lock guns. The crossbow seems not to have been well adapted for warfare and has been kept for hunting. The commonest forms of fighting

[2] *Journal, Asiatic Society of Bengal,* Vol. XXXVII, Pt. II, p. 161.

implements were spears and javelins. These were usually made with iron heads either of small bayonet-shape or elongated elipse-shape sharpened to a point. In the case of the larger spears the head measures about two feet in length and two or three inches across at the widest part of the blade. The shaft of some hard wood is five or six feet long.

The *Karen Thesaurus* distinguishes among three kinds of swords or "na," as they are collectively called by the people themselves. One kind is the two-edged sword with a sharp point ("na thweh hko"); the second is a blunt sword shaped like the tail of an eel ("na nya hti meh"), and the third is square at the end and can be used for cutting only ("na xu hko").[3] These swords were carried in sheathes of a type similar to those seen among the Shan, formed of two pieces of bamboo held together by rattan bands woven around them. No one knows whether or not these weapons are native with the Karen. They may have been copied from the Shan. Besides the three kinds of swords, the Karen used a long knife ("dah") for both defensive and offensive purposes, which is devoted nowadays to domestic employment.[4]

During the sixteenth century the Portuguese carried on an extensive trade in firearms in the East, especially in Burma. In this way the Karen tribes became familiar with flint-lock and match-lock guns, owning numbers of them. In numerous instances the stock of the gun had no butt to be held against the shoulder, as in the case of European and American guns, but a handle that was held against the cheek. Powder was "pounded out" in a mortar containing sulphur, saltpeter, and charcoal, all native products. The sulphur was often obtained from the deposits of bat dung found in the limestone caves that are numerous in the Moulmein district. Indeed, one of the common names for gun-powder was "bla-e," meaning bat dung. Inasmuch as lead mines have long been known in Burma and on the Chinese border, I presume that the Karen got the material for their bullets from these. When lead was not to be had, they substituted small round stones.

The approaches to the villages were guarded by burying sharpened bamboo spikes, hardened with fire, in the paths, leaving only the point protruding at a sufficient angle to catch the foot of the passer-by. These almost hidden spikes inflicted terrible wounds in

---
[3] For the weapons used in hunting see pp. 104, ff.
[4] *Karen Thesaurus*, Vol. III, 154; Cross, *Karen-English Dictionary*, 907.

the bare feet of the enemy who was careless enough to run into them.

In the early times the participants in a foray equipped themselves with armor and shields, although such protective contrivances are almost unknown at the present time. The armor was a sort of jacket of thick hides thought to be serviceable in warding off the strokes and thrusts of sword and spear. The name by which it was known was "t' xo." Shields, called "k' taw," were constructed of wood and covered with a tough skin. I have not been able to learn from any one what was their shape or just how they were made. However, Mr. F. H. Gates, the political officer of Karenni, gives us this bit of information on the subject: "A generation or two back these people carried a shield made of plank covered with buffalo hide and studded with brass nails." He adds that no specimens of these shields are to be obtained now.[5]

---

[5] *Report* of 1894-95, p. 22.

A SGAW KAREN ORCHESTRA, THARRAWADDY HILLS
The harp and the guitar are being played together.

## CHAPTER XVII

## MUSIC, MUSICAL INSTRUMENTS, AND DANCING

### Karen Music

The Karen use the pentatonic or five-toned scale, which has belonged to the Eastern nations since early times. This scale consists of the first, second, third, fifth, and sixth intervals of the modern octave. They appear to know nothing of different musical keys, but in starting a tune try one pitch or another until they have found the range suitable to their voices. They do not keep accurate time in their singing, but hold one or another tone as suits their fancy, introducing quavers on the long notes and sliding down or slurring from one tone to the next. Some words and phrases they repeat over and over again, thereby suggesting the repetitions in an anthem. As they sing in minor strain, their music has a quality of sadness.

On their instruments they play tunes that are not rendered vocally. This is especially true of the melodies they play on the pipes ("hpi ba"), rather than of set compositions. These pipes are capable of producing really beautiful music, consisting largely of improvised runs and variations, demanding no small skill.[1]

It is to be regretted that, with the acceptance of Christianity, the Karen have almost entirely dropped their own music for that of the West. Hymns particularly appeal to them. Perhaps this is due to their desire to leave their pre-Christian life altogether behind them, as well as to the more animated quality of our Western music. However, a few Karen melodies have been adapted to hymns and have been recently incorporated in their hymnbook through the efforts of the Rev. E. N. Harris, of Toungoo.

### Musical Instruments

The Karen have seven or eight primitive musical instruments, besides drums, cymbals, and gongs. Those in common use are the

---

[1] For this note on Karen music and the score of the accompanying "hta" I am indebted to Mrs. U. B. White, of Rangoon.

harp, the jew's-harp, the bamboo guitar or fiddle, the xylophone, the flute, the graduated-pipes, the gourd bag-pipe, and the wedding-horn. In the olden days every Karen youth possessed a harp ("t'na"), which he carried with him on all occasions. Even at the present time in the villages along the Pegu range one can generally hear these soft-toned instruments. Indeed, in the middle of the night one's sleep may be disturbed by the monotonous strumming on one of them by some wakeful old man, who is trying to beguile the slowly moving hours.

The body of the harp is hollowed out of a block of wood and looks not unlike a miniature dug-out canoe less than two feet long and about five inches in width. A strip of deerskin (of the barking-deer) is stretched across the open top, and lengthwise along the middle of this a piece of wood is fastened to which the strings are attached. The other ends of the strings are fastened to pegs that fit into holes in the arm of the instrument. This arm is curved somewhat like the prow of a boat and is inserted into the sharper end of the body of the instrument. Formerly the strings consisted of cotton fibre, but fine brass wire, bought at the bazaars, is now substituted for the cotton strings. (See frontispiece.)

I have seen a few harps that were made of bamboo, a large section between the nodes being utilized for the body, of which the open side was covered with deerskin extending well down along either edge and fastened with thong-lacing underneath. From one end of this body, and firmly lashed to it, was an arm of wood, the strings being strung from this across to a cleat fastened to the deerskin. This instrument is a very resonant one. In the Pegu Hills the harps have seven strings, the upper one serving only as a stay; but farther north five strings seem to be the rule, all being tuned and played.[2]

The jew's-harp ("t'xe") is usually considered the women's instrument, though there is a short one played by the men. When wooed by the youth with his harp, the maiden replies with her jew's-harp. This instrument consists of a narrow strip of bamboo a foot long and an inch wide at one end, from which it tapers gradually to a point at the other. The tongue is cut in the wider

---

[2] The Burmese harp is similar in form to the first one described above, but has thirteen strings, although the musical scale of both the Burmese and Karen harps comprises only five tones. For an account of Burmese music, see SIR J. G. SCOTT's *Burma, A Handbook of Practical, Commercial, and Political Information*, 352-357.

end. The specimens I have seen were hardened and blackened over a fire and looked like ebony. Old men have told me that in the days when raids by Burman dacoits were common, the scattered Karen who were hiding in the jungle, fearing lest some of their foes were still in ambush, would signal to one another by playing

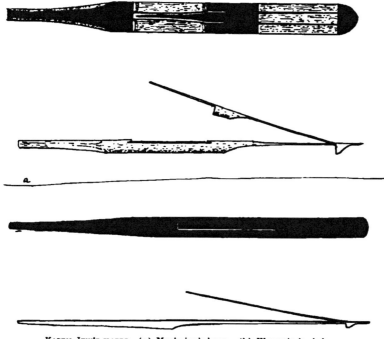

KAREN JEW'S-HARPS—(a) Men's jew's-harp. (b) Women's jew's-harp.

certain notes on these jew's-harps. Familiar with the sounds thus produced, which were unintelligible to their enemies, they were able to find one another and come together again.

A very primitive kind of guitar or fiddle ("thaw tu") consists of three strings stretched along one side of a hollow bamboo, which

A KAREN GUITAR           D.P.

has long longitudinal slits on either side of the strings to emit the sound. This instrument may be played with the fingers like a guitar or with a bow, which is nothing more than a smooth strip of bamboo. Nowadays the strings are brass wires fixed in slits at one end and held in place at the other by a cord around the barrel of the instrument. I am told that formerly the strings were made by cutting away the silicious surface of the bamboo and leaving a few fibres, which were then raised above the rest of the stock by running a knife under them and inserting little blocks as bridges at either end to hold the strings taut.

The "paw ku" resembles somewhat the African xylophone and is often made by individuals from green bamboos while stopping to rest by the roadside. After they have played a few strains on it they pass on, leaving it to dry up. It consists of eleven tubes ranging from seven and one-half inches to twenty inches in length and from an inch and a half to six inches in circumference. One end of each tube is cut off square at a node of the bamboo, while the other is sharpened like a quill pen. The distance from the closed end to the shank, where the opening begins, varies from two and one-quarter inches for the tube producing the highest tone to eleven and one-half for that producing the lowest. In addition to this series, there is a base pipe thirteen and three-quarters inches from the node to the shank and thirty-two inches to the point. This one is an octave below the third largest tube of the series and, when played, is struck with another pipe, which is as long as the fifth tube of the instrument. These two are called "klo" (drum) and "klo a deu" (drum enclosure), respectively. The player strikes the tubes of the xylophone with small mallets whittled out of bamboo, while the bass accompaniment is played, usually by a second performer, on the "klo." The tones are not unlike those produced by playing on different sized bottles. (See illustrations on p. 165.)

The "po dwa" is an open bamboo pipe about a cubit in length with three or seven holes down the side, as the case may be. It is not played with the instrument held in the position of the transverse flute or the military fyfe, but in a more or less vertical position like the flageolet, with the notched end of the instrument resting against the chin just below the lips. The player blows over the notch and secures the different tones by opening and closing the holes like a flute-player.

An instrument of graduated pipes, similar to the "Pan's pipes" known among the ancient Greeks, is familiar in the Tenasserim divi-

MUSIC, MUSICAL INSTRUMENTS, AND DANCING 165

PLAYING THE "PAW KU" OR KAREN XYLOPHONE
The man at the right is playing the bass accompaniment on the long tube, while the other strikes the other tubes, which are all laid out in order.

AN EXHIBITION PERFORMANCE ON THE XYLOPHONE
With the tubes spread out in groups of twos and threes, the performer has to exert himself to produce his tones.

sion. It comprises a number of slender bamboo tubes ranging from a foot or more to three or four feet in length, bound together in a bundle by rattans. "Hpi ba" is the name applied to the instrument by the Karen, who play it with considerable skill and use it frequently. It is said to be of Talain or of Siamese origin.[4]

MUSICAL SCORE OF A KAREN "HTA" OR POEM

The Toungoo Karen, either the Ker-ko or the Padaung, make an instrument, which suggests a bag-pipe, by inserting five bamboo tubes in a gourd. The player blows into the stem of the gourd and fingers the holes in the tubes to produce the different sounds.

---

[4] These graduated-pipes exhibit a striking similarity to those found in Malaysia, Borneo, and the Philippine Islands: Skeat and Blagdon, *Pagan Races of the Malay Peninsula*, Vol. II, p. 145; Hose and McDougall, *Pagan Tribes of Borneo*, Vol. II, p. 192, and the figures opposite p. 122; Cole, *Davao Tribes*, p. 110.

Illustrations of musical instruments used by the Bangala and Bajande tribes of the Congo region, including just such a harp as the Karen have, are given in *George Grenfell and the Congo*, Vol. II, p. 719. An instrument like the graduated-pipes of the Karen is shown in A. W. Niewenhuis's *Quer durch Borneo*, Vol. II, p. 142.

The wedding-horn or "kweh" has but three notes, but should be included in the list of musical instruments. It consists of a foot or more of the smaller end of a buffalo horn, or an elephant's tusk hollowed out and the tip cut off, so that a hole the size of a pencil is left through the truncated tip, and a reed (made nowadays of a piece of tin or brass) is inserted as a mouthpiece, on the concave side of the curve midway between the two ends. The player produces different tones by blowing or inhaling through the reed and by closing or opening the hole in the tip with his thumb. Sometimes these horns are ornamented by encircling the two ends with silver bands. The ivory instrument is thought to be a choicer one than that made of buffalo horn.

Drums, cymbals, and gongs of Burmese manufacture are often found nowadays in Karen villages.

## Dancing

Dancing of any sort appears to be very little cultivated among the Karen. The practice of walking or parading around the corpse at a funeral can hardly be called dancing, for the participants do not perform any special steps, or move in figures, or observe time and rythm apart from the chanting of their verses. No one has been able to tell me anything about dancing among the Sgaw Karen. Colonel MacMahon has, however, given an account of a ball held in his honor by the Tsaw-ku Karens in the Toungoo Hills. At this dancing party the whole company moved forward, backward, and sideways, swaying their arms up and down, except that they extended them backward when they courtesied. The women wore a special headdress of basket-work, like a brimless hat, which was adorned with beads and the wings of green beetles. This headgear proved to be a novelty, even to the members of other Karen tribes who constituted Colonel MacMahon's retinue.[5]

---
[5] MacMahon, *The Karens of the Golden Chersonese*, p. 291.

## CHAPTER XVIII

## BIRTH CUSTOMS, CHILDHOOD

### Birth Customs

Among the Sgaw Karen in the Pegu Hills and on the plains there appear to be but few special customs connected with the births of children. Offspring are desired, and a large family gives joy to the parents. A pregnant woman experiences but little lightening of her usual tasks and works up to the time of her delivery. The prospective mother is expected to omit bitter herbs and fruits from her diet, as these are thought to be harmful to her; while her husband avoids having his hair cut during her pregnancy, lest it should bring ill-luck and shorten the life of the child.

Old women usually serve as midwives and are sometimes believed to possess considerable skill in aiding delivery, although they are without special training for the function they perform. Custom is too deeply ingrained for them to profit much from their own experience. They resort to massage to hasten the birth, and in stubborn cases they tread upon the abdomen to expel the foetus. They believe in aiding nature rather than in letting nature take its own course, even in normal cases. For her services the midwife receives a rupee and a bundle of dried bark for the preparation of a head-washing solution ("t' yaw"). She uses the solution to prevent the eruption of some sort of itching skin-disease, after which she anoints herself with sandal wood. In case the delivery should be abnormal, the midwife would receive double wages. If the labors are unduly prolonged and she can not bring things to pass, she sends for a soothsayer or a medicine-man, who usually gives the suffering woman little else than a cup of charmed water ("hti th' mu").

When a woman dies before the child is delivered, it must be extracted before the funeral ceremonies are performed. In case this can not be conveniently done at the time, the operation is postponed until the body is carried to the place of burning or burial, the foetus being then removed through an incision in the abdomen. This operation is thought necessary, in order to prevent the reincarnation of the spirit of the woman from having a deformity in the abdomen.

If the child survives its birth, the umbilical cord and the placenta are wrapped in a cloth or placed in a bamboo joint, and buried in the ground or hung up in a tree. If the latter disposition is made of them, a large tree of one of the hardiest varieties is selected for the purpose, in order that the babe may gain strength therefrom.

Soon after the child is born offerings are presented to the spirit, and a string is tied around the child's wrist to keep its "k' la" from being enticed away. In some cases the cord is tied around the neck and loins as well as the wrist. These threads may be of scarlet to dazzle the eyes of the demons and prevent their seeing the "k' la" of the infant.[1] In Toungoo it is also customary to provide new cooking pots, water buckets, mats, knives, and a new ladder to the house, to render it more difficult for the spirits to find the child. Among the Brecs the husband goes into seclusion for seven days, during which he must speak to no one. He alone cares for the mother and child. Nobody is permitted to enter the house. Among the Padaungs the period of the husband's retirement is a month, and during a month and a half the whole family must live on rice roasted in bamboo joints, boiled rice being tabu. Although the villagers may not speak to the couple, the women are expected to brew a special liquor for their use during this period.[2] It is usual in these tribes for father and child to perform in pantomine the work that the child will be expected to do when it grows up. For example, the child's hand is put to a miniature hoe, with which the father strikes the ground. Dr. Mason speaks of this as taking place when the father returns from disposing of the placenta, but Dr. Bunker refers to it as coming later, when the father holds a feast for the child.[3] On the third day after the birth the father goes on a hunting expedition, the outcome of which is thought to indicate the relative success of the child's life. On the father's return from the hunt the child is bathed to remove all spiritual defilement from it, whereupon the father waves a splint of bamboo downwards over the infant's arm, as if fanning him, and

---

[1] *Cf.* Dr. Alonzo Bunker, *Soo Tha*, 21.

[2] *Cf. Notes on the Bwe Expedition*, by Capt. Coynder (Rangoon, 1894); also *Notes on the Bwe and Padaung Countries*, by Lieut. E. W. Carrick (Rangoon, 1895). These are Government publications.

[3] Mason in *Journal, Asiatic Society of Bengal*, 1866; Bunker, *Soo Tha*, p. 21.

says: "Fan away all illness, failure, stupidity, and wretchedness." Then fanning upwards, he says: "Fan on all prosperity, health, and power." After this he ties a thread on the child's arm and gives it the name that he and the mother have chosen for it.

Among the Sgaw Karen I find that no special naming customs exist. However, according to our Western ideas, a curious selection of names prevails. One little girl was called Miss Thunder because, as was explained to me by her father, she was born at the time of a thundred storm. The name of a personal peculiarity, a color, an ancestor (especially of one who was prosperous or powerful), a flower, an animal, or a month may serve as a personal name. I know of men who bear such names as Tiger, Eel, Pole Star, Gladness, Yellow, Teacher-come (the person with this last name was born on the day a missionary first visited his village), besides many others equally odd.

Nicknames are in vogue among Karen children, as they are among their fellows in the Western hemisphere. Nicknames of a special class are those given by parents to disguise their love of, and their satisfaction in, their offspring, in order to keep the demons away from the latter. Such names suggest parental contempt and lack of affection in the hope of deceiving the evil spirits into thinking that the parents can not be injured through the injury or loss of their children. This practice is illustrated by names like Stink-pot, Rotten-fish, Lame-dog, etc., which often stick to men through life.[4]

Although boys are much more desired than girls, the latter are not mistreated or abandoned, as they are in China and other Oriental countries. The Karen possess a considerable degree of parental affection. Only in extreme danger, as formerly in the case of raids, would parents desert a female child. My observation is that Karen parents are too indulgent to their children and do not exercise as much control over them as would be good for them. Twins are not uncommon among these people, and triplets are not unknown. Twins are considered as having only one "k'la" between them. If one of the pair dies, the early death of the other is feared. Its wrist is, therefore, carefully tied with a cord, and every precaution is taken to prevent the escape of the "k'la." I presume that

---

[4] Parents sometimes express their satisfaction over the male sex of a child by applying to him a nickname indicative of the presence of the male genitals. Such appellations, as terms of endearment, are regularly recognized names and carry no opprebrium with them.

BIRTH CUSTOMS, CHILDHOOD 171

triplets are also thought to share the "k'la" among them, but I am not sure as I have not made inquiry concerning such cases.

It is common for Karen women in Lower Burma who are recovering from child-birth, to observe the custom that prevails among the Burmese, namely, to have a fire on an improvised hearth or in a brasier set near the mat on which they lie. The fire is kept burning constantly for several days or a week after their confinement, to assist them in regaining their strength. The hotter their rooms are kept, the more quickly they are supposed to recover their strength.

## CHILDHOOD

The period of childhood is a short one among the Karen.[5] The baby early accompanies its mother on her journeys from place to place or to work, slung on her back by means of an old blanket or skirt. When she puts the infant down, she improvises a hammock out of this cloth by tying ropes to its corners and swinging it from the rafters of the house or the little hut in the field or from the branches of a tree. When the child grows a little older he plays about, while his mother is at work; and when he goes with her he rides on her hip. (See p. 172.) She does not always give up carrying her first child on the arrival of the second. More than once I have seen a mother struggling along with a smaller child on her back and a larger one astride of her hip.

The play of Karen children, more than that of the little folk of more advanced races, is imitative of the work of their elders. With little in the way of toys they gather a few bits of broken jars, which the girls utilize to cook rice in. The boys induce their father or some other male relative to make for them miniature bows and arrows, slings, and spears with which they assail dogs and crows, as well as small game along the edge of the jungle clearing. Streams afford places for them to play in the water or try for fish. With the sap of the banyan (bird-lime) smeared on a bamboo they may catch a crow for a pet. They tie together two bamboos, plantain stocks, or black bottles and lead them about as a yoke of oxen,

---
[5] On account of the fact that the Karen do not keep accurate age records, and also because of the shyness of the youth, it is difficult to obtain exact information as to when the children come to the age of puberty. The ages usually given me have been twelve for the girls and a year or two later for the boys. Two cases of arrested development of girls have come under my notice. Both of these died when they were reported to have been about sixteen or seventeen, and both were reported never to have had any periods. One appeared to be not more than a girl of nine or ten, while the other was larger but was emanciated and had defective eyes.

and in various ways manage to get a good deal of fun out of the few years elapsing before they have to assume their share of the labor in the field and the village.

Girls and young maidens are early trained to assist their mothers, especially in carrying up the water needed for domestic

CHILD RIDING ON ITS MOTHER'S HIP
The youngster does not like to face the camera so well as his mother. He is riding on her hip, which is the common method of carrying children all through the Orient. A silver earring can be seen in the mother's right ear.

uses. Their imitative play is, therefore, largely devoted to doing some of the things they see their mothers do. Besides this play at house-keeping they have other pastimes. Thus, when they hear the repeated calls, "tauk-te, tauk-te, tauk-te," of the ubiquitous "gecko" or spotted lizard, which lives in hollow trees and sometimes in the houses, they count off "richman, poorman, beggarman, thief," etc., in the playful attempt to discover to which of these groups their future husbands will belong, just as maidens in English-speaking countries count the petals of a daisy for the same purpose. They participate in running games, such as "tag," repeating rhymes in counting out the players and choosing the one who is to be "it." When the players are about to be counted out, they all squat on the ground near the one who is to say over the ditty, with their right fists extended in a circle. She strikes each fist as she utters a syllable, and the one whose hand is struck at the final word becomes the new leader or victim in the game.

There are many of these ditties in use by the children, some of which are composed of words which originally may have had meanings that are now lost, while some may be simply a string of resonant syllables like our own "eeny, meeny, miny, mo." One of these rhymes, which was written down for me in the Pegu Hills, runs as follows:

"T' ku, hki ku, paw ta lu, saw maw ku ku li, lu t' re, maw ku ta aw yu."

Others, however, take the form of a narrative, for example, the following which speaks of a Burmese Buddhist monk ("pongyi"), an object of terror to the Karen children. Hence, they say:

"Hop kyi klo hko neu weh lo
Leh aw hsa leu ta lu hko.
Pla wa law teh, hseh ba a hko."

Translated, this reads:

"The 'pongyi' with close shaven head, miserably hungry,
Went to eat his food on the ridge.
The unpoisoned arrow falls and pierces his head."

The children have other little songs which they use in play as, for instance, when in the villages on the plains they run on the logs laid from house to house to serve as walks during the heavy rains. One of their verses is:

"Paw paw to me law ten to di do."

Another version of this is:

"Paw paw pgha me law teh pgha di do."

The translation of the former is:

"Walk, walk the bridge. If it falls the bigger it is," meaning the bigger the bridge, the greater the fall. The rendering of the latter is:

"Walk, walk, the bigger the man, the greater the fall."

When playing with the chickens, children sometimes catch one of them and pretend to rock it to sleep, droning the while:

> "Hsaw hpo, mi, mi.
> N' mo n' pa leh hsu Yo.
> Heh ke so ne na p' theh tha wa ko lo.
> Aw gha lo gha lo.
> Me aw, hsaw hpo."

The translation of this runs,

> "Sleep, sleep, little chick,
> Your mother and father have gone to Shanland.
> They will come back, bringing you a supply of white betel-nuts.
> You can eat them one by one.
> Sleep, little chick."

Both boys and girls play with the seeds of the giant creeper ("maw keh"). These seeds, which are often two inches in diameter, look much like flattened horse-chestnuts or buckeyes. They come from the enormous pods, a yard or more in length, of the vine, *Estada pusoetha*, which grows a hundred yards or over along the tops of the forest trees.[6] The games in which these seeds are used are played in the dry season. An even number of players is required, divided into two equal groups or "sides." Each side must have the same number of seeds, which are made to stand on their edges by being set in grooves in the hard earth. The rows thus formed are from eight to ten feet apart, according to the age of the children playing. One player begins by spinning a "shooter" at the opposite row, aiming to knock down one or more of the nuts in it. Whether he succeeds or not, his opponent takes his turn, and the players thus shoot alternately back and forth, until one row or the other is entirely knocked over. The winning side is, of course, the one that first demolishes the other's row.

In another game played with these seeds the two sides are again equal in the number of players. However, only those on one side

---

[6] Burmese children also play with these seeds.

set up their seeds, while each of those on the other has one shooter, which he spins in turn at the row. If he hits one or more of the nuts, he wins them. When he knocks down all the seeds of his immediate opponent, he changes places with him. If he does not succeed in knocking all of them over, using as shooters all of the seeds he may have won, he changes places and sets up the seeds that he had at the beginning of the game. Sometimes these games are played by the children while squatting on the ground, but often the boy who is shooting will snap his seeds while sitting astride the back of another boy, after the manner of playing "ride the pony," which is sometimes indulged in by European boys.

Karen youths are accustomed to try their strength in boxing, though it is more properly wrestling. Especially in the Moulmein district is this developed as an art and the Karens there are reputed to be the best wrestlers in the country, so much so that even the Burmans concede their superiority. The contest is a sort of catch-as-catch-can affair, in which the object is not to throw the opponent but to scratch him so as to draw blood. The first drop of blood showing on a contestant means that he has lost the match. There seems to be few rules, for hands and feet are used indiscriminately. This art appears to have been practiced for a long time, for John Crawfurd in his *Journal*, in 1827, says that "a Karyen peasant was granted a village in perpetuity by the King [of Burma] on account of his peculiar skill in boxing. He was to teach the youth of this village his noble art."[7] This peasant seems to have come from Bassein.

---

[7] John Crawfurd, *Journal of an Embassey from the Governor General of India to the Court of Ava*, Vol. II, 164.

## CHAPTER XIX

## MARRIAGE CUSTOMS

In the early days it appears that a young man did not marry until he was twenty-five or thirty years of age. His parents, deciding that it was about time for him to have a wife, either arranged with the parents of some maiden or, as was more often the case, confided in some friendly elder and entrusted the matter to him. If they had a preference, they made it known; but not infrequently the mediator was permitted to select whomsoever he might think best. It made no difference whether the young persons had ever met or not. When the subject was broached to them, they usually consented; but if they refused, as they seem to have done sometimes, the proposed arrangement was dropped. The mediator in such an affair was known as the "t' lo pa."

Up to a generation or two ago marriage between a Karen and a member of another race was altogether tabu. This explains why the Karen have maintained their traditions and their social solidarity to so remarkable a degree. Moreover, it was an almost invariable rule among the Karen that the young woman should belong to the same tribe as the youth. Even to this day one who marries into another tribe is looked at a little askance and is spoken of as having married outside ("pgha htaw leu hko"). It was not uncommon for relatives, usually second or third cousins, to wed. First cousins very rarely married. In Shewegyin if a girl was a relative of the man, she must belong to his generation, that is, they must be first, second, or third cousins, as the case might be. She might be an inhabitant of the same village as her spouse or of another. While it was more common for the parents of the young man to begin the negotiations for a wedding, it was not a rare occurrence for the parents of a girl of marriageable age to begin them.

Child betrothals were not uncommon in the early days. Two families, who were on very intimate terms and desirous of prolonging their intimacy indefinitely, would arrange to have their children marry. Even young couples, who as yet had no children, would agree that, if favored by fortune, a marriage should take place between their hoped-for offspring, although such an agreement might be made at any time during the growth of the children. Such a pact was considered firmly binding on those concerned. The children might or might not be told of the arrangement. Later on, at any rate, the youth would learn of it; and it was expected, when the proper time came, that he would seek out his betrothed, even if she was then living in a distant village. Thra Than Bya tells of a couple who were thus affianced while living on the banks of the Irrawaddy River. During hard times the girl's parents removed from one place to another, until at length they settled near Moulmein. When the youth had reached man's estate, his father told him of his engagement and sent him to seek his betrothed. Knowing only her name and that of her father, he traced them from village to village until, arriving at the place where they then dwelt, the chief confirmed the fact and consented to the young man's entering into a rhyming contest with the maiden, when she should arrive at the feast that was being held there. Retiring into the jungle, the youth got himself up in disheveled array, returned, and addressed the damsel in poetic language, explaining briefly his mission. She repelled his attentions; but he persisted, saying that she belonged to him by right of their childhood betrothal. Thereupon she besought her parents to save her from such an undesirable husband. They imposed the condition that she should surpass him in the rhyming contest. Failing in the attempt, she humbled herself and invited him to her house, where her parents proceeded to celebrate her wedding with a great feast.[1]

Feasts, especially funeral-feasts, were the occasions at which youths and maidens met. They used to go to such gatherings in companies, each with its leader who was skilled in reciting or extemporizing simple verses. Being thus thrown together, couples often became engaged, pledging themselves in verses like the following:

Youth:   "I promise you, you promise me.
          We have promised each other."

Maiden: "After you have promised me and do not come,
          Cotton will grow on your grave.
        If you agree and do not come,
          Paddy will grow over your tomb."

---
[1] In the *Journal of the Asiatic Society of Bengal* for 1866, Dr. Mason mentions similar customs as existing among the Karen of Toungoo.

Youth: "We are pledging each other before the dead.
We shall not be worthy of offspring."

If later during the same festival either one of the pair wished to break the betrothal, they addressed each other in verse, saying:
"We promise each other in rhyme.
Now let us speak verse again.
May evil not come upon us,
Or upon our descendants."

Such verses are called "hta thi kwaw." Unless an engagement thus made was broken off the same night, the young man was under obligation to send a mediator to arrange for the wedding within a short time. If he failed to keep his pledge, his strength to resist an evil charm ("so"), would lapse, and he would go, it was thought, into a decline.

Many of these practices still obtain among the Karen in the outlying hill-country; and in choosing a bride no step would be taken without divination by the customary method of inspecting the chicken bones, except in the case of the betrothals effected by the young people themselves at the funeral-feasts. It sometimes happens that a young man, seeing a maiden who attracts him, mentions the circumstance to his parents, who approve his choice and send a mediator to her parents with an offer of marriage. As the services of a confidant are required sooner or later in nearly all cases, the omens are consulted and must prove favorable before he proceeds on his mission.[2] If on his way he should chance on anything that is inauspicious, such as the gliding of a snake across his path, the barking of a deer, or the report of a death, he will return home. Otherwise, he continues his journey to the house of the young woman's parents. The conversation that takes place there is carried on in verse characterized by figures of speech which suggest, but do not state explicitly, the purpose for which the mediator came. On entering the house, he sighs, perhaps, and remarks that he is in a trying position. The parents inquire what the matter is, and he answers with a couplet:
"Give me a white pullet,
And I shall feel better."

---

[2] See Chapter XXVII, pp. 280, ff.

The parents apprehend that he is asking for their daughter. If not ready to give her in marriage, they may answer:

"This white pullet we have but raised;
Never once has she cackled."

THE FRIENDS OF THE BRIDEGROOM
Except for the youth with the wedding horn, they are using Burmese instruments on which they are practicing preparatory to the wedding ceremony on the morrow.

The hint is sufficient, and the mediator promptly makes his adieu in plainer speech:

"You have not received me. Do not revile me.
The youth's parents will keep their son.

You did not consent, but you spoke kindly.
As for me, I am not discouraged."

In case, however, the parents are favorably inclined, but are in doubt as to who the young man may be, knowing that their caller has a son of his own, they ask him:

"Do you come on your own legs,
Or on those of another?"

He replies:

"On the legs of another."

Or they may be uncertain as to whether he intends his offer of marriage for their maiden daughter or the older one, an eligible young widow. So they ask him:

"Are you crossing a flat bridge or a round one?"

The expression "flat bridge" refers to the young widow, the other to the maiden. A "round bridge" is a log, for in the jungle a bridge is commonly nothing more than a log. A flat bridge is one made of planks. The significance of the two expressions as applied by the parents is obscure to me, but is subject to several interpretations. If there should be two unmarried daughters in the family, both eligible, the parents would inquire:

"Have you come for a basket of rice
Or only for a mortarful?"

The basket, being the larger receptacle refers to the older and, presumably, larger maiden.[3]

During his first call the mediator does not expect to progress far in his negotiations. If he has been favorably received, the family may kill a chicken and invite him to eat with them. He departs without knowing what the outcome will be, and the parents find an early opportunity to get the consent of their unmarried daughter to become a married woman ("mü pgha").

On his second visit a few days later the intermediary may find the father sitting at the front of the house and probably overhears him call out to the mother at one of her tasks within: "Here comes that male buffalo. Shall we tether him or let him go?" If she shouts back: "We might as well tether him," he knows that his proposal will be accepted. Even should she reply to the contrary, the caller would enter the house and pay his visit, but would make

---

[3] The Karens often use the word "larger" in referring to an older child.

no reference to the object of the call. This whole procedure illustrates not only a Karen, but also an Oriental, trait of character. The Oriental deals in indirect methods, rather than run the risk of saying something disagreeable.

Realizing that his mission is not in vain, the intermediary enters the house of the prospective bride's parents in joyous mood, fairly shouting the Karen version of "tra-la-la," which is "traw-le, wa-le, ho-o-o." They sit down and discuss the matter. Then the parents kill a fowl or a pig, and the guest stays for dinner in token that the bargain is sealed. After the date for the wedding-feast has been set, the intermediary returns to the young man's family and reports his success. As a rule the time of the feast is fixed by the maiden's parents, but it is sometimes determined by the youth's family.

The only month that is tabu for wedding-feasts is "La plü" (December). This is the month when the moon is most often eclipsed (swallowed by the dogs). To many the month seems as though it were killed and is, therefore, regarded as inauspicious for new life. Others say that it is the month when neither birds nor animals mate, and that it is unwise for men to undertake to start a new household. The favorite months for marriages are March and April in the dry season, because the harvest is past, the weather is good, and there is plenty to eat and drink. The date of the wedding must fall during the waxing of the moon, which augurs an increasing family. This important point being settled, the prospective bride busies herself less with the preparation of her own trousseau than with the weaving of a set of new garments for her future husband, including a white turban, a white blanket with a red stripe running through it lengthwise, and, in the olden days, a "hse plo" or single smock. The maiden's family prepare the rice, fish-paste, pork, and liquor for the feast. The prospective groom has only to make for himself a horn to be blown at the festivities. On the plains and in those places in the hills where each family has its separate house, a booth or "k'la pyeh" is built close at hand for the wedding-feasts.[4] This structure must be so placed as to have its entrance towards the tail of the "p'yo" or great dragon of the Karens. Not long ago I saw such a booth, which was enclosed on three sides and had a small open entrance to the east. The south side was entirely open. Access to the structure was had

---

[4] This booth is often called a "mandat." The name, "k'la pyeh," is from the Burmese. Perhaps the booth itself is of Burmese origin, but I do not know.

through the east door and exit from the south side. The dragon was supposed at the time to be lying with its head to the west and its tail to the east.

With the near approach of the wedding-day the friends of the groom gather at his village, blowing horns, beating on gongs and drums, striking cymbals, and chanting "htas." Early on the wedding-morn every one is astir. The rice is cooked and eaten by sunrise and, to an accompaniment of all the noisy instruments and with shouting and singing, the party sets forth. In the olden days, when the precepts of the elders were strictly observed, there was much drinking of liquor and boisterous sport on such occasions, but withal a certain decorum was not altogether lacking by reason of the halting of the procession from stage to stage and the reciting of appropriate verses. As the party is ready to leave the village they sing:

>"To-day is a good day.
>  We shall see a maiden as fair as cotton-wool.
> This is indeed a good day.
>  We shall behold one as fair as a cotton boll."

On setting forth, they do not overlook the unmarried girls of the village:

>"Here you have not loved me.
>   Listen to my wedding-horns blowing yonder.
>  Remain here. You have not esteemed me.
>   Watch us depart with our horns blowing."

On the journey they sing:

>"The wedding is timed at the coming of the rats.
>  Unless death intrudes, we shall prosper.
>  The marriage takes place when the rodents are here.
>  Unless death comes, we shall work and be happy." [5]

As they approach the bride's village a party greets them:

>"The 'the kaw' blossoms in the dark of the moon.
>  The moon waxes and wanes.
>  The 'the kaw' blossoms in the full of the moon.
>  The moon increases and declines." [6]

The above stanza refers to the maidens, still unmarried, who are waiting from one moon to the next. The groom replies:

---

[5] The years of full crops always bring a plague of rats in the hills. Thus, the time of rats is a time of prosperity.

[6] This verse, recited by the villagers, refers to the girls who have not yet married and are still waiting from one moon to the next.

"The mountains are great and lofty.
   My desire brought me, panting.
Reeking with sweat on the towering hills,
   My passion brought me, leaping and bounding.
I was wretched. I only trusted.
   Whether good or bad the omens, come I would."

The whole company now enters the village, and its members are offered drink. (See page 185). Meanwhile, the young men shout:

"You have expected a company.
   Can you feast such a company as we?
You invited a crowd.
   Can you spread a feast for all of us?"

The hosts disclaim making any preparation for the company:

"There is nothing to eat.
   Let us resort together to the betel-box.
As yet we have nothing else.
   Let us partake from the bamboo betel-box."

But the guests will not be satisfied with betel chewing only:

"Boil for us. Brew our drink.
   Feed us the white progeny of the pot.[7]
The hand raises food and drink,
   And the heart is satisfied."

The women now insist that with little or no paddy they can do nothing:

"Have you not looked at the supply of paddy?
   We women can prepare neither rice nor liquor.
Have you not seen the paddy?
   We can neither cook rice nor brew liquor."

But the young men do not relax their demands:

"Bring out your distilling pipe.
   That you have none, we do not believe.
Come prod us with your distilling tube.
   That you lack one, we are not convinced."

At length, the women consent to supply what they have:

"We have nothing worth bringing to serve you,
   But will fetch it, as ordered, though we suffer."

In some instances the intermediary acts as master of ceremonies for the young men, although they may choose another elder to serve as their leader. In Shwegyin, when the wedding party is about half-way to the village of the prospective bride, the elders

---

[7] This refers to the white kernals of the cooked rice, which are often spoken of as the "children of the pot."

halt the young men and instruct them in the proprieties of the approaching occasion, reminding them that they are going to a strange village where they will be entertained as guests. The hosts will serve them with rice and spirits. The elders remind them that the rice liquor that will be provided has been twice boiled and would intoxicate a horse or an elephant. They, therefore, advise moderation, telling them also not to hear any evil that may be spoken of them, to remain seated though others stand, to continue reclining though others sit up, to answer mildly though others speak roughly, and not to strike back should others slap them in the face. The elders require the company to say definitely that they will remember their advice, whereupon each one breaks a twig from a tree to be placed in a pile on the ground in token of the promise of all to conduct themselves properly and keep the peace.

A few years ago I visited a village in the Pegu Yomas at the time of a wedding. In the room of the bride's family they were preparing quantities of rice and curries. However, no liquor was in evidence. The bride herself was busy carrying water almost to the moment that the horns sounded at the village gate. The new clothing for the groom was resting upon the beam over the door. Now and again the horns and gongs could be heard in the distance. A party arriving from a village to the north waited outside the gate, in order to avoid the impropriety of preceding the groom's party, which was coming from across the valley, as the sounds reaching us from time to time from that direction informed us. As the groom's retinue ascended the hill, the waiting delegation hailed them with the din of their instruments, the other crowd giving vent in response with a volume of noise that showed them to be still unexhausted by the ascending of the hill. Brief intervals of silence followed by intermittent shouts and blasts of the horns indicated that the groom and his party were being welcomed by the elders.

As the procession again moved forward, we could catch glimpses of the red-bordered smocks or "hse plos" of the men. On their nearer approach we could see the elders in the lead, followed by the married women and after them the groom attended by his party of young men. They now advanced along the narrow paths by twos and threes with their arms around each other, jumping and frolicing as they came. The bright colors of their costumes were accentuated by the bright red bags slung over their shoulders and the long tassels hanging from these. The large silver earrings adorned the lobes of their ears, which were further decorated by

## MARRIAGE CUSTOMS 185

A Bridegroom's Company Entering the Bride's Village
Notice the young women leaving the house as they are entering it.

The Wedding Party
They are keeping still for a few minutes to have their photograph taken

bits of red and yellow wool or by beads. The women wore heavily beaded smocks above their richly colored skirts, numerous chains of silver and glass beads, and red and white turbans. Meanwhile, the horns were emitting alternate short and long tones of reedy timbre. When the guests began to gather at the foot of the ladder, a boy was there with a jar of water from which he sprinkled the feet of each one as he ascended into the house. Shouts of "traw le-o, traw le-o" mingled with the notes of the horns as the groom advanced to the doorway of his bride's parents. Here he was met by two young men, neither of whom had lost a parent (such is the requirement of the occasion), who poured the contents of two bamboo water joints over him, completely drenching him. They then assisted him to don the new garments provided for him by his betrothed.[6] The din produced by the merry-makers by no means ceased when they had entered the house. Indeed, it only seemed to increase, being punctuated now and then with a shout which served as a signal for the crowd to jump up and down on the plain bamboo floor, shaking the whole building until it seemed ready to collapse.

Meanwhile, the bride had long since retired into obscurity in a rear room. Any glimpse of her called forth all the noise the crowd was capable of. In Karen weddings, as in most Oriental nuptials, the bride keeps herself in the background as much as possible. I once asked to see the bride at a wedding on the plains and was told that she was back in the darkest part of the room. I remember that I gazed intently, but was not able to discern her.

The groom in his wedding-array occupied himself in cutting in two-yard lengths a long piece of white muslin and distributing these for turbans to the male relatives of the bride. On request the chief of the village permitted the young men to visit the different rooms of the village-house, for the purpose of merry-making under such restrictions as he saw fit to impose. After that they quieted down for the remainder of the day, spending most of their time in chewing betel, telling stories, and amusing themselves in other ways. Many of them went apart into a room to sleep, having had little rest the night before.

When a wedding is about to take place in a village nearly all the young women of the place disappear, leaving the day before the event for a visit to another village or retiring into the jungle. The

---

[6] Dr. Mason tells us that it was the custom for the bride to be conducted to the groom's house and to be there drenched with water: *Journal, Asiatic Society of Bengal,* 1866.

bolder ones may remain, but spend their time under the houses or in the deeper shadows.

After darkness has come on and the party has finished the evening meal, the young men make the round of the village, hunting for any of the girls who have had the temerity to remain. Those who are caught are subjected to good-natured badgering and perhaps to pretended abduction. Shouting, the noise of the instruments, and the slaps on the floor and sides of the house with bamboos split at one end into six or eight strips, accompany this hunt for the maidens. Such sport does not degenerate into ill-treatment of the girls, if they are caught, even though the men have indulged in liquor; but the fun is certain to be kept up all night, and sometimes the scant partitions between the living-rooms of the village families are removed, with the permission of the chief, to enable the visitors to circulate the more freely throughout the village-house.

Among the Shwegin Karen a vestige of wife-purchase appears to have survived. I am told that as night comes on the intermediary and the visiting elders place a jacket and skirt on a winnowing-tray and carry them to the parents of the bride as "ta k'ner" or "things that will win." The local elders, who are present with the parents, decline to accept the garments as being of too little value. The intermediary retires to return with some added articles—a headdress, bracelets, and beads. The parents and village elders are not yet satisfied, and the intermediary has to add a silver head-band, earrings, and a lump of silver to the things on his tray, before he is regarded as offering a sufficient price. A bottle of liquor is now brought out and drunk by way of sealing the bargain, and the village elders announce that "the price is paid." Among these same people it is customary for the elders, on the morning of the second day of the wedding-feasts, to send the bridegroom and his young men out on a hunt. The game taken must be brought back by the groom on his own shoulders and carried by him to the house of the bride. This hunt is his last with his fellows and his first foraging expedition for the household he is establishing.

On the last evening of the feasts a ceremony used to be performed that is rarely seen nowadays. I have been informed that it was the main part of the marriage-feasts, signifying the uniting of husband and wife. Its name was "Hpo nya mo, hpo nya pa," and meant "Children tease mother; children tease father." For this ceremony the bride prepared a cock and a hen, which were boiled whole, and she also cooked a pot of rice. These were placed in the inner room of the house. Thither the groom was escorted to his bride in the evening by his attendants, who chanted:

> "Go, escort the husband to the maiden.
> The mother looks on with smiles.
> The wild buffalo shall enter.[9]
> Tell the father to fasten the door.
> Lead the young man to her room.
> Let no one molest him.
> Take in the youth.
> Leave him undisturbed."

After the groom had seated himself near his bride, the rice and fowls were set before them. Each in turn took sparingly of the food, while the company looked on until the bride raised a morsel to her lips, when they shouted "Hpo nya mo! Hpo nya pa!" and began to scramble for the chickens, which they pulled to pieces and threw at the women. The latter returned the volley with shouts of "Hpo nya mo! Hyo nya ma!" This "teasing" of the future parents and throwing scraps of chicken at one another is said to have betokened the mutual expression of good wishes for increasing families for all those participating in the ceremony. The groom was then escorted back to the booth or the guest-room, where he spent the night with his friends.

Returning from our digressions in the preceding three paragraphs, the villagers early on the second morning of the wedding ceremonies prepare a feast of rice and chicken curry for their guests. Not less than two young roosters or two pullets are used in the preparation of this final feast, every part of the fowls being cooked, even the intestines, which have been carefully cleaned. Bits of stewed plantain stalks are included in the dish, inasmuch as the prolific nature of this plant is supposed to be communicated to those partaking of it, thus assuring the large families desired. A joint of bamboo full of liquor is also brought out. The bride and groom must then dip their fingers into the liquor and the food, while calling out "Pru-r-r k'la, heh ke" ("Pru-r-r k'la, come back"), two or three times. The elders now shout: "This day you twain, husband and wife, have become one spirit. May God take care of you. May the Just One watch over you. May the powerful Thi Hko Mü Xa (Lord of the demons) shield you. May you have strength to work and gain your livelihood. May you sleep in peace and eat the fruits of the land. May you have long life, ten children, and one hundred grandchildren." The elders next ad-

---
[9] A nickname for the intermediary.

dress the "k'la," as follows: "Pru-r-r k'la, return, return. Do not stay in the jungle. Behold your place here. Do not leave it. Go not away. Look at your own room. See your own place." A morsel of the rice, together with the heart and lungs of the fowls, is then placed upon the heads of the bridal pair, and the guests proceed to eat the remainder of the feast, finishing it before sunrise.

Thus far the intermediary has passed through the marriage celebration with the consideration on all hands belonging to one who has conducted successfully the negotiations between the parents of the groom and those of the bride. He has been the groom's personal attendant, has carried his principal's few worldly goods to the bride's house for, as among the ancient Hebrews, the young man leaves his father and mother to become a member of his wife's family. But now the intermediary finds himself suddenly deprived of his position of respect and becomes the butt of the night's fun. The foot of a pig killed for the feast is tied about his neck with a rattan, and its head is set upon a post of the house for him to bark at for the sport of the guests.[10] If he could lift the head down from the post, it became his possession. His success in accomplishing this was said to symbolize his skill in finding a suitable wife for his friend, which was likened to the scent of the old Karen hunting dogs ("htwi maw seh") in the chase. The guests now take their departure for their several villages, having spent two days, if not more as sometimes happens, at the celebration. No one whose feet were sprinkled on his arrival, is allowed to leave until the celebration is over.

After the departure of the guests, the intermediary remarks to the bride's parents: "I have brought you a son. Cherish him. If you have aught to say against him, speak it out now." On receiving a negative reply he continues: "I have given him into your hands. I have done my duty, and my task is finished." One of the village elders tells the intermediary that after seven days he will be free from blame in case anything evil transpires concerning the groom. The bride's parents present him with a pair of fowls for his services, which he carries home and keeps, unless by reason of illness he must sacrifice them to recall his wandering "k'la."

The groom lingers about the village during the day after the guests have gone and in the evening is escorted by some of the elders to the bride's room. Formerly in some localities it was cus-

---

[10] In some places the pig's head was hung about the intermediary's neck, and he went about barking at one or another of the company, as the spirit moved.

tomary to sprinkle the bridal floor with rice to give the pair a fruitful married life. Possibly the showering of rice on newly married couples in the West had originally a similar significance. However, I have been told that in the olden times couples often refrained from living together for months or even a year or two after their marriage.

Many tabus were formerly observed by parties going to a wedding. If they heard of a death, passed a funeral, or came into contact with anything connected with a burial, the intermediary at once halted his companions and directed them to recall their "k'las." If a snake crossed their path, he stopped them and addressed the reptile: "You follow your path, and we will follow ours. Our way is short and pleasant. Yours is long and evil." If they happened to hear the call of the red-headed woodpecker, which is considered a bird of ill-omen, he would cry out: "You may be sick and die. It is nothing to us. Let the white ginger burn you." If they came upon a dead wild animal, the intermediary reminded the company that death, having taken its victim, would not touch them. Chancing to meet another wedding party, the two groups exchanged the greeting: "May you be free from all evil, and may you have peace." If either company had liquor with them, they all drank together.

Certain tabus made it necessary for the whole party to sit down where they were and wait until they believed the danger was past. They did this when they heard the call of the plover, the cry of the barking-deer, the "tauke te" of the lizard, or the scream of the woodpecker. When about to renew their journey after an interruption of this kind, they pretended to spit something out of their mouths, saying: "Let all evil remain on you." A sneeze would halt the entire retinue until the leader was assured that no more sneezes were to follow.

According to modern usage the groom is supposed to remain in his wife's house three, seven, or any other number of days required by her parents. After the specified interval has elapsed, he is free to go about as he pleases; but he seldom returns to his own village, except for a brief visit. The general custom is for the husband to settle down with his parents-in-law, a practice that looks much like a survival from the matriarchal stage of the Karen's past.

Should the marriage prove unsatisfactory to the wife or her parents and they wish to sever the connection, they must purchase their release by paying the husband an ox or one hundred rupees.

KAREN GIRLS OF THE PLAINS, THARRAWADDY DISTRICT
They have put on their best and brought out their umbrellas and handkerchiefs for display.

CHRISTIAN CONVERTS, NGAPE EH VILLAGE, THARRAWADDY DISTRICT
A village near the plains, hence the combination of Karen and Burmese costumes.

In case the young man is dissatisfied with the union he has formed, the price to be paid by him is much larger, namely, three hundred rupees, one change of clothing, bracelets, earrings, and other jewelry. Because the man and his parents have the initiative and exercise the right of choice in effecting a marriage, the justice of the above arrangement is obvious.

I have been repeatedly assured that in the early days, when the Karen people lived unto themselves, moral lapses were uncommon among them, and that the lot of young persons found to be holding improper relations with each other was a hard one. Their sin was regarded not only as an offense against their household gods, the "Bgha," but also a crime against the community, inasmuch as it was supposed to cause sterility of the earth and, hence, loss of crops. The sinful ones were brought before the elders, who, having eaten two fowls that were cooked whole for them, required the couple to sacrifice a large animal, that is, a buffalo, an ox, a pig, or a goat. The blood of the slain creature was sprinkled on the ground "to cool it off" or, in other words, to remove the curse that rested upon it. The elders then resorted to extreme methods to shame the offenders, who were driven from the village, sometimes after having been stripped naked. As they were not allowed to mingle with the rest of the inhabitants perhaps for several years, they either went to some distant village to live, or built themselves a hut in the jungle.[11]

---

[11] On the subject of adultery and its relation to divorce among the Karen, see p. 148.

CHAPTER XX

FUNERAL CUSTOMS

When a Karen is ill, his sickness is thought to be due to some action of the malevolent spirits of the unseen world or to the wandering of his "k'la" (life principle or psyche). His malady may be due to an accident, an attack of indigestion after eating too many green mangoes, or an infection of some sort; but, according to his belief, some invisible spirit has been offended by a slight and is the real cause of his disorder.[1]

The seven-fold "k'la," which presides over the life of every person from the time of his birth, will, the Karen believes, determine the time and manner of that person's death. Notwithstanding the fact that one or another of the many causes of death will sometime effect the dissolution of every member of the race, the Karen makes offerings to delay as long as possible the inevitable end. Most propitiatory feasts require the presence of every immediate member of the family, in order to render the feasts acceptable to the spirits. If the sick person seems to be sinking, his relatives will all remain and try to be at hand when he breathes his last.

Karen funerals are by no means solemn occasions. On the contrary, they afford the greatest opportunity for the people to enjoy themselves. I have heard it said that when a considerable time has elapsed since a death in a particular region, the young people long for someone to die, so that they may have a jolly time. The question has often been raised why the Karen, who are not without family affection, conduct themselves in what to Occidentals is a very unseemly manner at the funerals of their dearly beloved ones. Possibly some light is thrown on this question by the story of the fabulous White Python. According to this story, after the python had been compelled to release "Naw Mü E," it took vengeance by killing men in great numbers by discharging its venom on their footprints. It took pleasure in hearing of the suffering and sorrow it was causing the human race and, therefore, redoubled its efforts. The peo-

---
[1] See Chapter XXIII, pp. 239-245, and Chapter XXIV, pp. 249-254, 257.

ple, fearing lest they should become extinct, sought to overcome the python by guile. They determined to try the plan of deceiving the serpent and its menials by ostentatious feasting and festivity when a person died through its malevolence, instead of mourning over the victim. This subterfuge proved to be successful, for the servants of the python reported to their master that the people were no longer succumbing to its poison, but were rejoicing over their newly won immunity. At this the enraged serpent discharged all of its venom and thereby lost the power it had formerly possessed of causing the death of human beings.

This tale reveals the Karen's profound fear of the mysterious causes of death. He is unacquainted with the modern sciences of physiology, pathology, hygiene, etc. Some unknown power removes his parents or his children, and he strives to fortify himself against it. The White Python of the tale typifies the evil spirits, who are continually lying in wait for him and the members of his family. His object seems to be to counteract their baneful influence, even in the hour of its manifestation, by concealing his sorrow and indulging in ceremonial feasting and forced hilarity. Such appears to be the significance of the story of "Naw Mü E" and the fabulous White Python.

The people have their own explanations of their mode of conducting funerals. One is that certain of their sports assist the spirit of the departed to avoid the pitfalls in his path as he journeys from this world to his proper place in the next. They are employing the appropriate means "to make his way cool," as they express it. Being inhabitants of a tropical region, the word "cool" is the Karen's synonym for comfortable and pleasant. Another explanation given by the Karen for his method of conducting funerals is that he aims to cheer the hearts of those who are bereaved. Being without a solace to overcome the sting of death, the mourners are the more ready to fill their minds with such absorbing sights and sounds as will expel the sad remembrance of their loss. The reaction comes later, but the Karen's habit of living in the present has enabled him to reduce that to a minimum.

When a person dies, the relatives, if not all present, are immediately called by sounding the big bronze drum or "klo a' ko" (the hot drum or drum of discomfort). The pounding of this drum communicates to everyone within hearing the news that a death has taken place, just as the tolling of a church bell in the early days of New England carried the tidings of death to the villagers. For a short time the relatives indulge in weeping, but soon begin to prepare the corpse for burial or cremation.

On the plains the body is bathed, but not in the hills. East of Moulmein on the Siamese border the face is brushed over with an infusion of acacia pods and tumeric for the purpose, as the people assert, of washing it and giving the soul a good start. They then repeat the following words: "You have gone on before. We have been left behind. May it also be well with us." As a receptable for the body the Bwe and some of the other hill-tribes about Toungoo used to hollow out a log coffin, as do the Chinese. But by far the greater number of the Karen wrap the body in a mat. While preparing this mat they offer a brief prayer:

"Let the shade of the dead depart.
Let the corpse of death and hades sleep on this mat.
Approach not. Come not near."

The two thumbs and the two great toes are tied together, but the string with which they are bound is immediately cut. After a blanket has been spread over the mat the body is placed on it and wrapped up in the two coverings, which are bound around at three places with red and white rope. These bands are connected by another rope running lengthwise of the body, which serves as the means of lifting and carrying the corpse. A bamboo water-joint and a betel-box [2] are placed upon the body, and the following words are spoken: "Chew your betel. Smoke your cigar. May your body eat, and may your 'k'la' eat as well." In Shwegyin those in attendance about the corpse address it, saying: "Do not take the path leading into the forest. Return to your resting-place and your pleasant home." Then they put the body in the guest-room and, having cooked rice and a duck curry, they place a portion of this food by it and say: "If your spirit and your 'k'la' have not departed, may they come and eat." Meantime, the beak, wings, and legs of the duck are dried a little by the fire and laid by the corpse, the following words expressing their purpose in so doing:

"Let the beak become a canoe for him.
Let the wings become his sail,
And the legs, his paddles."

Placing two bits of liver on the eyes of the corpse, they utter the wish: "May these become bright eyes for you, to see clearly your way as you go back."

---
[2] For an account of betel chewing see pp. 72, 73.

Sgaw Karen Young Women

In some sections of the country the village elders try to keep the children away from the dead, lest their "k'las" should be induced to follow its "k'la." In order to divert the attention of the latter from prevailing on the shade of some living person to follow it, the elders pretend to pick up fruit about the room where the body is lying and to put it into the skirts of their garments.

In the Pegu Hills it is customary to prepare a bier for the body. This is a low bamboo frame ("thi hso law") with a bamboo framework above, over which a blanket or several garments are spread to form a canopy ("ta t' su"). By this means the spirit is supposed to be assured a cool and shady journey to its next abode. The body is usually kept only from one to three days, at the end of which time bits of the finger and toe-nails are pared off and a lock of the hair is cut to be placed in a tiny mat and substituted for the corpse during the remaining days of the funeral rites, and the "mourners" march around them as they would around the corpse itself.

A ceremony, called "ta le me" or the lighting of the way, takes place in the evening. The Karen people seem to think of the realm of death as quite the reverse of this world. I have sometimes thought that they locate it beneath the earth, but am not sure whether they ascribe a location to it or not. Their conception of the conditions prevailing in the other sphere as opposed to those existing in this one, is shown by the following observance: Two young men take their places on opposite sides of the corpse, one holding a candle between his first and second fingers, as a cigar is held, the palm of the hand being downward. He passes the candle to his fellow, who passes it back, the recipient taking it between the third and fourth digits. The candle is then thrown down beneath the house, while the young men raise their hands and point to the sky, saying to the corpse: "The roots of your trees are there," and then to the ground with the words: "There are the tops of your trees." Pointing in the direction of the source of the neighboring stream, they call it the mouth of the river and then pointing to its mouth, they speak of it as the source.

After this the company file around the body, chanting a "hta" (poem) to the sun. In Siam it is the custom to march around to the left, making the circuit three times, after which the participants begin to recite the following version of this "hta," entitled "The Face of the Sun":

> "The sun is dark; dark is the sun.
> The moon is dark; dark is the moon.
> The face of the sun is black. We point to the plantain.
> The tops of your trees are the roots.
> The mouths of your rivers have become their sources."

> "The face of the sun shines.
> The sun rises and reveals himself.
> The moon ascends and displays herself.
> They sink into the great river,
> Setting among the fragrant flowers,
> Where the perfumes are most satisfying."

No regular order of funeral ceremonies appears to be observed throughout the Karen country. Not only do different tribes have their particular customs, but also various groups within the same tribe differ more or less from one another. This wide variety of rites renders it almost impossible to ascertain what the original customs were. On the plains, where the Karen have come into contact with the Burmese, the old customs have largely disappeared and are known only through the reports of old men. Even in the hill-country some of the ancient customs have been discontinued, so that one rarely sees a funeral nowadays at which all of the rites mentioned in this chapter are observed.[3]

Nevertheless, it seems to have been a universal custom for the elders to take a leading part in the ceremonies by chanting a poem in which they declare that the spirit of the deceased has left this sphere for another and a better life in the spirit-world. A poem of this import is still recited in Siam and is probably not widely different from that which was familiar to the various tribes in the early days. It runs as follows:

> "On the other side of the great river[4]
> The apes call loudly to each other and cry.
> They cry, 'tis said, because death comes so readily:
> Men vanish like water rolling from the caladium leaf;[5]
> They enter life suddenly and die quickly.
> One by one they tread in the steps of God's sons.
> They return whence they came as attendants of God;
> They spread his mat and roll his cigars."

---

[3] At a funeral which the writer attended in the Pegu Hills in 1917 only a few of the elders, and a young man who had come from Papun, could repeat the "htas" which were used in the ceremonies. The young folks of the village itself could only be persuaded to take part after much talking, and then they appeared to be ashamed and shy. Only one night did they attempt to recite the poems, and the next morning the corpse was taken out through the side of the house and carried to the burial place where, they told me, no further rites were observed.

[4] This fabulous great river is supposed to separate this world from the next.

[5] A drop of water rolls from the axil of a caladium leaf like a drop of mercury.

"The Lord of death, does his work swiftly.
The servants of Death are prompt in their task.
By the light of dawn they sharpen their spears.
In the ev'ning glow they whet them again.
They ponder where they will go to fight.
They choose whom they will overcome.
They steal through the vales and over the hills.
They vanquish the sons and daughters of men.
Into the huts of the poor, among the fowls,
Into the great houses and into the guest-rooms,
Where the oblations of brass and silver are seen
And the fowls are killed and offered, they come."

"Go, kill a black chicken.
Prepare it and offer it.
Go forth, and offer it on the main road,
At the intersection of the main roads.
If the curious person should eat it,
We would say that our grief has gone to him;
That he has carried it a great distance.
Let not evil's combings fall on us.
Let them fall 'midst the trees of the woods
Or elsewhere: the country is spacious."

Other verses are chanted, among them the following taken from what is known as a great poem ("hta mo pgha"):

"In the beginning when men first worked,
They toiled as their discernment led them.
From the beginning they worked for you;
They worked; they talked; they chanted."

A small poem ("hta hpo") supplies its lessons also:

"No more will you wear the beads,
But be draped in tendrils of the banyan.
Instead of the jacket and loin-cloth
You will wear the leaves of the banyan.
Go hence, eat the sour fruit of hades
And honey from the comb of the bees."

"Go, eat the salt fruit down in hades.
Go before and eat of the honey.
The dead, who face toward the ridge-pole,
Leave all of their children behind them.
They die and must look up the ladder,
But leave all their labor behind them.
Their death makes life not easy for us:
They send us on many an errand;
Our feet and our backs become weary."

Many are the poems that are chanted during the nights of the funeral-feasts. The Karen divide them into various groups, such as the great poems ("hta do"), which are their nearest approach to our classical epics; the small poems ("hta hpo"), which are less dignified than the former; the poems of hades ("hta plü"), in which the words and sentiments are often in keeping with the character of the deceased, praising the respected and condemning the dishonored; poems showing Death the way back to his abode ("hta thwe plü"); poems for the king of hades, in which his name, "Hkü Hte," is mentioned in every line, while in one ("hta yeh law plü") of this group the Karen name for hades is as often repeated; extempore verses ("hta na do") sung in rhyming contests on the last night of the funeral-feasts between the most skillful improvisers of the companies from the different villages represented, and, finally, the love poems, in which the story of the romance between the lover and the maiden is chanted by the leaders of the groups of the young people.

The funeral observances held during the daytime are as boisterous as those held at night. Several of the former consist of jumping the pestles ("ta se kle"). The pestles are the stout sticks with which the hulls are pounded from the rice in wooden mortars, but bamboos are frequently substituted for these in the jumping games about to be described. Four of the pestles or bamboos are placed on the ground in the manner indicated by the accompanying

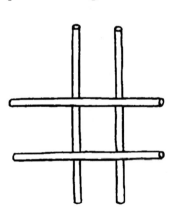

illustration, and four young men take their stations on the sides of the figure thus formed, grasping the ends of the sticks. Three times in succession they knock the pestles on the ground and the fourth time they knock them together. While this is going on a fifth young man jumps in between the projecting ends of the parallel sticks, first on one side, then on another, and the fourth time into the center of the square and out again, if possible, before they are clashed together. The game requires quickness of action and produces great merriment, especially when the jumper's feet are caught. Should they be caught, his failure to clear the sticks is regarded as a bad omen, showing that the spirit of the dead man has encountered some obstacle on its journey to its next abode. It is, therefore, incumbent on the jumper to try the center leap over again until he gets through safely.[5]

The next game in order is that of "pounding the pestles" ("ta to kli"). In this game three young men, each provided with a pestle or bamboo stick, take their places at equal intervals about a central spot on the ground, which forms the target at which they strike in turn. A fourth youth must jump first from one side and then another to the center and out again before each stroke falls, and the fourth time also when the wielders of the sticks strike together. In this game the jumper runs considerable risk of getting hit on the feet, unless he is very spry in his movements.

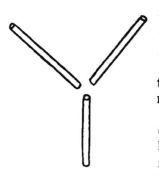

A third game with the pestles is called "stretching the neck" ("ta leh kah"). The four pestles required in this game are held in "criss-cross" fashion as in the first jumping game, but as high as one's shoulders. A young man stands beneath them, and another stands at one corner waving a naked sword above them. The four holding the ends of the pestles strike them together at brief intervals, while the youth beneath them must thrust his head up between the ends of the sticks and withdraw it again before they close about his neck, or the swinging sword touches him. Having done this on three sides in succession, the fourth time he must attempt it through the square in the middle. If he is successful in making the circuit three times without getting "his neck stretched," the assembled company are entitled to feel satisfied that it is well with the soul of the departed.

"Climbing the fruit tree" ("htaw the tha") is a very different kind of game from those described above, involving no physical risk inasmuch as it is a performance in pretending. A conventionalized picture of a tree with a knot part-way up the trunk, two

[5] Dr. Nieuwenhuis tells of a rice-pounder dance in Borneo performed by the women, who skip into the center and out again between the simultaneous strokes of the rice pestles. This dance is not unlike the funeral game described above. He also shows a picture of wrestling in Borneo, a sport evidently conducted like wrestling among the Karen. See plate 13, p. 137 of Dr. Nieuwenhuis's *Quer durch Borneo* (Leyden, 1907).

pairs of side branches and a central branch, each terminating in two twigs bearing a fruit and leaves, is drawn on the inside of a winnowing-tray. (See page 203.) Betel-nuts or small coins are laid on the sketch to represent the fruit. The man designated to "climb the tree" must receive his instructions from a woman sitting opposite. He begins by asking her: "In climbing the tree, how shall I go up?" To which she replies: "Go up to the big knot." Question and answer follow until he has passed his hand from point to point to the tip of a twig, secured the fruit there, and brought it to earth. This is repeated over and over again, in a way that would prove insufferably tedious to a Westerner, until the last fruit has been gathered. The assembled Karens seem never to tire of this game and regard it as a kind of offering to the departed friend.

A ceremony ("ta w maw") participated in by both the young men and maidens is that of blowing bamboo tubes, rattling bangles, and parading or prancing, rather than dancing, around the corpse. In Shwegyin this ceremony is performed at night. In other places it used to be performed in the daytime at the place of burial, but has largely disappeared in recent times. The young men cut for themselves pieces of small bamboo with the joint in the middle, leaving the ends open, and, provided with these, take their places around the corpse alternating with the maidens, who wear bangles of little round bells or rattling seeds on their wrists. The participants, now facing towards the body and now away from it, parade around it, keeping step to the mingled but pulsating tones of the whistles or open tubes blown by the men and the rattle of the bangles on the swinging arms of the girls. At the end of this noisy parade the men tear their bamboos open with their teeth and throw them down with a loud shout, in which the girls join while shaking their arms vigorously. The spirit of the dead, when it hears this shout, knows that its welfare has not been forgotten by the friends remaining behind and believes that it will be able to avoid all demons along its path. The friends expect this ceremony to speed the departed on his journey.

If the deceased is a very old person who has left all of his children and grandchildren married and with homes of their own, a special observance is celebrated in his behalf. This is called the "taw kwe tah" or the "taw klaw taw." I am not able to interpret these terms. Nowadays the ceremony is very rarely observed, and in the earlier times it seems to have been observed on the plains, but

## FUNERAL CUSTOMS

not at all in the Pegu Yomas. I have been told that on one occasion when this ceremony was to be performed at Letpadan, those concerned had to get permission from the township officer there and

A Sketch of a Tree Used in the Funeral Games

that they spoke of it as "collecting taxes for the soul." A company of young men disguise themselves, several of them in women's costumes and carrying fish-nets, one as a blind man, and another as a lame one. They circulate among the neighboring villages with much shouting and laughter, calling on the inhabitants to contribute sundry supplies. The members of the party who are impersonating women, go under the houses and pretend to catch fish in their nets. By such methods they manage to gather all they can carry of fruit, vegetables, and other kinds of food, which they consume on their return to the place where the funeral is being held. This ceremony is performed more frequently when the bones of the deceased are exhumed than at the time of his death.

After the ordinary daylight observances and the chanting of the poems in the evenings have been completed, the body is removed through an opening made for the purpose in the side of the house and is carried to the place where it is to be burned or buried. In the olden days it was usual to burn the body, but latterly burial is the common practice. The children used to be confined or tied up at home during the removal of the corpse. This was to prevent their being scared by the gruesome sight, thus causing their shades or "k'las" to withdraw from their bodies and make them sick, or to keep their "k'las" from being enticed to follow that of the dead person with the same result.

In Siam three beds of leaves and twigs are made along the path to the place of burning, the bearers stopping at these piles as though to put down their burden and rest, but allowing it barely to touch the bed when they raise it again and go on.

In those cases in which burning is resorted to, the body is placed upon a pile of fagots three or four feet high and more wood is piled on top. Dry bamboo torches are applied at two or more places and, after the fire is blazing, the body is pierced with long sharpened bamboos to allow the juices to exude and so hasten the process of incineration. Before the body has been wholly consumed, charred pieces of the bones and particularly of the skull are raked out, held near the fire, and addressed with the words: "If you are hot, sit by the fire." After this water is poured over them and they are told, if cold, to bathe and drink water. These injunctions to the bones again illustrate the curious conception on the part of the Karen that the conditions prevailing in the next world are just the reverse of those existing in the present one.

If the full funeral rites have been performed, the bones are ready to be deposited in the family burial-ground. If, however, the cremation has taken place before the performance of the full ceremonies, the bones are usually placed in a basket or wrapped in a cloth and taken home to be used again when the full rites are celebrated. This carrying home of the relics and celebrating a funeral later is called "ta hu taw pgha a' hki." It is done both on the plains and in the hills. If the person dies in the rainy or the harvest season, the practice is to dispose of the body quickly and hold the burial rites, namely, the games and recitation of the poems or "htas" at a more convenient time.

On their way back from the burning-place the people stop at intervals, look back, wave their hands, and call out: "Pru-r-r k'la, come back, come back." They are summoning their own "k'las" to keep them from remaining behind with that of the dead person. In order to prevent the "k'la" of the deceased from following after them, they set up branches of trees in the path, which is their method of warning friends not to take a certain path. In Siam the funeral party resort to the additional precaution of opening the trunk of a big rotten tree in the jungle the next morning and summoning the "k'la" of the deceased to abide in that. Having provided an offering of rice and water for the nourishment of the spirit here, they address the tree as follows:

"O Rotten Tree, you know hades and the land of the dead.
Be kind enough to show the deceased the way thither."

But few localities are left where the Karen still keep up their old burial-places. These localities are in the hills and on the eastern border of Burma. In these regions an elder of the bereaved family, who is familiar with the burial-place, takes the bones and valuables of the deceased, such as beads, ornaments, etc., to the spot and deposits them with the ashes of his ancestors. A man in the employ of a timber contractor told me of a chance visit made by him to one of these sacred burial-places. With a Karen driver he was in search of a working elephant that had strayed away. After crossing two or three mountain ridges and the intervening valleys, the Karen remarked that they were approaching his ancestral burial-spot and consented to lead his companion to it. They climbed to the top of the next ridge, where the ground was covered with huge boulders. Threading their way among these, they emerged into a grassy plot in the midst of which lay a boulder larger than the others, and, after clambering to the top of this rock, they found therein a deep hole in which the family relics of the elephant driver were deposited. His companion thrust the shaft of his spear nearly its whole length into the hole, the mouth of which was not more than four of five inches in diameter, and, poking about, could hear the jingling of silver, probably bracelets, beads, rings, and other jewelry. It is said that hollow trees and the limestone caves that are so common in the hills of Burma and Siam, contain many such hidden treasures. In the Pegu Hills the people appear to bury the relics of their dead wherever fancy dictates and to pay no further attention to the spot. Indeed, as a whole the Karen raise no monuments over their dead. When the remains of a woman are buried, not only her trinkets and ornaments are buried with her, but also her pigs and fowls which, as her peculiar property, are killed and deposited with her relics.

Both in the hills and on the plains it is the custom to dig up the bones of the dead who have been carried off by epidemics, as well as of those who have died at inconvenient times, and hold ceremonies over them. It is said that in Shwegyin December ("La plü"), which is the month of eclipses and of the dead, is the time when these ceremonies are usually performed. On the plains the months of the hot season are those chosen for these rites.

When the bones are brought back to serve as the center of the burial ceremonies, they are placed in a little basket and set within a small enclosure. In the Pegu Hills they are put under a small canopy, but on the plains the receptacle for them is made in the form of a miniature pagoda ("hko so law") or a little hut ("hko saw"). The hut is a model of a house with its ladder, water pots, etc. The basket containing the bones is put into the hut, and one end of a string is tied to the basket and the other let down into a water jar under the miniature house. This arrangement makes it possible for the "k'la" of the deceased to go down for a drink whenever it is thirsty. Early in the morning one of the elders carries a firebrand out to the hut, which is usually situated outside of the village. There he lifts out a piece of the bone and heats it with the glowing brand, saying: "If you are hot, sit by the fire." Then he pours water over it and tells it to drink and bathe, if it is cold. This he does in turn with each fragment of the bone. Finally, he puts the firebrand under the hut, calls back his own "k'la," and returns home. On top of the hut an image of a parrot is left, in case the deceased is an unmarried person; but for married persons two such images are set up. These birds are supposed to help carry the spirit of the deceaseed to its next abiding-place. As long as the bones are in the hut the friends take food to the "k'la" every day.

If the deceased is unmarried, the friends sometimes chant poems deriding him for dying before he has left any offspring to perpetuate his stock on earth. When they are ready to carry the hut to the grave, they remove the image of the parrot ("t'le") and bury it at the fork of the roads with its head towards the jungle, probably so that it will fly in that direction and carry the "k'la" of the deceased into the woods. On their return the love poems ("na do") are chanted by the young men and maidens, and early next morning the hut with the little basket of bones inside is taken to the back of the usual burying-place and left there. The funeral party stops long enough to say: "We have brought you here with all your belongings. Remain here." On their way home they do not forget to call their "k'las" frequently, lest these should be tempted to stay behind. In the case of the burial of married persons the mourners cook eggs, rice, and curry and spread a feast near the hut. They request the spirit of the dead to come and eat and then to depart to the king of spirits, "Mü Hka," and not to return. The hut and its contents are then removed to the burial-place and left there. The closing ceremony is one performed over the bones at noon of the last day of the rites, its object being to discover whether the "k'la" of the departed has yet reached the land of delight whence it will not return, or whether it is still wandering around and, therefore, liable to entice away the "k'las" of its relatives and friends. This final ceremony is called "t'yaw lo ke a' k'la." A slender bamboo or stock of elephant grass is stuck in the ground obliquely near the foot of the hut, and from its top is suspended a newly spun cotton string on which is tied a piece of the charred bone of the dead person and below it a bit of cotton wool. Four or five more pieces of bone separated by bits of the wool are strung on the cord, the end of which is attached to a gold or yellow bracelet. Directly under the bracelet a cup containing a boiled duck egg and a lump of cooked rice is set. The relatives now sit down and chant a poem or "hta," in which their love for the deceased is expressed. Then each member of the family strikes the cup and bracelet a gentle blow and, calling the dead by name, asks his spirit to return. If nothing unusual happens, they know that it has arrived at its destination and will never come back again. If, however, the string vibrates considerably or breaks, as may happen, when somebody taps the bracelet there is great lamentation for they are then convinced that the "k'la" is present and has descended the string. Hence, offerings of food must be continued to prevent the "k'la" from exercising its enticing power on that of some living relative.

The "k'las" of the children are thought to be especially susceptible to such influence, and among the Bwes extraordinary precautions are taken to protect the children. The Bwe grandmother, who is head of the "Bgha" feast, wraps a pair of fowls in a number of garments, each of her grandchildren supplying one. She then calls back the spirits of the children to prevent them from being attracted by the "Mü xa." After the necks of the fowls have been wrung their flesh is eaten by the family, while the "Mü xa" are supposed to feed upon the essence of the chickens.

The Karen bury their children soon after death, and seem to take no further notice of their passing. When parents have had the misfortune to lose several of their offspring shortly after birth, they believe that the spirits from some vague region have sought mortal birth through their instrumentality, simply to gain the ornaments and trinkets that Karen are in the habit of giving to their children. Having secured these coveted possessions, the spirits return to their former abode with their undeserved rewards. The Karen call this fleeting existence "ta plu aw ka," which means "gaining something by entering life." Parents thus taken advantage of, as they feel, have recourse to a revolting method of terrifying a spirit of this greedy type. After a child has died and been carried to the burial-place, the indignant father thrusts a spear or sword through and through the little body or slashes it with a "dah," that is, a long knife, in the hope that the spirit, seeing how badly its temporary mortal tenement is being treated, may fear to come back again.

Our study of funeral customs among the Karen shows that, in the case of adults at least, funerals are festal and feasting occasions. Much rice and pork curry are consumed and, in the olden time, liquor flowed freely. In earlier times when people of different villages met at a funeral, a spirit of rivalry was shown in the improvising and chanting of the poems and sometimes in other ways. I have in my possession an old bronze funeral drum, which was reputed to be the sweetest sounding drum in the hills at the head of Thonze Creek.[6] On its rim "dah" cuts appear which are the lasting marks of a fight in which rival groups of villagers engaged

---

[6] See Chapter XIII on Bronze Drums, pp. 121-123.

long ago, because some of those present expressed a decided preference for the musical tones of this drum over those of other drums belonging to members of neighboring villages.

Although many who took part in some of the old funeral celebrations were undoubtedly under the influence of liquor and in a corresponding state of hilarity, funerals do not seem to have become the occasion of feuds or even of drunken brawls. Young people came together on more intimate terms at funerals than was permitted at other times, and some of their poems would not bear reproduction in print. Probably at times their conduct also went beyond the bounds of propriety, but such lapses seem to have been rare and bitterly regretted. However, it is clear that Karen mourners succeeded in drowning their sorrow and believed that by means of their festivities they had sent the spirit of their dead rejoicing on its way to its future abode.

## CHAPTER XXI
## RELIGIOUS CONCEPTIONS

### THE THREE CONCEPTIONS

Among the Karen we find traces of three distinct religious conceptions, which have left their impress upon the people. The principle underlying the most primitive religious ideas is that of an impersonal power or force residing both in men and things, but which is all-pervasive, invisible except as it betrays itself by its effect on certain things, and invincible in that it can only be overcome in a particular person or thing by a more powerful manifestation of itself in some other object.[1] The Karen designate this force "pgho." It is the equivalent of what the Melanesians know as "mana" and is defined in the *Karen Thesaurus* as a certain more or less unknown force believed to be all about and which can not be overcome.[2] It may reside in certain individuals who, by its aid, are enabled to accomplish unusual tasks. It can be imparted to objects which, by its power, become charms potent for good or ill. The deities are said to possess "pgho" and on that account to be able to do wonderful things. It is also spoken of by the people as revealing itself in the infinite attributes of "Y'wa," the eternal God, but this is, of course, an adaptation to Christian teachings. However, it is in the realm of the magic, rather than in that of religion, that this power is particularly exploited. Those who are able to perform magical deeds are called "pgha a pgho," that is, persons of "pgho."[3]

The second religious conception attained by the Karen was the animistic. They entered upon this stage of religious belief when they began to assign personal attributes to the various powers about them, conceiving of every unknown force as a more or less distinct personality. Thus, they personified the vegetative force in the crops as the goddess "Hpi Bi Yaw;" they conceived of the agency that brought the dry and rainy seasons (the monsoon in reality, of course,) as two different demons, each ruling in the upper air dur-

---
[1] This view was first brought to the attention of scholars by Bishop R. H. Codrington in his work, *The Melanesians*, pp. 227 ff. Compare also J. E. Carpenter, *Comparative Religion*, pp. 80, ff. for a brief but full discussion of the subject.
[2] The *Karen Thesaurus*, old ed., Vol. III, p. 489.
[3] In speaking of the attributes of "Y'wa" the people say: "Y'wa a pgho a pkhaw." The use of the couplet gives a more finished form of speech.

ing a period of six months to the exclusion of the other; they assigned a lord ("k' sa") to every mountain and river, and they invested every utensil and object about the house and the animals out-of-doors with separate ghosts ("k'las"). Some of these imaginary beings are beneficent, such as the "Mü xa" or celestial spirits that preside over births; but most of them are malevolent and have to be appeased by continual offerings, sacrifices, and tabus. To keep on good terms with these innumerable spirits consumes a large part of the time and thought of the Karen.[4]

The third conception in the religious traditions of the people is embodied in the "Y'wa" legend, which tells of the placing of the first parents in the garden by "Y'wa," the Creator; their temptation to eat of the forbidden fruit by a serpent or dragon, etc. This story so closely resembles that of the ancient Hebrews, as also certain western Asiatic traditions, that one finds it difficult not to believe that all these traditions somehow had a common origin. Were the "Y'wa" legend marked by distinctive features, we might regard it as one exhibiting only a general resemblance to other traditions extant in other parts of the world, but its parallelism with the account in Genesis precludes this view of the case.[5]

At any rate, the "Y'wa" legend has exercised a strong influence upon the Karen people. To be sure, it did not supplant the ancient animism of the tribes any more than Buddhism has displaced spirit worship among the Burmese. Nevertheless, it was accompanied by the prophesy of the return of the white brother with the Lost Book, which inspired the Karen with the hope of a better future and furnished an admirable foundation on which Christian teachers could build in promoting the development of the Karen nation which, during the last hundred years—the period not only of Christian missions but also of the British conquest and administration of Burma—has been truly remarkable.

## The "Y'wa" Tradition

The contrast between the animistic and the "Y'wa" conception of the creation of the world is illustrated in the lines of the following "hta" or poem:

> "When first the earth was made,
> Who worked and built it?
> When it was first formed,
> Who was the creator?"

---
[4] See Chapter XXII on Supernatural and Mythical Beings, p. 223.
[5] See pp. 10-12.

> "When first the world was created,
> The edolius and the termite toiled together.
> When the earth was first formed,
> These two helped each other and made it."

The "Y'wa" conception appears in the last stanza, given below:

> "When first the earth was formed,
> It was God ('Y'wa') who formed it.
> When first the world was fashioned,
> It was God who fashioned it."

In some of the omitted parts of the poem we find the thought expressed that the edolius and the termite were co-workers with God in creating the world. It should, perhaps, be explained that the termite is the white ant, which builds high mounds all over the country; while the *edolius paradiscus* is a black bird, a little smaller than a crow, with two long tail quills having tufts of feathers at the ends. Why this bird should have been given a part in the work of creation does not appear.

Characterization of "Y'wa" as the Eternal One is herewith given in two translations from an ancient poem, the first of these being by an unknown person of an earlier time and the other by Dr. Francis Mason.

> "God is eternal, He alone [existed]
> Before the world was made; His throne
> Interminable ages stood,
> And He, the everlasting God.
> Two worlds may pass, and yet He lives.
> Perfect in attributes divine,
> Age after age His glories shine." [7]

The rendering by Dr. Mason is as follows:

> "God is unchangeable, external;
> He was in the beginning of the world.
> God is endless and eternal;
> He existed in the beginning of the world.
> God is truly unchangeable and eternal;
> He existed in ancient time, at the beginning of the world.
> The life of God is endless;
> A succession of worlds does not measure his existence.
> God is perfect in every meritorious attribute,
> And dies not in succession on succession of worlds." [8]

---

[6] Rev. T. Than Bya, D.D., *Karen Customs, Ceremonies, and Poetry*, p. 51. The Karen name for the edolius is "hto hklu." Dr. Mason speaks of it as the Moulmein nightingale: *Burma*, p. 219.

[7] This version is printed in D. M. Smeaton's *The Loyal Karens of Burma*.

[8] Mason, *The Karen Apostle*, ap., p. 97.

Besides being called eternal, God is described as "all powerful" and as "having the knowledge of all things." He created man and "woman from a rib of man," and he made the animals and placed them on the earth.

The power mentioned in the old poems as opposed to "Y'wa" and as having brought evil into the world is "Naw k' plaw." In later poems the name given to him is "Mü kaw li," which is a term of reproach used on account of his often being supposed to assume the female form, in order to accomplish his deceptions on the human race.[9]

He is said to have been a servant of "Y'wa" at first, but to have been cast out of his lord's presence for offering him a gross insult. The other servants of "Y'wa" have ever since cherished the desire to destroy "Mü kaw li," but have never accomplished their purpose. Hence, he continues to roam about, deceiving mankind and spreading death among them, until he shall finally be put out of the way by "Y'wa" himself. He is the direct author of evil and of the curse that has fallen upon the earth which, before his contemptible conduct, had produced rice with kernels as large as pumpkins. It was through his malicious instructions that the people learned to make sacrifices to the "Bgha" and other demons.

The Karen legends and poems give the story of the fall of man in their own picturesque language, which has been translated into English by Dr. D. C. Gilmore, who has brought together the several versions extant in various parts of the country. For the most part I shall paraphrase and condense Dr. Gilmore's translation; for the original narratives, whether in prose or verse, are full of repetitions, variations in insignificant details, and other peculiarities incident to tales that have been handed down by word of mouth.

The Lord "Y'wa," father of the human race, spoke to the first pair he had created: "My son and daughter both, your father will make an orchard for you, and in that orchard there will be seven kinds of trees bearing seven kinds of fruit. Of the seven kinds there

---
[9] The derivation of the names of this being are interesting. "Naw" is the usual feminine prefix of the names of all females, and "k' plaw" signifies quickly, in reference to the suddenness with which his power to tempt one was exercised. The later name, which has now come into universal use both among non-Christian and Christian Karens as the designation of the Devil, is composed of "mü," meaning woman; "kaw," signifying the state of or pertaining to, and "li," denoting the female *locus impudicus*. This combination constitutes a term of the utmost contempt and refers to the insult which Satan visited upon "Y'wa" when offerings were being brought to him. The Devil's offering was a flower on which he had micturated. His act was discovered and aroused the anger of the entire celestial company.

CLIMBING THE COCOANUT-PALM

Often they climb the palm without any aid whatever. But in this case the boy has bound his feet together loosely with a Burmese loin-cloth ("longyi") to enable him to grip the trunk more easily.

is one that is not good to eat. Do not partake of it. If you eat of it, you will fall ill; you will grow old; you will die. Do not eat it. Now, whatever else I have made, I will give it all to you. Behold it and eat it. Once in seven days I will come and see you. Obey me in whatever I have commanded you. Keep my words. Do not forget me. Worship me every morning and evening."

By-and-by the Devil, in the form of a great serpent, came and engaged them in conversation, asking them what they were doing and what they had to eat. They replied that their father had provided them with more than sufficient food and escorted him to the orchard, where they pointed out the several varieties of the trees and told him the flavor of the fruit of six of the varieties. Concerning the taste of the seventh, they admitted their ignorance, inasmuch as they had been warned by their father not to eat of it. Thereupon, the Devil informed the pair that their father did not wish them well, that the fruit of the forbidden tree was the sweetest and richest of all and, moreover, would transform them into gods, enabling them to ascend to heaven, to fly, and to burrow under the ground at will. He declared that the Lord God was envious of them, while he, the Devil, loved them and was telling them the whole truth as they might easily prove by partaking of the forbidden fruit.

The man was not persuaded by the plausible words of Satan, maintained that they would comply with the orders of their father, and left the intruder. But his wife, "Naw I-u," listened to the Devil's seductive voice, was half-persuaded and sought assurance by inquiring whether she and her husband would really fly if they ate of this wonderful fruit. The Devil again insisted that he loved them dearly, and that he was trying to convince her of the truth. When she ate the fruit, the Devil laughed and told her to give some of it to her husband; otherwise, if she should die, she alone would perish, or if she should become like a goddess, she would be left without a companion. She did as directed and, after considerable persuasion, her husband also partook of the fruit, to the delight of Satan.

On the day following the eating of the forbidden fruit the Lord "Y'wa" came to see the disobedient pair and laid his curse upon them, declaring that they would grow old, sicken, and die; that their offspring would pass away at all ages, and that some of their descendants would have no more than half a family, that is, six children. Not only was the curse of "Y'wa" visited upon them, but also upon their first child, as was manifest by its falling sick. As "Y'wa" had forsaken them they appealed to the Devil, who replied that they must obey him to the end and promised to instruct them in the customs of his father and mother. Accordingly, he caught and killed a pig and examined its gall-bladder, explaining that if this organ were well rounded, the omen would be favorable; but if thin and flabby, there would be little hope for the recovery of the child. In case the child regained his health, they were to make a demon feast. Inasmuch as the little one did get well, they celebrated the feast according to instructions. Not long after another child was taken sick and, although they consulted the prescribed omen, there was no improvement in its condition. They, therefore, appealed again to the serpent, who told the father to catch a fowl which was to be used in calling back the spirit of the sick one. "Mü kaw li" placed the fowl, together with a bundle of chaff, a bundle of rice, and a bundle of potsherds, in a net, which he carried into the jungle, followed by the parents. There he plucked the feathers from the fowl and laid them, together with the three bundles, in the middle of the path. He then prayed: "Spirit, Spirit. The spirit has gone to hades. The spirit has gone to hell. Release the spirit." Next he cooked the fowl and tried its bones, to see whether they were soft or not. But he would not commit himself as to the favorableness or unfavorableness of the omen, telling the parents that they must watch and wait, and that meantime he would treat the case in every possible way. Nevertheless, the child died, and the Devil could give the bereaved ones no other consolation than that when the chicken bones were found in the future to be like those he had tested, they would know the omen to be unfavorable. He also taught them a charm to be used when there was sickness in the family, and, in connection with the charm, they were to wind seven threads.[10] Having wrought all this mischief and failed to furnish any certain relief from it, the Devil departed; while the man and his wife took up the task of teaching their offspring the ceremonies and charms in which he had instructed them.[11]

---

[10] See p. 221.

[11] The form of the tradition which is found among the Gaihko tribe is more explicit than the versions found elsewhere. The original ancestors of the human race are by them called "Ai-ra-bai" or "E ra bai," and "Mo ra mu" or "Moren meu". (Among the Sgaws they are called, respectively, "Saw Tha nai" and "Naw E u"). From the first pair they count by name thirty generations to the time of "Pan dan man," when the people attempted to build a

There can be no doubt but that the above legend of the fall of man [12] has been largely responsible for the readiness with which the Karen people have accepted Christianity. It led them to believe that they began their existence as a race under the care and protection of "Y'wa," which their ancestors soon forfeited by their disobedience in following the deceptive advice of "Mü kaw li." They believe that their present practices originated from an evil source and should be abandoned; but their veneration for their ancestors and the customs established by them, in addition to their fear of worse consequences should they depart from time-honored usage, makes it exceedingly difficult for them to give up the old ways. They acknowledge the goodness of "Y'wa" and their obligation to worship him; but they feel so hedged about by a multitude of demons who will bring calamities upon them and devour their souls that they placate these, while believing that "Y'wa" will not harm them even though they should not render homage unto him.

They illustrate their predicament by the story of a family occupying a hut near a field during the cultivating season. While the father and mother were absent at work, the children were terrified at home by a tiger that sprang from the bushes and made off with the sow. At nightfall the children told their parents what had happened. Before going into the field next morning, the father built a high platform of bamboos on which he placed the children and the motherless pigs, telling the children not to climb down during the day lest the tiger should again appear. The beast returned as expected and filled the air with its angry roaring, until the children threw down one of the pigs in the hope of quieting it. From time to time during the day its roaring was recompensed in the same manner, the children, meantime, watching the path with straining eyes for the return of their father and mother and listening intently for the sound of the bow-string which should tell them that an arrow was speeding on its way to put an end to the tiger. Thus "Y'wa" was apparently leaving the Karen people to their fate, while they were keeping on good terms with "Mü kaw li" by means of

---

pagoda which should reach to heaven. When the pagoda was half built, God came down and confounded the speech of the people and they became scattered. The father of the Gaihko tribe was reputed to be "Than man rai," who came westward from the Red Karen country in which they had all previously dwelt, and with eight chiefs settled in the valley of the Sittang River. Dr. Francis Mason doubts the antiquity of this legend, for it certainly shows the marks of Hebrew influence. (Dr. Mason in *Journal, Asiatic Society of Bengal*, 1868, Vol. XXXVII, p. 163).

[12] The above paraphrase is based on the translation of the legends by Dr. Mason as printed in the *Journal, Burma Research Society*, Vol. I, Pt. II, pp. 36, ff.

offerings and ceremonies and were hoping for the return of the white brother with the Lost Book.

## Beliefs Concerning the Soul and the Life Principle

The Karen distinguish between the "tha" or soul and the "k'la" or life principle (shade) of every human being. They think of the soul as the seat of their moral nature, endowed with conscience, that is, the power of apprehending right and wrong, and with a personality that persists after death. The soul is responsible and is judged for the acts in the flesh. The "k'la" is more intimately associated with one's physical existence. It is the force that keeps one alive and well. As it is being constantly solicited by demons and more or less by the "k'las" of dead relatives to leave the body, it needs the protection of charms, offerings, and medicines.[13] As the "k' la" comes from a previous existence to inhabit the body at the time of birth and departs into a new existence at death, so also it leaves the body for brief periods and at frequent intervals, as during sleep. If it remains away longer than usual, its absence causes the sickness and even the death of the body. As the "k' la" may be away visiting friends or on other errands during the sleeping hours, it is not safe to waken a sleeper suddenly. His "k' la" may not have yet returned, in which case he could not long survive. One Karen told me that he had dreamed of seeing various persons in heaven and hell and naively remarked that his "k' la" must have journeyed to those abodes during his sleep. Another Karen, whose wife underwent a surgical operation at a hospital in the city, asked me whether the ether cone was not used to extract and hold her "k' la," in order to render her unconscious, the "k' la" being restored to her to enable her to regain her faculties. The "k' las" of children are supposed to be peculiarly susceptible to being enticed away by those of the dead. Hence, it is customary to tie children up in the house while a corpse is being carried out. I have experienced considerable difficulty in inducing the inhabitants of outlying villages to let me take their pictures, for fear their "k' las" would be carried off along with the photo-

---

[13] A full study of the Karen "k' la" and "tha" was made by the early missionaries to determine which of these two words should be used in translating the word, soul. "Tha" was the word finally chosen. The results of these studies are recorded, those of Dr. Wade, in *The Karen Thesaurus*, new ed., Vol. I, 442, ff, and those of Dr. Mason in the *Journal, Asiatic Society of Bengal*, Vol. XXX, Pt. II, 195, ff.

graph.[14] In the early days when white men were still a strange sight to the people, they would beat their breasts and call their "k' las" to come back, evidently fearing that the latter would follow in curiosity after the strangers. A friend of mine had a similar experience among the Karen of Siam only a few years ago.

The people think that a wandering "k'la" may remain invisible or assume the form of the person himself. Stories are told of these wandering ghosts. A man who had been absent from his village met the apparition of his wife on his way home. It informed him that it was going to see its mother, but it consented to spend the night with him in the jungle. As they had no food, the ghost, which was supposed by the man to be his wife in person, went back to their house and took what food it wanted from the cooking pots, without revealing itself at all. Next morning the man and his ghostly wife took their separate paths, the former being greatly shocked on arriving in the village to find the burial rites of his wife in progress. Realizing that it was his wife's "k'la" which he had met in the jungle, he wished that he had called it back. Another story relates that a husband was so incensed at seeing his wife (the apparition being really her "k'la") wandering abroad that he struck her in the face. This act had the desired effect, for the "k' la" hastened back to its deserted body and thereby put an abrupt end to the funeral ceremonies, which were already in progress. This wandering propensity of the "k'la" leads to other complications than those already mentioned. The elders are authority for the statement that even though a couple are living together as man and wife, their "k' las" may form unions with those of other persons, especially during the hours of sleep. Even the efforts of a necromancer to summon the wandering "k' la" of a sick person may result in attracting the "k' la" of some other person to occupy the deserted body, in whose behalf the efforts are being put forth. The new occupant may remain only while generous offerings are made to it, and the sick person is sure to experience a serious relapse when it leaves.

It seems to be believed also that the "k' las" of human beings may take on other forms, such as those of insects. Animals have "k' las" which can do the same thing. Sometimes when moths are

---

[14] Sir J. G. Frazer quotes Dr. Nieuwerhuis, who tells of a similar experience among the people of Borneo: *Golden Bough*, Vol. III, p. 99. Some of the Karen object to having their photographs taken on account of their fear of sympathetic magic, that is, they fear that an accident to the photograph would cause a similar one to the original.

A Hill Village in Transition
The family rooms have become separate buildings, each with its own ladder.

A Karen Village on the Plains
The Karen do not set their houses in an orderly arrangement, but each man builds where he likes within the village plot. The taller trees are cocoanut-palms, the others are "toddy-palms." Notice the pots put up to catch the sap from which the toddy is made.

flying about a light people say: "Let the "k' las" of beasts and other creatures fall into the flame, but let the 'k' las' of men fly carefully and save themselves."

Inanimate objects have their "k' las," as well as the lower creatures. Ownership in such possessions is duly observed by killing the pigs and fowls of a woman when she dies. The remains are thrown away or given to foreigners, who do not share the superstitions of the Karen. The paddy-cleaning implements and clothing of the deceased are either burned or buried with the corpse, unless they are laid on top of her grave. In like manner the oxen belonging to a man who has died are killed and disposed of, while his personal effects are burned or put in the grave with him. Otherwise, the owner's "k' la" might return to the village for his property and thereby bring calamity on the inhabitants.

The idea seems to prevail among the Karen that the "k' las" enter and leave their bodies through the fontanel on the top of the head. In case a child falls and cries the mother will blow on this spot, in order to keep the life principle from escaping. However, the customary method of preventing the escape of the "k' la" is to tie a string around the wrists, either one or both of them, after fanning up the arms to blow the "k' la" back. Anybody may perform this act, but the services of elders or necromancers ("wi") are preferred.

Another conception of the "k' la," quite distinct from that set forth above, is that it is a seven-fold spirit inhabiting the body, whose death it is constantly striving to accomplish through one or another of seven methods, namely, insanity, licentiousness, epilepsy, oppression, diseases, accidents, and injury by wild beasts. Even from the birth of a person the seven-fold "k' la" accepts the responsibility of causing his or her death and is engaged in constant struggle with that person's "so" (personality or character) for the mastery. As long as the "so" is strong, it serves as the individual's guardian angel; and he remains immune both from the attacks of the seven-fold "k' la" and from the magic arts of witches and necromancers. However powerful the charm that may be employed against him, his dominating "so" will ward it off; but if his "so" should become weak, he will soon lose his immunity.[15]

---

[15] See Dr. J. Wade's account in *The Karen Thesaurus*, new ed., Vol. I, pp. 450, ff.

## The Continuity of Life

The Karen do not appear to have conceived the idea of an immortal life. They speak of "k' las" in "plu" (hades) as dying, when the "k' las" are believed to enter an intermediate stage of existence, becoming "sgheu." These "sgheu" are represented as something like eggs or bladders filled with a vaporous substance. When, later, these vapor-filled objects burst, their contents spread over the fields; and the developing flowers of the paddy and other plants are thereby fertilized, for the vapor contains the fructifying principle. When the grain is eaten as food, its life-giving power is communicated to the blood. Thence, it is imparted to the seminal fluid, by means of which men and animals are enabled to propagate life. The transmission of life from shades or ghosts back to life again is expressed in Karen speech by the root "lo," which signifies to expose or open one thing to the influence of another. Inasmuch as the fecundating of the paddy takes place in the rainy season, the "Law hpo," a company of demons who regulate the rainfall, are supposed to act as agents in bringing it about. When the kernels are forming in the heads of the paddy, the Karen are wont to say: "Bu deu htaw li," which means literally, "The paddy has conceived." [16]

---

[16] See Chapter XXII on Supernatural and Mythical Beings, p. 230.

# CHAPTER XXII

# SUPERNATURAL AND MYTHICAL BEINGS

In the Karen demonism the spirits are nearly all malevolent, and it takes a large share of the time of the people to keep on good terms with them. In the hills and remote regions these mythical beings still hold sway; but the average Karen on the plains of Lower Burma retains only a vague and dubious belief in these powers, which have lost their control over him for the most part, now that he has come into contact with many outside influences. The fullest account of these spirits is given in the *Karen Thesaurus* and the writings of Drs. Francis Mason and E. B. Cross. It is from these records, written in the early days before the Karen were disturbed by civilizing influences, that I have chiefly drawn the materials for this chapter.[1]

These numerous beings may be divided into three groups or divisions: first, those spirits that are thought to dwell apart, to possess human attributes, and to control the destiny of men and events; second, the spirits of mortals that for some reason have been condemned to wander about and that have relations, usually evil, with living men; and, third, a number of hetergeneous spirits that never were mortal, but still can influence men at various times and places. The members of this class are not so generally recognized as those of the first class.

In the first group are the "Mü xa" and the "Hti k' sa kaw k' sa," both of which are conceived of as being companies of divinities; "Naw k' plaw" or "Mü kaw li," who corresponds to Satan; "Hpi Bi Yaw," the Karen corn maiden; "Hkü Te," the ruler of hades, and "Teu Kweh," the rainbow.

The "Mü xa" seem to be a race of celestial beings, of whom "Mü xa do" (literally, the great "Mü xa") is the king. They appear to have existed prior to men, but good men may after death become members of their company and dwell with them in the upper regions of the air. They are not malicious, although offerings are

---

[1] Dr. J. Wade, *The Karen Thesaurus*, ed. of 1915, Vol. I, pp. 455-484; Dr. F. Mason, *Journal, Asiatic Society of Bengal*, Vol. XXXIV, Pt. II, pp. 195, ff; Rev. E. B. Cross, *Journal, Oriental Society*, Vol. IV, (1854) pp. 312, ff.

made to them lest their anger should be aroused by some untoward act on the part of men. Their special task is to preside over births. Their king occupies himself with the creation of men, but, being interrupted continually by various demands upon his attention, he turns out many defectives, cripples, and badly colored ones. This poor workmanship led men in the past to revile the "Mü xa," who, consequently, no longer show themselves to mortals. They have the power to unite the souls of those whom they have predestined to marry. Those thus paired are vouchsafed prosperous and happy lives; but if they succeed in mating with others than those intended for them, incompatibility and adversity surely follow. The "Mü xa" are often addressed as though they were the parents of mankind and appear to hold places comparable to that of Zeus or Jupiter among the gods of the ancient Greeks and Romans. They are often spoken of in Karen lore as dwelling on Mount "Thaw Thi," as Zeus in Greek mythology had his abode on Mount Olympus.[2] In the celebration of family rites and feasts the "Mü xa" are recognized by having words addressed to them, although the family spirits, commonly designated as "Bgha," are often thought of as the powers to be propitiated at this ceremony. In some sections of the country the "parents of mankind" are supposed to receive offerings in their extended hands, which are thereby cleansed. They are then expected to return to their celestial abode, the hope being that they will not descend again to the dwelling-place of mortals, lest, by some mischance, they should become offended and bring misfortune upon men. They are believed to be able to assume any form they wish and to render themselves visible or invisible at will.[3]

One member of this group, called "Mü xa hkleu," is thought to preside over the much-venerated banyan *(Ficus religiost)*. It was under a banyan tree that Gautama Buddha received his enlightenment. The banyan is, however, held sacred by most of the tribes of Indo-China, even though they are not Buddhists. No doubt the wonderful vitality of the seeds of this tree which germinate anywhere, especially in the crotches of other trees and in the head of the palm, later enveloping, killing, and thriving on its host, has helped to evoke the veneration of the peoples familiar with the banyan. According to the Karen legends, the rhinoceros ("ta do hkaw") is the beast on which the guardian spirit of the banyan tree is accustomed

---

[2] See Chapter XXV in regard to Mount "Thaw Thi," pp. 262-264.
[3] For a description of the rites tendered to the "Mü xa" see pp. 248, 254, 260.

to ride when searching for the "k' las" of human beings. Any person who kills one of these animals arouses the enmity of the spirit.

The "Hti k' sa kaw k' sa," or "lords of the water and land," or "lords of the earth," are the deities who rule over the lands of the earth. They are superior to the spirits that preside over rivers and mountains and have tempers that are easily disturbed. Ill-spoken words, as well as improper and immoral actions, easily offend them; and they take vengeance on persons guilty of such misdemeanors by sending tigers, snakes, and various illnesses upon them. They are sometimes confused with the king of hades, who also passes judgment on the sins of mortals. One way to avoid angering the lords of the earth is to scrape a little rice from the top of the pot while cooking and lay it aside as an offering to them. Concerning their relation to these divinities, the people say that if they transgress in their language while in a distant land, the lords of the earth will kill them before dark; but if guilty of swearing or using indecent words in their own country, they can assuage the anger of these spirits by making an offering of rice and water at the foot of a tree and uttering the following prayer: "O Lords of the earth, we are ignorant people. Whatever transgressions we have been guilty of in using harsh or obscene words, do not, O Lords, hold them against us. We will make offerings annually. If we do not die, you shall eat of our food every year and of our children's offerings generation after generation."

Every tree, river, lake, and, indeed, almost every natural object is supposed by the Karen to be inhabited by its "k' sa" or divinity. These local spirits, however, are regarded by many as constituting lower orders of the divinities of the first group. When a man selects the location for his field, he must perform certain ceremonies to win their good will. The simplest of these is to place offerings of rice and water at the foot of some large tree in the plot chosen or to go through the ceremonies described in the chapter on Agricultural Pursuits and Other Occupations.[4] There are also the annual sacrifices to these spirits that have been described fully in the chapter on Propitiatory Sacrifices and Healing Offerings, pp. 234, ff.

The nefarious work and character of "Naw k' plaw" or "Mü kaw li" have been sufficiently revealed in the narration of the story of his temptation of the first parents of the Karen race in the

---

[4] See *ante*, pp. 76, ff.

orchard that was planted for them by the great and eternal God, "Y'wa." (See pp. 214-216.)

The divinity that presides over the cultivation of the paddy is known as "Hpi Bi Yaw." The legend relating to this goddess states that she and her spouse, in the form of pythons, slept on the paddy pile of a certain man and thereby caused the increase of his grain until it filled three bins, but that the ungrateful wretch killed the male serpent, bringing a curse upon himself as the result of which his supply gave out at the end of three months. In the attempt to buy enough grain to furnish food for his family he was reduced to poverty. After this "Hpi Bi Yaw" taught an orphan how to raise abundant crops in return for offerings which he made to her. As the other people were ignorant of what was expected of them, she first destroyed their crops and later caused their death, thereby instituting the custom of sacrifices in her honor.

Another legend in regard to "Hpi Bi Yaw" relates that in the guise of a dreadful old hag she begged men, who were seeking food in the jungle during a famine, to share with her. They refused; but an orphan, following in her path, took pity on her and was rewarded by being instructed in all the arts of raising paddy. Beginning with three kernels, which he took from the stomach of a dove, he grew both the early and the ordinary varieties of rice, as well as the glutinous rice. With a small knife given him by the goddess he was able to clear away the jungle-growth from his field at a stroke. Returning home with him, she directed him to boil a pot of water, and into it she shook an ample quantity of rice for the meal from her finger-tips. Through her favor his field surpassed all others in productivity and was cut by one sweep of the sickle. The grain was transferred from the field to its bin by magic, and, although stolen by the villagers, was restored by the goddess's dancing in the empty bin. During successive years she befriended the orphan and even dwelt in a hut in his field during the cultivating season, until he became prosperous enough to marry. The very next season, however, the orphan's wife became jealous of the goddess, came to the field, and beat her with a bamboo pole, until the divinity managed to escape from her assailant by changing herself into a cricket and hiding in a crab's burrow. "Hpi Bi Yaw" became so incensed at the outrageous treatment she had received that she has never returned since to aid any mortal; but offerings are made to her, and the rim of earth that encircles the entrance to crabs' burrows is placed on top of the paddy pile and in the bin in her honor.[5]

"Hkü Te" is the lord of the region of death, the king of hades. His origin is explained as follows: A couple dwelling in the spirit

A BWE KAREN CHRISTIAN VILLAGE, TOUNGOO DISTRICT
The Karen still love to build their houses as close together as possible.

realm once plotted to slay and devour their son-in-law. Accordingly, they turned themselves into giant winding creepers hanging across the road by which their intended victim was returning from his field, carrying a basket of paddy. Instead of attempting to pass under the vines, as he was expected to do, the son-in-law severed them with his sickle. One of the creepers, the wife, immediately flew upward to the sky and became a rainbow, while the other penetrated the earth, resumed his original form as a man, and became king of hades. There he receives the souls of mortals and rules over the dead. As judge of those under his authority he grants permission to the ones that have lived worthily to enter the higher realms, but he condemns to the lowest hell those of base lives. No offerings are made to this Karen Pluto.

---

[5] See *ante*, p. 62. An account of the ceremonies performed in connection with the cultivation of paddy occupies pp. 54-62. The myth concerning "Hpi Bi Yaw" resembles more or less that of the Irish and Scotch corn maiden, Kernaby, and suggests that of the Roman Ceres and the Greek Demeter: Sir J. G. Frazer, "The Spirits of the Corn and of the Wild," in *The Golden Bough*, Vols. VII and VIII.

"Hkü Te" is to be seen as a rainbow in the west occasionally. At such times, according to one version of the legend, he is lowering a tube through which to drink the liquor provided at wedding-feasts. When a rainbow appears in the west early in the morning, the king of hades is again in the sky, this time setting up a funeral post ("t le") for his children.[6] From this it seems that he has had several offspring, but his wife has never borne him any since their son-in-law thwarted their plot against his life in the remote past. The funeral post is intended to remind men that many persons have died without receiving proper burial ceremonies. Such neglect entails some sort of a calamity. Hence, the Karen are stricken with terror when they observe the rainbow arching the western heavens early in the morning, especially if this sign is accompanied by thunder and earthquake. Under such circumstances they will not go to their work, for it is tabu.[7] If a Karen should point at such a rainbow, he would at once thrust his finger into his navel in order to avoid the loss of the offending member. This act is called "ugh de de."

The people say of the rainbow in the east that at the time "Teu Kweh," wife of "Hkü Te," became the bow of promise in the sky she was pregnant, and, being now separated from the earth, she is seen from time to time in the east going to draw water for herself. The souls of women who die with child are supposed to have no other means of obtaining drink, except from the rainbow divinity. When two rainbows appear in the east, the upper and larger one is her husband, who is visiting with her.

The second group of spirits among the Karen comprises those who have spent some time on earth as human beings, but have not gained entrance into the realm of the dead because they were denied funeral rites either on account of their bad character or on account of their having died by violence. Hence they are doomed to wander about, avenging themselves upon mortals. As they are supposed to be particularly occupied with this mission at nightfall, the Karen think it imprudent to be out during the early evening.

This division consists of three groups of beings. The first are "Th' re ta hka," or ghosts of those who have died violent deaths or have been carried off by epidemics of cholera, smallpox, etc. and could not, therefore, be given proper funeral ceremonies. They are believed to bring violent deaths and epidemics upon mortals, prob-

---

[6] See Chapter XX on Funeral Customs, p. 200.
[7] See Chapter XXVIII on Tabu, p. 289.

ably in revenge for the manner of their own taking-off. The second group is made up of those who were notoriously evil in the earthly life and suffered capital punishment for their crimes, and of those who as chiefs were known to be tyrants. This group as a whole is called "Ta mü xa." [8] Its members appear in the forms of giants and goblins or of Burman "pongyis" (Buddhist monks) and are usually seen by sick persons whose spirits ("k'las") they are seeking and on which they subsist.[9] These demons are attended by dogs in the form of woodpeckers. According to a legend two men, who were detained in the forest until night, heard a woodpecker call, and immediately thereafter they heard some ghosts say that the dog had barked. One of the men shouted, but they could distinguish nothing but some remark about monkeys, followed by the sound of a bowstring. The pair being thus discovered by the woodpecker, which was evidently with the demons, were stricken with a chill and died the next morning. Consequently, when a Karen hears the scream of this bird of ill-omen, he calls out:

"Shun me; stay far off.
Go thine own way; keep thine own road."

The third group of the ghosts of mortals consists of those who, through some accident, have been deprived of the funeral ceremonies. This group was discovered ages ago through the distressing experience of a certain patriarch, who came upon the body of a Talain who had been struck by lightning. He carried off the skull, took it home, and put it up over his fireplace. During the night the death's-head assumed human form and wandered all over the house, thereby striking terror into the members of the family. Before morning it resumed its former shape. The ghosts of people thus accidentally killed and left unburied are called "Ta t' hka" or "Ta s' hka." They inspire the Karen with horror, a fact taken advantage of by some miscreants who work evil on their enemies by means of a skull kept for the purpose. However, such working of evil falls within the realm of magic.[10]

The third general division of spirits comprises a heterogeneous lot of divinities, who exercise more or less influence on the life and prosperity of men. Some of these may have been inherited from

---

[8] The Karen designation of this group differs in pronunciation from that of the celestial beings (Mü xa) not only in having three syllables, but also in that its last syllable has the grave or heavy tone, while in the latter case "xa" is given the rising or light tone.
[9] For the rites in connection with these, see p. 240.
[10] See Chapter XXVI on Magic, p 274.

older tribes in the country, but have become the common property of the Karen for several generations back.

The Titan Atlas of the ancient Greeks, supporting a globe, has his counterpart in "Hsi gu maw ya" or "Maw ya," as he is sometimes called. He is a brother of "Y'wa" and holds the world on his shoulders. When he grows weary, he shifts it from one side to the other and thus causes earthquakes. Sometimes the beetles that feed on the refuse of human beings report to him that they are starving, because there are no more people to supply them with food. This so angers him that he shakes himself and produces a series of earth-tremors. As these phenomena are common in Burma, the Karen seek to quiet them by shouting out: "We are still here. We are still here." Work is tabu during the day on which an earthquake occurs.[11]

The semiannual change of seasons can not but attract the attention of the people living in Burma. For the Karen a company of demons, the "Law," is responsible for the wet season and another group, the "Hku de," for the dry season. The former, who are sometimes named the "Law hpo" (signifying a company of them), are believed to have cities and dwellings in the upper regions, whence they regulate the rainfall and reveal themselves in the thunder and lightning. The flashes of lightning are nothing less than the flapping of their wings and the thunder is the rattle of their flying shafts against their foes, the "Hku de."

The "Law" are also regarded as the source of the fructifying power in all plants and trees that form their fruits in the wet season. The grain is said to be conceiving when the kernels are developing, and the "Law hpo" are said to be the husbands who bring this about. Their function is to provide the plants, especially the paddy which is heading during the latter part of the rainy season, with the "sgheu" (the life-giving principle), that is, the vaporous substance that comes from the land of the dead and revives all life on the earth.[12] The scarcity of domestic animals among the Karen is attributed to these demons, who are alleged to have raised such a stifling dust by shooting their shafts against the rocks that the creatures took refuge in the jungle and became wild before they could be caught again.

The enemies of the "Law," the "Hku de," are also demons of the upper air with a human appearance, but no abiding-place. Dur-

---
[11] See Chapter XXVIII on Tabu, p. 289.
[12] See Chapter XXI on Religious Conceptions, p. 222.

ing the period when the "Law" are supreme, these divinities betake themselves to the clefts and fissures of the rocks on Mount "Thaw Thi"; but towards the end of the wet season they begin to gather their forces together for a mortal combat with their opponents. The flashing of spears is seen in the forked lightning, and the force of the blows exchanged is revealed in the roar of the thunder. The "Law hpo" are unable to hold out against the onslaught and withdraw for six months to the fissures and rifts in the rocks from which the "Hku de" came forth. A half-year later the "Law" will vanquish the present victors.

The "P'yo" are demons, usually in the form of dragons or serpents, that blow the water up from the ocean and produce the clouds from which the rain descends. They sometimes take on human form, and in this guise they figure in many Karen tales. They preside over the deep pools of streams, whose flow may otherwise be reduced to the merest trickle. The king of the crocodiles, "Maw law kwi," is said to be one of these demons.

Eclipses, like the clouds, are supposed to be caused by demons; but the eclipse-producing demons were once the dogs of a certain mythical personage who tried unsuccessfully to recover his stolen elixir of life from the moon. These dogs are "K' paw ta thu" and "T' hke mo bak."[13]

There are other mythical beings of whom the Karen have more or less vague ideas, for example, the two daughters of "Y'wa" who came to earth in order to improve the condition of men. A prophet discovered their identity and urged the people to build a temple for their worship. The Pwo Karens not only failed to follow this advice, but also disregarded the proprieties so far as to begin pulling out their gold and silver hair ornaments. The goddesses became so disgusted with this rude treatment that they hastened back to their celestial abode, nevermore to be seen by mankind.

A large group of malevolent beings, much feared by the Karen, are the "Ta na." These are witch-like in their operations, but possess the power to assume almost any form at will in order to harm mortals and are superhuman. They are not to be confused with the Burmese "nats," although they have certain resemblances to them.[14]

---

[13] For the tale of the origin of eclipses see Chapter XI on Measures of Time and Space. Karen Astronomy, p. 59.

[14] See "Shwe Yoe" (Sir J. G. Scott), *The Burman, His Life and Notions*, Chap. XXII, pp. 299, ff.

The origin of the "Ta na" is explained in two ways. According to one of these accounts, a basket containing all manner of living creatures was once set before the human race. The people were commanded to partake of them all, lest, if any were left, they might be themselves devoured by the survivors. But the "Ta na" clung so closely to the bottom of the basket that they were overlooked and have been able to terrify mortals ever since. The other explanation of the origin of these beings is that they were a sort of supernatural stomach belonging to certain persons and subsisting not on ordinary food, but on the "k'las" or spirits of human beings. The stomachs were capable of detaching themselves, in order to go in search of their special kind of nutriment. They may perhaps be compared to the old conception of the nightmare in English folklore, except that this demon confined its activities to the sleeping hours of the victim. The depredations of the horrible "Ta na" are related in many stories, of which the following may serve as an illustration:

A man was awakened one night by a figure, which he took to be that of his nephew in the act of massaging him. Next morning the nephew denied all knowledge of the incident and requested his uncle to strike him, if he was again detected in so strange a procedure. The next night there was a recurrence of the incident, but the uncle refrained from hitting his nephew, as he supposed the apparition to be. On the third night, however, he cut off the head of the troublesome visitor; and after dawn a headless corpse was found in the village, which the uncle regarded as proof that the "na" had assumed the form of his nephew in the effort to obtain his own shade ("k'la").

In another instance, one of the "Ta na" gave a slave girl the appearance of her mistress and *vice versa*. As a result of this exchange of characters the husband sent his wife into the fields to drive the birds from the standing grain. The wife, making friends with the birds, easily induced them to let the paddy alone; while she sent a dove to her mother to fetch some fragrant oil, by means of which she was at length restored to her own form and station.

One of the measures sometimes taken by a Karen to protect his field from the ravages of the birds, is to impale a tuft of grass on a sharp stick in token of the kind of treatment he declares himself to be visiting on the demon itself. The latter is thereby duly warned to stay away from the field.

As certain "na" dwell in the water, persons who go in bathing must take care not to offend them. Otherwise, the bathers are liable to sudden illness.

A monster called "T'nu" appears destined to play the part of destroying angel among the Karen after the righteous shall have disappeared from the earth. He will then exterminate the wicked. He is represented as going about with a huge crossbow.

There is a race of giants, known as "Daw t'ka," who, like the "Ta na," feed on the "k'las" of mortals. They are greatly feared by the Karen, especially in Siam where the people refuse to send their children to school in the neighboring district of Moulmein, lest these spirit-eating giants may devour them.

In the Shwegyin district "Ta t' hkaw hkaw" (the one-legged one) is a demon with the form of a female with but one leg on which she hops along the jungle paths, occasionally falling over. If one answers her call for help and assists her to arise, her ill-temper causes her to give no other acknowledgment of the service than a slap in the face of him who renders it. The Brecs offer the alleged bones of this creature for sale to the women of other tribes, who prize them greatly as charms.

From the foregoing account it will be readily seen that the life of the Karen has been dominated by superstitious beliefs in unseen and malicious powers, which seem to be always in waiting to take offense and do some harm to his crops, his family, or himself. In the succeeding chapter his efforts to propitiate and keep on good terms with these myriad demons are set forth.

## CHAPTER XXIII

## PROPITIATORY SACRIFICES AND HEALING OFFERINGS

The rites and sacrifices of the Karen people seem almost innumerable. As we have seen elsewhere, their offerings are designed to placate the evil powers and win the favor of the good. It is difficult to discover the exact meaning of the numerous ceremonies; for the people are reticent about them, fearing that the demons may overhear and learn their motives or other matters connected with the rites that may anger them. Often persons who are performing some ceremony do not pretend to know its meaning, frankly admitting that they do not understand but are simply following the customs of the elders. Offerings that seem nearly alike to the foreign resident in Burma have their special significance for the Karen, being made to different demons, or at special times, or as preventives, cures, etc. The religion of the Karen is not one of love and worship, but largely of fear of the occult powers by which they believe themselves to be surrounded. Their ceremonies and offerings are, therefore, inspired by personal and utilitarian motives, namely, to avert danger and bring good fortune. Hence, it is not uncommon for the ritualist to make his offering not to a single demon but to "all you evil spirits." Since the "k'la" or life principle of human beings is supposed to be the normal food of these spirits, sickness is to be avoided or cured by offerings of the most savory foods, drink, and other things that may tempt the hungry demon from the person whose shade it is trying to devour.

For convenience we may divide the propitiatory ceremonies into three classes. One group comprises those acts of homage, sometimes elaborate, in which the demons are invoked with sacrifices and rites, as in the case of the offerings to the lords of the land and water ("Hti k' kaw k' sa"), to the "Mü xa," and to the "Bgha" of the particular family. The second group consists of the rites used in placating evil demons who may be feeding upon the "k'la" of a sick person. These take the form of offerings and appeals to the wandering shade to return to its proper abode. The third group is that in which the offerings are made to the shade itself, when it has left the body of its own volition or on account of a sudden fright, and is liable to become lost in the jungle. In such cases the "k' la" must be lured back and induced to remain in the body it normally animates.

The "Hti k' sa kaw k' sa" are the powers that rule the earth and that most abhor the sins of lust.[1] It is to these powers that the Sgaw and Bwe tribes make a periodic sacrifice ("Ta lu hpa do" or the great sacrifice), ordinarily once in three years, but when the crops fail because of their sins, as they think, as often as once a year. The sacrifice serves the double purpose of honoring the lords of the land and water and purging the people of their carnal sins. When, therefore, the tribes enjoy a prolonged period of prosperity, they consider themselves morally acceptable to the powers and delay their sacrifice for four or even five years.[2]

## A. THE GREAT SACRIFICE OF THE SGAW

Among the Sgaw the great sacrifice is ordered by the most influential chief of the country, his directions being given to those chiefs who are willing to acknowledge his superiority and by them in turn to their villages. The time being appointed, a suitable spot near a good stream is chosen to which every family is expected to bring a boar and a white fowl, while the chiefs each bring a bullock or a goat. An altar of bamboo with seven posts on each side is erected, the roof of which consists of seven tiers each smaller than the one below, like that of a Buddhist palace. Posts are set round to which the sacrificial creatures are tied. On the day named for the ceremonies a jar of liquor is placed at the foot of each post, and a young man is appointed by each chief to kill his animal after a prayer has been uttered by the great chief. During the prayer the young men stand holding their "xeh" (sickles) over their victims, while the chiefs place their hands on the animals. The prayer is as follows:

"O Lords of the land and water. O Lords of mercy. Lest the country should be stricken and the grain destroyed; lest the people should be distressed and a pestilence come upon them, we put our sins on these buffaloes, oxen, and goats.[3] From this day henceforth may it please you to disregard our sins. Let

---

[1] See page 225.

[2] Dr. Mason in the *Journal of the Asiatic Society of Bengal*, Vol. XXXIV, pp. 212, ff.; Rev. T. Than Bya in *Karen Customs*, pp. 20, ff.

[3] In these ceremonies one can readily see the similarity to that of the scapegoat of ancient Israel. (Lev. 16:21-23). For a full discussion of this widespread idea, see Sir J. G. Frazer's article on "The Scape Goat," in *The Golden Bough*, Vol. IX.

illness not come upon our people. O ye Great Spirits that rule the heaven and the earth, receive our offerings and have mercy upon us. From now on may our land be fruitful, may the work of our children prosper, may they keep well. Forget our evil deeds, which bring distress. May these things come to pass because of the offerings that we are now making."

The young men hamstring the animals and cut their throats as soon as the chiefs remove their hands. The blood is poured around the place of sacrifice. The gall-bladders are examined to see if they are full and well-rounded. If so, the sacrifice is thought to be acceptable. Otherwise, it is evident that the sins of the people are not yet absolved and will not be, until they provide satisfactory animals. Assuming, however, that the first offering proves to be acceptable, the hair is burned off of the animals. Their heads and feet are cut off and laid upon the altar, and seven bamboo water-joints are fastened to its posts. When the flesh is cooked the great chief goes to the altar, takes some rice and meat on a silver tray, fills all of the bamboo joints and puts some of the food down at various places on the altar. He then eats a morsel himself, after which each of the others eat in turn.

While this ceremony is in progress, every one must confess his sins. If there is any doubt about a person, he must remove it either by the water ordeal or by that of climbing a tree. The water ordeal consists of two parts. First, the person doubted and the one doubting him take each a plantain stem and toss it into the swift current of the river. The chief notes which stem is thrown up higher by the water. Second, this part is far more serious: it consists in pushing the two men under the water and holding them there by means of forked sticks across their necks. The first one struggling up for air is accounted the loser. If he is the same one whose plantain was tossed lower than that of his opponent, he is regarded as surely guilty.

In the ordeal of tree climbing the contending men are sent in turn up a tree that has been cut around the foot until almost ready to fall. The climber must ascend to the top and throw down a garment so deftly as not to touch any one of a number of spears set up around its base. During the test the tree must not sway or creak, much less fall. The one who performs this feat with the least disturbance to the tree is the winner.

## B. The Bwe Sacrifice

The Sgaw offer their great sacrifice in January.[4] The Bwe, however, make their offering in July when the paddy is well started. They sacrifice one hog in a central spot of the village lands, first erecting a booth under a eugenia tree, which they consider sacred. Four elders act as priests, their functions being hereditary.[5] Each man cuts three bamboos, one to represent a post of his paddy-bin and the other two to show the height he wants the grain to be in his bin. Then he makes a miniature bin, a long pen, a trap, and a snare. When the people assemble, only the most prosperous elders sit with the priests in the booth. No women are allowed to be present.

The leader takes a sprig from a eugenia tree and raises it in his clasped hand to heaven and prays, the others doing likewise. The leader then spears the hog; and, when the blood flows, all seize their bamboos and cry out: "May my paddy be as high as these bamboos." Some declare that they have caught many rats in their traps and others that they have snared many wild fowls, in proof of their purpose to protect the growing grain. Others dance and shout, while some beat gongs or blow bamboo pipes.

The hog is then carried to the village to be cooked. Each man also provides a fowl. When all the food has been prepared, it is brought back to the booth; and, after a prayer much like that quoted above, they set out the food but eat none of it. On their way back to the village they dance and sing and spend the night in revelry. Next morning they return to the booth, and the priests begin to eat of the food left there, all being allowed to partake; but any one who considers himself unholy must not eat, for the food is sacred. Not only persons guilty of immoral conduct, but also men whose wives are pregnant are under tabu.

After the feast, when they have again danced their way back to the village, the chiefs draw two joints of water for each family and carry them into the village. The families are then called out on their verandas and each family group, including the women and children, is sprinkled with water from one of the joints brought for it. The other is carried to the field next morning by the head of

---

[4] So far as I have been able to ascertain, it seems to have been many years since one of these great sacrifices has been observed by the Sgaw Karen of Lower Burma. I have been able to get no contemporary accounts of such a ceremony. As to the length of time since the Bwe have held such a sacrifice, I can give no definite information.

[5] See p. 247 on priests among the Bwe.

the family, and its contents are sprinkled on the grain. This rite is supposed to cleanse the families from evil and to produce good crops. The four priests officiate under special names, of which three signify, respectively, lord of the village, messenger, and

KAREN GIRLS POUNDING PADDY IN A MORTAR OUT-OF-DOORS

keeper of the village. I do not know the meaning of the fourth title. During the ceremony they wear embroidered tunics, longer than ordinary garments. From the people they receive gifts of beads and ear ornaments. In some villages a bullock is substituted for the hog, and in one of the Mopgha villages near Toungoo the inhabitants require a coal-black bullock, being willing to pay a large price in order to obtain one.

## C. The Small Sacrifice of the Sgaw

Besides the great sacrifice offered by the Sgaw to the lords of the land, they also make a small sacrifice ("Ta lü hpo") to the same powers. A few men—the exact number being determined by divination—build a little booth in the jungle and clear three paths leading from it. They sacrifice a white fowl, letting some of its blood into a bamboo joint containing liquor. Some of the blood is smeared on the outside of the joint and on the posts of the booth, and feathers from the fowl are stuck to it. A kind of broom is made by splitting a bamboo, with which they beat the booth, while praying: "O Lords of the land and water. Let the sick member of my family change places with this fowl. Forgive his sins and free him from disease." Sometimes they address their prayer to the water-witch: "We are offering thee the blood of this fowl. Eat this and go thy way. Do not come near us." After cooking and eating the fowl, they color a little cotton thread yellow and wind it about their water-joint. Having returned home, they draw water and sprinkle some of it on the sick person. A piece of the colored thread is then tied around his waist so that the demon may identify him as the one for whom the offering was made. They must not permit any one to accompany them on their sacrificial journey or to converse with them.

## II. Offerings for the Sick

The small sacrifice described above is one of the offerings for the sick, but because it is made to the lords of the land rather than to the evil spirits who entice away and feed upon the "k'las" of human beings, I have grouped it with the offerings to those deities. Certain demons are malicious and require placating and diverting to keep them from indulging in this practice, which results in the illness and perhaps the death of the persons involved. Divination may indicate that some particular demon, for example, one of the water-witches ("Na hti") or one of the ghosts of tyrants that dwell in the jungles ("T're t' hka"), is engaged in this nefarious work. If so, the rites peculiar to that demon must be executed in an effort to induce it to leave the village and follow the person carrying the offerings to some lonely spot in the jungle, there to remain and partake of the aroma of the feast, much as one would entice a pig from rooting in the garden to follow an ear of corn back to its pen. Having gone through this performance, the carrier stealthily returns, trying on the way to deceive the demon into believing that he has taken some other trail by blocking the one he has actually followed, and fondly thinking that he has removed the cause of the sickness of the member of his household.

I am led to believe that many offerings are made in remote districts that belong in this group, although I have obtained no accurate account of them. The recital in the succeeding paragraphs will suffice, however, to convey a general idea of the nature of these rites, in all of which, when the ceremony is concluded, the wrist of the patient is tied around with a string to keep the "k'la" from getting away again.[6]

The offering made when the "T're t' hka," or ghosts of evil tyrants that inhabit the deep jungles, wander into the village and attack the "k' la" of some one, is called "Ta taw law ta." This rite requires the weaving of a small basket, in the bottom of which cotton is laid, and on this four lumps of cooked rice, one colored black with soot, another yellow with tumeric, the third red with amotta berries (from the *Bixa orellana*), and the fourth left white. A chick is tied to the basket, being made secure by binding both its wings and its feet. Finally, sprigs of yellow and white cockscomb are laid in the basket.

The basket thus fitted out is carried beyond at least two ridges of hills to a place from which it is believed the demon will not be able to find its way back. There the basket is set down with its contents, and the following petition is offered: "We are bringing you red and yellow rice and yellow and white flowers, O Great 'T're t' hka.' Go back to your own place. Keep away from us." The performers of this rite may sweep a spot under the basket and pick up a clod of earth near at hand. Calling the "k'la" to follow them, they leave the chick and rice with the basket to be the food of the ghost and return home. As they go along they break off branches, which they place in the path to throw the demon off their track, should he attempt to follow them.[7] On arriving at the house, they

---

[6] It is not uncommon to see a black line tatooed about a Karen's wrist, the obvious purpose of which is to serve as a permanent hindrance against the escape of his "k'la," thus preventing sickness.

[7] In traveling if one who goes ahead wishes to warn those following not to take a certain path, one puts branches across its entrance. Thus, notice is given that the path is "killed" and not to be taken.

call out to ask whether the patient has recovered or not, and, on being assured that he has, they ascend the ladder and put a bit of the clod in the hole of his ear-lobe, believing that they have taken ample measures to promote his recovery.

In performing the ceremony called "Ta hu law pa law," a bundle containing a handful of chaff, a piece of broken pot, and a few chicken feathers is used to touch the sick person, while "Ta mü to xa, Ta yu ta pleh" are addressed as follows: "O Spirits and very bad Witches, we are cooling your anger lest you look with longing eyes on this person. Restore and heal him. Go back to your places, east, west, north, or south. Return to your own abodes." The bundle is then borne out along a path indicated by the omens and left there. The person carrying it pretends to retire into the jungle, but really returns home.

In the rite known as "Ta taw the hka heh" the patient's friends carry to a considerable distance a little basket containing a chick and a prepared betel quid. A similar petition to that given above is then uttered, and the chick is split in halves and replaced in the basket, which is hidden in some hollow tree or rock crevice. Again a plea is made, the basket and its contents are left behind, and a circuitous route home is followed, the bushes along the way being cut in order to convince the demons by the marks of the knife that they will be cut by it, should they follow after.

The rite performed when the water-witches are supposed to have enticed a "k'la" away is called "Ta lu hti htu hti." A fowl of one color must be carried down to the water, where a small altar is erected of two rows of twelve posts each, the two rows converging like the rafters of a roof. The fowl is killed and its blood smeared on the posts, four feathers being stuck on each of the corner posts. The lords of the water and the lakes, the water-witches, are then besought, in case the sick person has invaded their province in any way or they have caused his illness, to partake of the fowl, sweet liquor, and rice that are provided and allow the "k'la" to return and the person to recover. The petition closes with the words: "Do not look with longing eyes upon him, but eat your feast here." The sick man's friends then cook and eat the fowl and return home.

It appears that sometimes the water-witches are offended by a person who is in bathing and cause him to become ill with cramps or indigestion. In such a case rice, saffron, and spices are placed upon the head of the offender and then taken to a rock at the waterside. The witches are summoned by repeatedly striking the rock and urged to enjoy their feast there.

The ceremony, "Ta di law kweh leh," is performed with a bundle containing a handful of chaff, bits of broken pot, a piece of bamboo, some scrapings of gold and silver, and a fowl. After the patient has been touched with this bundle, the demons of "Plü" (hades), the king of hades, and the Great Elephant ("Ta do k' the, ta do k' saw") are addressed as follows: "I am exchanging the sick person for a big bird and a big fowl, for quantities of gold and silver. Let his shade depart. If you hold him, go." The bundle is then carried out along the road and laid down, and the fowl is plucked. The latter is brought home, the bushes along the way being beaten with a bamboo with split ends, while the "k'la" is summoned to follow. On arriving near the house, the friends call to those within to see if it has returned. On receiving a favorable reply, they enter, tie up the wrist of the sick person, and cook the fowl.[8]

A different form of the above ceremony is described by Thra Than Bya.[9] According to his account, the friends carry only a fowl to the place on the road and there place a dead leaf on a little mound of earth, after which they call the "k' la" to return. Then they take the fowl home and cook it, and, after the sick one has eaten a morsel, the rest of the family partake.

Another form of the offering by the roadside is called "Ka law ta." In this instance a bamboo post about four feet long is set up, the upper end of which is split and the splints spread apart by weaving in and out a piece of bamboo. Upon this a little mat of loosely woven bamboo is laid, on which are placed three chicken feathers, a few pieces of egg shell, and a roll of cotton blackened with charcoal at three points. The feathers seem to represent a fowl and the cotton a pig, for the one making the offering says, addressing the demons in general: "I am giving you a pig and a fowl. Do not come near me any more. Help me and heal me." This offering differs from any of the others mentioned in this chapter in that it is sym-

---

[8] I am told that now, with the waning of the faith in these old customs, the person who has taken out the offering occasionally becomes angry if the people in the house do not give a favorable answer concerning the return of th "k' la" and the improvement of the patient, and refuses to repeat the ceremony, as he is supposed to do.

[9] Rev. T. Than Bya, *Karen Customs*, p. 30.

bolic, and also in the fact that the patient performs the rite in his own behalf.

### III. OFFERINGS TO THE "K'LA" ITSELF

Sometimes the auspices indicate that the "k' la" of an ill person has departed by reason of fright or from some other cause than being enticed by a malicious demon. The place to which it has gone and the method by which it may be won back are also shown by the omens. In such cases the appeal and offerings are made to the "k' la" itself.

In performing the rite known as "Ta kweh k' la hpa do" (the great ceremony of calling the "k'la"), two black fowls, namely, a cock and a hen, must be killed by wringing their necks. Their internal organs must be cleaned and replaced and the birds cooked whole. They are then laid on a tray on which are three Malay apple leaves, seven lumps of cold rice, and a cup of fragrant water.[10] The tray with its contents is set at the head of the stairs or ladder, and a lighted candle is placed there. A white cotton thread is carried from the tray to the foot of the stairs and fastened. The fragrant water, after being blown upon by the head of the house, is sprinkled on the family and on the stairs.[11] A lump of rice is then charmed and thrown down the stairs, which are beaten with a stick, and the "k' la" of the invalid is summoned. The call is: "Pru-u-u k'la,[12]—heh ke, heh ke. (O Shade, come back, come back.)" If for any reason it is thought that the shade has not heeded this call, the operation is repeated until the family feels assured that it has returned. They then immediately break the string by means of which it has ascended the stairs and throw it away, lest it should again escape. With other pieces of string they tie up the wrists of the sick person and the other members of the family, meanwhile calling the "k' la" to remain. The patient is bathed all over with what is left of the fragrant water and is then expected to recover.

The rite of "Ta kweh k' la," or inviting the "k'la" to return, is performed in the house, like the one described above. The family

---

[10] The leaves named (those of the "thabye" or *Eugenia malaccensis*) are generally used for this purpose, but I do not know why.

[11] When the Karen on the plains perform these ceremonies, in which the wandering "k'la" is expected to return to the house by the ladder, they retain the old-fashioned notched log that has served from time immemorial as the means of entrance to the house, but that is being superseded in modern houses by flights of stairs. They think the "k'la" will more easily return by the kind of stairs to which it has been accustomed.

[12] "Pru-u-u-" is a sort of trill which the women use in calling their children, pigs, or fowls, as well as their "k' las."

elder takes the stirring-stick from its hole in the fireplace post and strikes the top of the house ladder to attract the attention of the "k'la," which he begs to return, saying: "Pru-u-u we, pru-u k' la, come back, whether you have gone to the west, east, north, or south; come back, whether you are in the bush, jungle, or ends of the earth; come back to your pleasant dwelling, to your comfortable home. I will prepare delicious pork and fowl for you. Eat of your rice and drink of your liquor. Do not wander off any more." Then the animal specified in the divination is killed—pig, fowl, goat, ox, or buffalo—and if a fowl, its bones are examined for the omen, which is favorable in case the holes are even in number. In case one of the animals has been indicated, the performers of the rite look for a rounded gall-bladder. If the auspices are unfavorable, they must repeat the whole operation until they find the conditions satisfactory. The animal is then cut up, cooked, and the feast proceeds. During these ceremonies every member of the family must be present.

The rite, "Ta waw k'la" (driving back the "k'la"), has some features not found in the one described in the preceding paragraph and is performed in the jungle and along the paths where the ghost has disappeared, as revealed by the divination. The man of the house splits the end of a bamboo pole into four splints and spreads them into a crude broom, which he takes to the place where the "k'la" became lost. With a prayer similar to that quoted above he calls the wandering "k'la" and beats the bushes all the way home. Before entering, he asks the usual question about the return of the ghost and receives the usual answer. Mounting to the house, he beats the top of the ladder with the stirring-stick, repeating the invitation to the "k'la" to return and then beats the posts of the fireplace, asking repeatedly if it has come back and getting the same reply. Finally, the animal or fowl is killed and the omen declared. In case it is favorable, the feast proceeds.

The rite for the return of a "k'la" thought to have been driven off by the wind is called "Ta yaw ke a k'la." A bracelet is suspended by a string from the tip of a slender bamboo over a cup containing a little sticky rice and a hard-boiled egg. The elder strikes the cup with the stirring-stick and begs the "k'la" to come back out of the winds, the storm, the firmament, from near the stars or the moon, and eat the egg. The string supporting the bracelet is usually poorly spun, and the suspended object twists back and forth until finally the string parts, and the ornament drops into the cup. A person standing near claps a cloth over the receptacle to confine the "k'la." If an air-space is found at the end of the egg, it is a sign that the shade has returned; if not, the experiment must be repeated.[13]

The ceremony, "Ta hpi htaw ke a k'la," is in order when a person's sickness is attributed to the detention of his "k'la" under the water or in a swampy place. The auspices having shown the necessity for this rite and the kind of creature to be sacrificed, the performers of the rite throw up a little mound at the foot of the ladder with a sharp bamboo stick or other implement, and set upon it in order bundles of glutinous rice and jars or bamboo joints of liquor. The victim, say a fowl, is plucked, and, after the shade has been attracted by making a noise, it is addressed as the great "k'la": "If you have been drowned in the water or are anywhere under the mud or the ground; if you have been led astray in the water or the mire," says the leader, "I beg you to come back to your pleasant dwelling, to your comfortable home. Come eat delicious pork and toothsome chicken. Come and partake of sweet liquor and white rice." The victim is struck on the head with the stirring-stick, killed, and the omens examined. If these prove to be favorable, the fowl is cooked and the feast is held. As is usual in such ceremonies when the shade is believed to have returned, the wrist of the patient is tied with string to prevent its wandering again. A piece of the string, together with a morsel of the rice and meat, is placed on the fontanel ("hko hti") of the patient, which is considered the seat of the "k' la."

### Prophets and Elders

The propitiatory sacrifices discussed in the first section of this chapter are evidently tribal functions and are, therefore, inaugurated by the chiefs. Formerly men called "wi," especially designated as prophets, were consulted to interpret the auspices. On occasion they went into trances in order to reveal secrets. Their office in most of the Karen tribes was for life or while they maintained a good character, and it involved a knowledge of the ancient poetry of

---

[13] See p. 207 of Chapter XX (Funeral Customs) for a similar method of determining the presence of the "k' la" of the dead.

Photo by Dr. Bunker
A BWE KAREN PROPHET

A HUT ERECTED IN A FOREST CLEARING BY A SELF-STYLED PROPHET AS THE CENTER OF A NEW KAREN RELIGIOUS CULT OF SHORT DURATION

the folk by which the traditions and customs were handed down from generation to generation. Among the Bwe, who seem to have esteemed priests more than the other tribes, there were four of these prophets who presided over the great sacrifice, the eldest being regarded as high priest. When one of them died, the elders assembled and chose which of his sons should inherit the office. Then, earrings, a headband, richly ornamented clothing, and a silver-mounted sword were secretly prepared for the ceremony of installation. A delegation of the elders took these gifts to the house of the chosen one, an elder going ahead to ascertain that he was at home. The party, being assured of his presence, surrounded the house to prevent his escape, which he must feign attempt. The presents were then cast before him. If he really desired to escape, he must do so before the house was surrounded.

In case the elders did not find the chosen successor at home, they laid in wait for him either by the path approaching the house or within the house itself. Sometimes an elder climbed up under the roof, hid himself until the man returned, and then dropped the gifts at his feet. The appurtenances of the priestly office, having been presented, could not be refused.[14] In some instances a "wi" was also a chief, serving thus as a leader in the tribe and in its magic. In any case he was a most important personage and was held in awe by the people.[15] Only a few of these men now remain.

The healing offerings dealt with in the second and third sections of this chapter fall generally within the province of the village elders, or are often performed by the members of the family of the sick person, for almost everybody knows more or less how to make the offerings, though this is not so true at the present time as it was a generation ago.

---
[14] Bunker, *Soo Tha*, pp. 66, ff.
[15] For the "wi's" connection with magic, see p. 275.

## CHAPTER XXIV

## FEASTS TO THE "BGHA"

### THE CEREMONIAL OF THE FEASTS

"Mü xa do" (the great "Mü xa" or king of the "Mü xa") is the demon most intimately connected with the affairs of men. He may serve as their guardian and protector if properly propitiated with offerings; but he is more often feared as the author of all kinds of evil. Some Karens, especially in Shwegyin, regard him as a household deity to whom the family offer their sacrifices called "ta aw Bgha" (to eat the "Bgha"). He is addressed as "Thi Hko Mü Xa," and is evidently regarded as the lord of demons.[1] In most parts of the Sgaw Karen country, however, the "Bgha" is mentioned as being distinct from "Mü xa do" and, in a special way, as the tutelary god of the family by whom it is reverenced and feared. It is supposed to subsist upon the "k'las" or shades of the members of the family, if it is not provided generously with pork and chicken; and even then the family's immunity may not be assured. In their prayers and offerings the people sometimes associate the "T'reh t' hka" with the "Bgha," the former having, as I understand it, no connection with the family. Perhaps this is a precaution taken in the hope of appeasing whichever spirit may be responsible for the misfortune they are trying to alleviate.

A veneration of ancestors is manifest all through the family ceremonies treated in this chapter. The ancestors are thought of as taking an interest, although not always a friendly one, in the affairs of living men. The Karen do not, however, indulge in ancestor worship to the extent that the Chinese practice it.

The family "Bghas" are said to be eternal. As new unions take place and households are set up generation by generation, each family finds itself provided with a "Bgha" of its own. But what the relation of the new crop of "Bghas" is to that of the preceding generation, no one is able to explain.

The grandmother or the eldest female in the direct line of the family presides as the high priestess at the "Bgha" feast of the

---
[1] Dr. Wade in *The Karen Thesaurus*, new ed., Vol. I., p. 469.

whole family. She is the "Bgha a' hko." This custom seems to hark back to the matriarchal stage of development among the Karen, as also does the fact that the groom goes to live with the bride's family. Why a woman should hold the place of honor at the "Bgha" feast has been "explained" to me in two ways, namely, (1) that a female was the first person to fall under the influence of "Mü kaw li" (Satan) in the orchard, and (2) that as the woman is the more susceptible to sickness, she properly has more to do with the offerings and should take the leading part in making them. The Karen maintain that the elders are responsible for these explanations and that the ceremonial of the "Bgha" feast has come down from time immemorial.

There are three kinds of "Bgha" feasts. The most familiar kind is that observed by the members of the immediate family when one of their number has fallen sick, in case divination shows that his illness is due to his having offended the "Bgha." In such a case the family must at once join in a feast. The second kind of feast is that observed as a preventive of possible sickness and as a means of keeping on good terms with the "Bgha." This is known as "ta aw bwaw a' tha" (eating to strengthen one's heart). The third kind of feast is that participated in by all the kindred, when the most elaborate rites are celebrated. Such a feast is called "ta aw saw ke saw na." While there is a general resemblance among the feasts held all over the Karen country, the various tribes and even parts of the same tribe differ in the details of their observances.

In the case of an illness found by divination to be due to the "Bgha," the ceremonial of the feast among the Sgaw Karen of the Tharrawaddy district and in the Pegu Hills, is as follows: After a pot of rice has been set on the fire to boil, a fowl is caught and killed, and its feathers are burned off in the fireplace. It is then cut up and cooked with salt and a chili and placed on the table or family tray. The father, mother, and children in the order of their ages severally partake of a morsel, after which they eat their meal together. If the parents of the father and mother are living, the feast is held in the morning; but if they are dead, it is held in the afternoon. On the following morning a pig is caught, brought into the house, and its legs are tied together. It is then killed by strangulation or by wrenching the neck, care being taken not to break any of its bones or bruise its skin lest some of its blood should be spilled. The body of the pig is then run through lengthwise on a spit, its bristles are burned off, and it is then carried into the house and laid at the head of the sleeping-mats. The father and other members of the family touch the side of the animal with the tips of their fingers. In Shwegyin and Siam this rite is still observed, but in many other localities it has been discontinued. The pig is now ready to be cut up and cooked, after which the members of the family each taste of the meat in turn, avoiding eating anything from the hind-quarters that day and from the fore-quarters the next, in case their grandparents are living. If, however, their grandparents are dead, they may eat from any part of the animal. After having thus each taken a morsel, they complete their meal. If any is left after the feast, it is not uncommon nowadays for the family to invite in some of their neighbors to finish the remainder. This is contrary to the old practice among the Karen.

In the remoter regions, where the complete ceremonial is still observed, its main features differ but little from those described above, but the details are much more fully observed, and I will, therefore, describe the ceremonial as it is carried out in those areas. The rice having first been cooked, the water from it must be poured into the fireplace and the pot set down in the wet ashes, while the chicken is caught by the wife who brings the fowl into the house and hands it to her husband. He holds it under his arm, strokes its beak toward the point, and says: "Take away sickness. Remove weariness and swellings. Give me life and health for a hundred years." Then the wife and each child in turn stroke the chicken's beak, while the father repeats the same prayer for each one. He next wrings the fowl's neck, scalds the bird in a jar of water, plucks its feathers and carefully puts them in a receptacle by the fire, and removes the intestines and places them with the feathers. The flesh is cut up, cooked, and served, each member of the family taking a morsel. The father now places a small quantity of the rice and chicken on a tray and summons "the great ancestors of old" to partake. Meantime, the family eat the feast, after which the father throws away the offering. The pig is eaten on the following day, but in Siam two days are allowed to elapse before this part of the feast is celebrated. In preparation for this event the father goes into the jungle after an early breakfast, taking with him one of his children or, if he has no child, calling some other boy to accompany him. He carries a small basket and his "xeh" or sickle. He returns with two pieces of bamboo, each two full joints in length, some plantain leaves, and a pole long enough to serve as a spit for the pig. He cuts one of the bamboo pieces into two sections in which to cook the rice and curry, and splits the other bamboo into withes. After the rice has been cooked, the mother mixes a little of it with chaff, puts some of it in a small pot and a lump of it on top of the pot, besides sprinkling water on the fireplace.

A SGAW KAREN GRANDMOTHER

Later the lump of chaff and rice is used as a bait in catching the pig that is to become the offering. Two withes of the outside and two of the inside of the bamboo are used in tying the feet of the animal, and one more of each kind to bind the feet together. Other withes are wound around the snout, one turn being passed through the mouth, which is thus closed securely. The pig is now carried into the house and laid on plantain leaves spread on the floor, a winnowing-tray being placed in front of it along with the pot of rice and chaff and a small bamboo cup ("maw"). Three times in succession the father touches first the pig and then the pot with the tips of his fingers, while addressing the "Bgha" as follows: "Avert all sickness from me. Let me be well and live a long life. I am feeding you with pork. Therefore, help me." The same petition is uttered as the other members of the family touch the pig in their turn. The father then strikes the animal three times with his "xeh" and stabs it thrice with a knife, but not to a greater depth than the width of four fingers. The killing of the pig is completed by binding its snout in a wet cloth to smother it and by wrenching its neck. The withes are now removed from its feet, and the carcass is carried to another part of the room and washed. After being laid again on the plantain leaves, an opening is made in its belly for the purpose of examining the gall-bladder. If this organ is plump, the omen is favorable and the feast may proceed. Otherwise, another pig must be sacrificed on the following day, and if necessary another, until a gall-bladder is found that meets the required conditions.

A satisfactory offering having been obtained, the intestines are removed and the carcass is impaled lengthwise on the sharpened stick brought from the jungle, and the bristles are burned off at a new fireplace built for the feast in the inner room of the house. After the body is washed it is butchered: first the head and stabbed shoulder being cut off in one piece, then the hind leg on the same side, next the fore and hind legs on the other side. The carcass is now opened down the front and down the middle of the back, the side that was stabbed being first removed and prepared. The wife puts the currypot on to boil, while her husband cuts up the meat, including the heart, liver, and lungs, some of which is dropped into one of the bamboo joints over the top of which a plantain leaf is tied. The other bamboo joint is filled with rice, and both vessels are set over the fire and watched carefully to prevent burning. However, the vessels must not be removed from the fire before their contents are thoroughly cooked, else the offering would be offensive to the "Bgha."

The rest of the pork is cooked in the currypot, which the wife has set on the fire. The wife must clean out the intestines, which she does outside the house. When she brings them in, the husband brushes off any ashes that may be on the top of the little pot and covers the mouth of it with a plantain leaf. He makes little holes in the covering and inserts short pieces of bamboo down into the pot obliquely, so as to hold the cover on. He then pours water in through these holes. He now makes a sort of standard, called "thi keh," out of a strip of bamboo. The bamboo is split into three strips, but not entirely separated. They are bound together at three points with withes, and then the two outer ones are broken between the bindings but only enough to make them stand out like arms akimbo. The lower ends of each of the side strips are bent out and then brought back and inserted in a hole, or under the lowest withe around the stock. This is set in the pot. What the significance of this is, neither my informant could tell me, nor do the reference books help one to find the meaning of it.

When the food has been cooked, the husband empties the rice on one tray and the pork on another; and the members of the family—father, mother, and the children in succession according to their ages—each take a morsel from both trays. Then the father takes a swallow from a pot containing water or liquor, being followed by the others in due order. He also pours out two cups of the liquid for the ancestors of the family and throws the rest away. He collects into a bundle the withes used in tying the feet of the pig and hangs it on the end of one of the floor joists at the rear of the house. Finally, he washes his hands and returns to join his family in finishing the feast.

In case the grandparents are living, they are summoned to the "Bgha" feast and arrive on the evening preceding the event. After breakfast next morning the preparations are made much the same as described above, but include the providing of three little bamboo cups ("maw") and the construction of a tiny model of a house ("hi hpo hkeh") about a foot long, which is set in front of the pig and in which the favorable gall-bladder of the animal is placed, together with its heart and the lung and kidney of the side that has been stabbed. The organs of the other side and any blood remaining in the abdominal cavity are placed on a tray. Only the flesh of the stabbed side is used at once. While it is cooking, the wife pounds some rice, moistened with a little water, until it is reduced to fine flour. Two of the cups are filled with a mixture of this flour, chopped pork, and a little blood, and hung over the fire to cook. The wife washes the intestines of the animal, while her husband arranges the "thi keh" as before and dishes out the food for the family. When all is ready each member of the household partakes of a morsel and sip of liquor, the grandfather and grandmother coming after the children. This ceremonial being completed, all eat together. In the afternoon the intestines are cooked and eaten. Next morning the husband removes the heart, lung, and kidney from the miniature house, cuts them up, and cooks them. These are eaten, the room is cleaned, the little house is thrown away, the grandparents return home, and the sick person for whom the feast has been held is supposed to recover.

In some places the intestines of the pig and the blood-stained plantain leaves are put in a basket and hung on a tree in the jungle as an offering to "Thi Hko Mü Xa," the lord of the demons.

The second kind of "Bgha" feast is not preceded by divination. It is held not to cure sickness in the family, but to prevent it. When one of the parents begins to worry lest illness may visit the family, the "Bgha" is feasted and venerated and the hearts of the family are thus strengthened, as they express it. Hence, this feast is called "Ta aw᾽ bwaw a' tha." The ceremonial does not differ from that described above.

The third kind of feast is that in honor of the great "Bgha," in which all the kindred by blood participate. It is, therefore, called the feast of the whole family ("ta aw saw ke saw na"). The eldest female of the family, the grandmother if living, or if not her eldest daughter or granddaughter, presides as chief priestess or head of the "Bgha" ("Bgha a' hko"). If the feast is held annually, it occurs in April or May; but the priestess may fix a time at her pleasure when she feels that the "Bgha" should be honored and propitiated. Those required to attend this feast of the kindred are the full brothers and sisters of the priestess, her sons, daughters, and daughters' children; but her husband, brothers-in-law, sisters-in-law, and their sons, together with her sons-in-law and the sons of her sons, are excluded and eat their feast with their own kindreds.

The eligible members of the family having assembled, the grandmother holds a pair of fowls, male and female, by their heads and says: "O Lord of the demons, we are offering to thee the flesh of fowls and pigs. Free us from all illness." After wringing the necks of the chickens, she orders their feathers to be burned off preparatory to cooking them with salt and chili only. Rice is also cooked. These viands are set out and the priestess eats a morsel, followed by her sons and each of the other relatives in the order of their ages. They are then ready to consume the feast of chicken and rice. As in the case of the other "Bgha" feasts, a repast of pork follows.

A pig is caught after dark, its feet are tied together, and it is carried up into the house where the whole family is present. It is laid on a plantain leaf on the floor in front of a miniature house set at the head of the grandmother's sleeping-mat. Placing her hand on the pig, she prays: "O Great Family Spirit and Spirit of the jungle ('Thi Hko Mü Xa, t' re t' hka'), we are offering you the flesh of fowls and of a swine. Do not harm us. When our children go out, if they happen to come near you, let them pass unmolested." Then each member of the family touches the side of the pig and afterwards the plantain leaf. After the animal has been beaten with the side of an axe or back of a sickle, but not hard enough to kill it or break any of its bones, it is strangled by pouring water down its nostrils while its head is wrenched to one side. The abdomen is cut open and the body smeared with the blood. The gall-bladder is removed, and, if it is full and round, the other internal organs are taken out. If the gall-bladder is flabby, they must repeat the sacrifice on succeeding days until they find a pig that affords the favorable omen. They are then ready to transfix the carcass with a spit, burn off the bristles at the special fireplace in the inner room, cut the body in twain lengthwise, and hang the upper half with the head over the miniature house. The lower half and intestines are now cooked with salt and chilis and served. The grandmother takes her morsel and the rest follow her example in turn, while she again utters the prayer to the great family spirit, after which they all eat heartily.

Next morning they cook the head and the portion that was hung up the day before, the shoulder of the lower side being the last piece to be cooked. This piece is carried into the jungle in a basket, where another prayer to the great "Bgha" is repeated. The ceremony is concluded by bringing back the shoulder, together with a clod of earth, giving a bit of this meat to each member of the family, and placing a little earth over one of the ears of each. In some parts of the hill-country the people place a pot of liquor in front of the tiny house and cook bamboo sprouts with the pork. After the cooking, the heart, liver, and spleen are taken out of the vessel and sparingly served with a little rice on three plantain leaves. The grandmother and the other members of the kindred

KAREN VILLAGERS, THARRAWADDY DISTRICT
Only the old men retain the Karen costume. On the plains practically all Karen men dress as do the Burmans.

supply themselves with pieces of plantain leaf and in turn help themselves from each of the three leaves while praying: "O Lord of the great spirits, do thou, who carest for us, prevent all sickness and sorrow from approaching us. May we be protected from injury by sharp sticks of bamboo and wood, by the arrows and spears of our enemies, and from all evil that may befall us. Wilt thou be our shield and defense." Through a small bamboo tube the grandmother-priestess drinks a little liquor from the pot, as do her relatives in their turn. She then points a newly sprouted plantain leaf at the skull of the pig, which has been hung up over her mat, and repeats the last prayer. Then all drink a little more of the liquor and are ready to follow the example of the priestess in partaking of the feast.

The earthen pot, in which the pork has been cooked, is intended to remind the kindred that they are children of the earth; while the bamboo joints, in which some of the offerings have been prepared, serve to keep before their minds the temporary character of their bamboo houses and utensils.

### Customs Incidental to the "Bgha" Feasts

Certain customs and tabus incidental to the "Bgha" feasts should be noted. Unless all the members of the family are present at such a ceremony, except those excluded from the feast, the offerings are thought to be objectionable to the "Bgha." If a person absents himself from a feast that is being held to promote the recovery of a sick relative, he is suspected of desiring the continued illness or the death of the sick one. Or his absence may be interpreted as an effort to bring calamity upon some member of the family. Such charges are made against the member of a family who becomes a Christian and remains away from the ceremony. The others allege that he no longer retains his affection for his kindred and is willing to bring illness and disaster upon them by his absence, which angers the "Bgha."

While the feasts are in progress, no stranger is permitted to enter the family-room. When I first traveled in the hills, I noticed that as I passed through the corridor of a village-house some member of a family stood in the doorway of one or another of the family-rooms to prevent my entering. This seemed strange, in view of the fact that I was usually received with cordial hospitality. On inquiry I found that the guarding of the door was to keep me from unwittingly rendering their offerings futile. The advantage of the village guest-room then became clear to me. There I and other strangers could be entertained, and there the men who were ineligible to attend the feast of the family they had married into could congregate and visit, while their relatives were participating in the "Bgha" ceremony.

The idea of sacrifice is undoubtedly at the root of the "Bgha" feasts. According to the explanation of an old Karen woman, when one has offended the family spirit or, as the people say, has "hit the 'Bgha'" ("pgha ba Bgha"), one has fallen on the worst possible fate; for the demon will seek to devour the life principle ("k' la") of the unfortunate one, unless propitiated by offerings of chicken and pork. The "Bgha" is supposed to be satisfied with the "k' la" of these sacrifices, which constitute the best eating within the knowledge of the Karen people. Even those who no longer fear their "Bgha" will call in the members of their family and make a feast, principally on account of their own enjoyment of it. In such cases they add the spices for a curry, instead of cooking the meat with only salt and chili. The Karen, especially those of Shwegyin, declare that fornication, adultery, and incest anger the family spirits more than any other offenses. Such acts of immorality incite the "Bgha" to curse the soil, blight the crops, and send epidemics among the people. Once aroused, a "Bgha" will assume the form of a tiger or snake and wait for its victims, in order to destroy the "k'las" of the offenders and other inhabitants of their village. In case of a poor season and bad crops the elders become suspicious and sometimes succeed in scaring young persons into a confession of their secret sins. Unusual offerings are required to appease the offended demon, these being—according to one list in my possession—first, a buffalo, next, an ox, and finally, a chicken and a pig. All the family must unite in an earnest prayer that these offerings may prove acceptable to the "Bgha" and avert any further calamities from them. The great fear of blighted crops, and of other evils not less feared because unknown, tends to keep the Karen a chaste people, which they certainly are for the most part.[2]

The traditional explanation of the use of the chicken bones and the pig's gall-bladder in divination, and of pork and fowls in the family feasts, is that the chickens and pigs ate most of the fragments of the God-given book which the white brother delivered to

---

[2] See pp. 30, 139, 142, 148, 192, 225, 288.

the Karen back in the mythological age, and which the latter carelessly burned when he set fire to the brush that he had cut from his field. What offerings more acceptable to the "Bgha" could be made than the creatures that had absorbed the wisdom of the divine book?[3] That the pig is regarded as a vicarious sacrifice is shown by the rite in which the members of the family touch the side of the animal, while the "Lord of the spirits" is asked to protect them from sickness and sorrow. However, the Karen do not charge the pig with a message to the great spirit, as do the Kenyah and Kayan tribes of Borneo;[4] nor do they put their sins on the pig, as did the ancient Hebrews on the head of the sacrificial bullock or on the scapegoat.[5] In Toungoo the dog is substituted for the pig in the family rites, the tradition there being that it ate some of the fragments of the book of wisdom. The Rev. E. W. Blythe is authority for the statement that the cat is also offered to the "Bgha" in Toungoo.[6] The Bwe and Red Karen tribes, among whom the ox, buffalo, and goat are the common domestic animals, use one or another of these creatures, according to the manifestations obtained through divination.[7] I am told that in Shwegyin there are some localities where the people do not sacrifice animals of any kind, but make offerings of flowers only.

The leaves used in the feasts must be those of the wild plantain ("ya"), which is found everywhere in the jungle throughout Burma; for the tradition is that it was this variety of plantain which "Htaw Meh Pa," the mythical ancestor of the Karen race, cut off in blazing the trail for his people to follow on the way to a more fruitful land.[8]

The miniature house ("hi hpo kheh") is intended as a resting-place for the "Bgha," when it comes to enjoy the feast provided for it. This tiny structure is set in the inner room where the pig is killed, the sacrificial fireplace built, and the feast held. This fireplace is a sacred family altar apart from the place where the cooking is carried on daily. The inner room affords greater privacy to the family during the feasts. The Pwo Karen have special trays and dishes for their feasts, which are kept sacredly for this purpose.

---

[3] Colonel A. R. MacMahon, *The Karens of the Gold Chersonese*, pp. 140, ff. For the story of the Lost Book see p. 333.
[4] Hose and MacDougall, *Pagan Tribes of Borneo*, Vol. II, pp. 60, ff.
[5] Leviticus, 16:21-23.
[6] Rev. E. W. Blythe in *The Rangoon Diocesan Quarterly*, 1917, p. 9.
[7] E. O'Riley in *Journal, Indian Archipelago*, 1859, p. 16.
[8] See *ante*, p. 5.

I remember being asked by a family, who had become Christians and were discarding the old ways, to destroy these utensils for them. They had not yet freed themselves of their fears sufficiently to perform an act that seemed to them like desecration.

Families who are about to adopt Burmese customs or to accept Christianity, generally dispose of all their pigs and fowls, with the

Utensils for the Sacred "Bgha" Feast of a Pwo Karen Family, Bassein District.

exception of two or three of the latter and one of the former. When the time for a feast arrives, they make the usual preparations; but before the pig is killed, one of the elders will put his hand on its side and inform the "Mü xa" that the family are about to make their last offering and beg the demons to dismiss them and allow them to go in peace. This rite is called "Ta aw k' tew kwi Bgha" literally, "eating to finish the 'Bgha'." The statement that this is the final offering is repeated in every address to the spirit uttered during the course of the feast. If the parents of the head of the family are living, they construct a little house and put into it offerings of rice and meat in order to satisfy the appetite of the "Bgha." Families who thus terminate their relations with their special divinities, observe the tabu of not keeping pigs and fowls again for a period of three years. Not all families who become Christians observe this rite, for many times they make the transition by simply forsaking the "Bgha" once for all.

## CHAPTER XXV

## MOUNT "THAW THI." RELIGIOUS CULTS

### The Sacred Mount

In Karen lore mention is often made of the sacred mountain, "Thaw Thi," which was early thought to be identical with the fabulous sacred mountain of the Buddhists, "Myenmo Taung." When, however, Dr. Mason went to Toungoo, he found that "Thaw Thi" was the dominating peak of the range of hills separating the valley of the Sittang from that of the Salween—a peak evidently held in reverence by the Burmese who call it "Nattaung," that is, the mountain of the "nats" or demons. Of this range "Thaw Thi" is the most impressive peak, although it is a thousand feet lower than Mount "Pghaw Ghaw" four miles to the north, which rises to a height of 8,607 feet above sea-level and from which a wonderful view may be had over the surrounding hills. Of these two peaks "Thaw Thi" is thought to be the wife and the more important. Its summit is a wide clear space which, the people believe, is swept clean every morning by the goddess "Ta La," who has her abode there.[1]

Several traditions concerning the mountain suggest that it may have been a place of veneration of the people in its neighborhood. One story connects Mount "Thaw Thi" with the flood that submerged the world, except the ridge along the top "as much as a comb."[2] When the flood receded, the peacock pheasant ("pgho ghaw") alighted on the summit now bearing its name. Another legend represents "Thaw Thi" as being considered the highest mountain in the world, whose sides abound with all kinds of game, these creatures being constrained to render homage to this kingly mountain. Hence, all the beasts and the birds of the air, including the tiger, bear, crocodile, wild dog, dragon, vulture, and adjutant, ascend in procession to do reverence.

---

[1] See p 289.

[2] Dr. Mason, who is quoted in MacMahon's *The Karens of the Golden Chersonese*, 242, ff., is authority for this interpretation. A similar meaning was given me in Toungoo, but the spelling of the name of the bird and of the word meaning "as much as" differs a little from that commonly employed. These differences are probably due to local usage.

Mount "Thaw Thi" also figures in some of the ancient folk-tales of the people. For example, one version of the story of the patriarch "Htaw Meh Pa" locates his home there. The den of the White Python is still pointed out on one side of the mount. It was to this den, according to the tale of "Ku Law Lay" and "Naw Mü E," that the fabulous serpent carried off the latter, whose husband dug holes there in trying to rescue her. These holes are also still shown.

When, in the middle of the nineteenth century, evangelists began to travel in the Toungoo district they discovered that the people living in the villages near Mount "Thaw Thi" indulged in various more or less elaborate rites on the peak. They had leaders or prophets in each village who interpreted the signs and set the time for the annual pilgrimage to the summit, where they sacrificed pigs and buffaloes, made offerings of wood and water, and built cairns of stones. A recent visitor to this spot reports that the cairns may still be seen, as also the broken pieces of the jars and bottles which once held the offerings; but that the paths are now overgrown, inasmuch as the former ceremonies have been long discontinued. Only a few old men recollect the pilgrimages to the summit made in their boyhood days. Some of these say that the people ascended the mountain to await there the appearance of the god, "Y'wa," in order that they might commune with him;[3] while others connect these rites with the Karen goddess, "Ta La," who they say dwelt there and must be propitiated at her own shrine. That "Y'wa" was venerated on the mountain is confirmed by the following poem, which Dr. Mason found in Tavoy, more than three hundred miles from "Thaw Thi" itself:

> "'Y'wa' will come and bring the great 'Thaw Thi'.
> We must worship, both great and small,
> The great 'Thaw Thi', created by 'Y'wa'.
> Let us ascend and worship.
> There is a great mountain in the ford.
> Can you ascend and worship 'Y'wa'?
> There is a great mountain in the way.
> Can you go up and commune with 'Y'wa'?
> You call yourselves the sons of 'Y'wa'.
> How often have you ascended to worship him?
> You claim to be the children of 'Y'wa'.
> How many times have you gone up to worship 'Y'wa'?"

That so conspicuous a peak as Mount "Thaw Thi" should have been regarded as the abiding-place of the great god, "Y'wa," and

---

[3] Rev. E. W. Blythe, of Toungoo, in *The Rangoon Diocesan Magazine*, (1917) Vol. XXI, No. 11, pp. 98, ff.

become an object of veneration among the Karen is not difficult to understand in view of the prevalence of animism among Oriental peoples. Other great mountains in the East have been reverenced by the inhabitants of the region round about.

## Religious Cults

Like the Jews, who two thousand years ago were constantly expecting the Messiah and followed after those who set themselves up as such, the Karen seem to have been ever ready to accept the teachings of some self-constituted prophet. Dr. Judson met with a person of this sort north of Moulmein in 1832.[4] The names of a number of these religious teachers, including a few women, are known. The founder of one of these cults, which attained a remarkable vogue and is known as the "Maw Lay," began his labors in the village of Pli hta, which lies about fifty miles north of Shwegyin, where they still point out the original pagoda and the huge stone steps leading up to it, reputed to have been built by the founder of the sect. The teaching was eclectic, as is generally true of other cults of this sort, embracing in this case the "Y'wa" and other traditions of the Karen, together with some elements of Buddhism and some of Christianity. The concluding sentence of the myth concerning the incarnation of the reputed author of this religion relates that when he appeared among the white men he was called Jesus Christ, and that when he appeared among the Karen he was known as "Maw Lay." The new cult originated about the middle of the last century and spread rapidly into almost every district where the Karen are found. At one time its adherents seem to have numbered some thousands, and a few of them still remain. They have a regular form of worship, consisting of a liturgy, hymns, and offerings of food and water.

Later movements of a similar nature, but more influenced by Christianity, have gained a large following chiefly among the non-Christian Karens, to whose national feeling the leaders have undoubtedly appealed. Conspicuous among these religious leaders has been Ko Pisan, also later known as Ko San Ye, who came from Papun or Shewegyin, entered the Baptist Mission, and for some years at the beginning of the present century exercised a considerable influence toward a real religious revival. Later he withdrew from his Baptist connection and started an independent Christian church, which has survived its founder and now has a membership

---

[4] Dr. Francis Mason, *The Karen Apostle*, p. 96.

of between six and seven thousand persons. The future development of this movement will be watched with interest for, under the direction of a few trained preachers and others, it affords an excellent opportunity for the Karen to show what they can accomplish in the way of religious progress by themselves.

If they can maintain their ideals, administer the affairs and discipline of their church, and increase its membership, while continuing friendly relations with other Christian bodies in Burma, they will be worthy of all praise.

Contemporaneous with the founding of the independent church by Ko San Ye, a former priest of the Church of England started the "Hkli Bo Pa" cult in the Toungoo Hills, basing his preaching on a misapprehension of a passage of Scripture. He has instituted a form of worship with peculiar practices, has been excommunicated from the Anglican body, and has since been carrying on his labors with only indifferent success.

VILLAGE SCHOOL CHILDREN WITH THEIR TEACHER
The Karen on the plains in the Prome District have become Burmanized. These children are wearing their hair trimmed Burmese fashion.

# CHAPTER XXVI

## MAGIC

The division lines between religion, magic, and science, as these matters appear to primitive peoples, are hard to trace. In truth, the three fields so overlap and interpenetrate that it is almost impossible to tell where one begins and the other leaves off. However, religion for them may be defined as consisting of the socially recognized practices and conceptions belonging to the tribe or group and relating to the supernatural powers or forces. Through their conceptions and practices the people try to enter into relation with these powers for their own welfare. Magic may be defined as the art of influencing the action of spirits and occult powers for the purpose of serving private ends. This art may involve resorting to secret and sinister means for an anti-social purpose. As many, if not most, of the magical rites are concerned with matters of health, the realm of magic includes a portion of that of science, especially of medical science, which makes use of the effects of roots, herbs, and minerals on the human body, as well as of other treatments, which form the beginning of a real scientific knowledge.

The underlying principle of Karen magic seems to be the "pgho," that all-pervasive impersonal power which is so potent for good or ill. By observing certain ceremonies and incantations the individual is thought to be able to induce the "pgho" to take up its abode in some person or object and have it accomplish the end he has in view.

The belief in the power of magic doubtless grew out of incidental observation and primitive experimentation with the unseen forces surrounding all human life, in which coincidence of events was ignorantly seized upon as establishing a necessary connection between them. That the magical power of an alleged charm rests on very insecure foundations is illustrated in an experience which I had with a Karen, who brought me two magical stones about the color and size of horse-chestnuts to be tested. The Karen had inherited these stones, which had long been regarded in his family as charms against injury by weapons. He wanted me to fire my gun at them; but I had one of my native helpers fire the gun, in order to preclude the deduction on the part of the owner of the stones that a foreigner's handling of the gun had prevented the working of the charm. The discharge of the weapon knocked the stones to bits to the great surprise of the owner, who exclaimed repeatedly that the stones were worthless after all. Such decisive demonstrations of the uselessness of magic were, of course, lacking in the olden time, and the failure of a charm to accomplish what was desired could always be explained by some unfavorable circumstance, such as the omission of some necessary rite or the ill-humor of the spirit whose coöperation was necessary. It should be remembered also that the absence of the accustomed charm produces an adverse psychological effect on those depending on them. I am told that both Karen and Burman boys who play football, have a "medicine" to protect them from injury and to bring victory. Without this talisman, which has its counterpart in the mascot of some American baseball and football teams, the players are apt to do poorly and lose the game. In like manner a Karen, who attributes his indisposition to the evil influence of some one who is bewitching him, is likely to become worse through the power of suggestion; just as his fellow-villager, who has placed himself under the protective charms and remedies of the medicine-man, often derives benefit from his own faith in their efficiency.

In some outlying Karen districts there are still persons of both sexes among the Karens who profess to maintain communication with the powers of the invisible world. Of these "wi," so-called, one group has dealings with the powers of evil, while the other looks to "Y'wa," the eternal God, for the revelation of unseen things. The latter group is sometimes designated leaders of religion ("bu hko," heads of the feasts). The prophesies of the deliverance of the Karen from the Burman yoke and of the coming of the white brother were uttered by some of these "wi." The members of the former group are believed to be able to see into hell and to bring evil forces to bear on men. They go into trances and work themselves into a state of frenzy, writhing on the ground and frothing at the mouth until they have received a message. Then they calm down and deliver their oracle in verse. They are reputed to have often deceived their patrons. They are at enmity with the prophets of the second group. Their influence is limited to those of weak "so" or personal powers.[2] Not only have strong-

---
[2] See Chapter XXI on Religious Conceptions, p. 221.

willed persons been able to resist their magic, but also in some instances have put the magic-workers to death. These "wi" are not supposed to be easily persuaded into exercising their sinister influence. It is said that they reserve their offices for the client who has suffered a real injury, or one whose distress is revealed by his tears, or one against whom seven malicious attempts have been made. Usually they are men of high-strung nervous temperament. Occasionally, other persons think themselves possessed of magic power ("pgha pgho") and try to use it for good or ill in influencing their own or some one else's life. However, a casual practitioner of the art must observe proper reticence in regard to such matters, or run the risk of falling into disrepute or of exciting the envy of some more experienced "wi." Many persons living in Karen villages at the present time are usually spoken of not as "wi," but as "k' thi thra" ("medicine-teachers" or doctors). They are very backward about referring to their art.

A class of persons supposed in the early days to be gifted with magical powers, consisted of the orphans and other unfortunates who were driven from the villages and compelled to live by themselves in the jungle.[3] In Karen folk-lore many tales recount episodes in which an orphan exercises his uncanny powers, usually in defense of some weaker person whom he saves or helps to get the better of his foes. One such story tells of a chief whose village had been raided again and again. Having no orphan magician at hand to aid him, he was beaten every time; while the victorious villages were every one of them blessed in having such a champion. The chief, anticipating another raid, sent his daughter away because he had no one else to give in ransom, should he be vanquished again. She ran through the jungle until she fell exhausted, and next morning was found by an orphan, one of seven brothers, near whose hut she had fallen. She related her story to the aged grandmother of the seven, and they were so captivated by her that they determined to aid her father in recovering the bronze drums and other treasure that he had surrendered, in order to save his village from destruction. Before the grandmother would consent to her grandsons' enterprise, she required them to make a trial of their strength. This they did by each catching a tusker elephant in the jungle, grasping him by the fore and hind legs and using him as a huge kind of battering-ram in knocking down a clump of bam-

[3] See pp. 133, 134.

boos. Quite satisfied with this demonstration of their magic power, the grandmother allowed them to go on their mission. In the battle that followed the seven orphans severally engaged the champions of the seven victorious villages and won back for the maiden's father the treasure that he had been forced to pay over in the previous raids. The oldest of the brothers then received the hand of the chief's daughter in marriage, having cleared himself of the curse that had rested upon him as an orphan.

Why such extraordinary powers have been attributed to the once despised orphan is not known. At first he was feared for the bad luck he might bring to the other inhabitants of the village, if allowed to remain within the stockade. That he did not perish as an outcast in the jungle must have been regarded as a sort of miracle by the village community, whose members had always lived and worked together in close interdependence. They must have looked upon him with awe and believed that he was protected by some powerful influence, not only from the evilly disposed "Bgha" but also from the dangers of the forest. It was, therefore, natural enough to regard him in course of time as a person who had "pgho." In these later days orphans appear to have been considered less extraordinary persons, as indicated by the following couplet:

> "In olden times the orphans had magic.
> Orphans now must talk" [like other persons].

The "k' thi thra" or "medicine-teachers" constitute another group that should be mentioned among magic-workers. It is true that they possess a rude knowledge of the efficacy of roots and herbs, but they also sometimes dispense disgusting and filthy concoctions. The Karen, like other primitive peoples, regard sickness as due to some mysterious force or "mana" and believe that all medicine, even that prescribed by European physicians, operates to dispel or vanquish this force. They expect a dose to cure immediately and discredit a medicine that must be taken repeatedly. Hence, in general, they prefer their native "medicine-teacher" and his nostrums to the educated physician and his medicine, the therapeutic effects of which are beyond their understanding. Doubtless, some Karens do distinguish between the charm and the drug, but most of them seem to cling to the idea that the drug has more or less of the charm connected with it.

Magic among the Karen, as among other primitive races, is divisible into white and black magic. The former is the beneficent kind, involving the use of certain rites, practices, and conceptions by which one tries to protect one's self against unknown powers and forces. White magic may be divided in turn into three varieties, namely, defensive, productive, and prognostic magic.

As suggested by its name, defensive magic is employed to safeguard one from injury and to prolong one's life. Charms are used, such as the wild boar's tusk without a nerve cavity, to prevent the possessor from being wounded by the firing of a gun or the bolt from a crossbow. The tusk charm is called "soh."

The boar's tusk must be the tusk of an old and fierce animal (for the older the animal, the smaller the cavity), which was, therefore, hard to kill. This, according to Karen belief, renders its owner equally hard to destroy. Sometimes the tooth of an ancestor is worn, in order to gain the reputed courage and strength of the latter. A female wears such a charm around her neck. A man may wear it set in a finger-ring. The latter method of wearing the tooth would not serve in the case of a woman or girl, for unavoidably it would be brought in contact with her skirt and that would be disrespectful to the dead, thus destroying the value of the charm. A lock of hair or the parings of nails from a corpse are also frequently worn to prolong the life of the wearer.

A certain plant of magic power, called "k' thi baw tho" or "tiger medicine" is said by the Karen to confer such immunity upon him who uses it that he may enter a den of fierce tigers at any time without the least fear.[4] It is also reported that by burying the root of this magic plant at the bottom of a hole seven cubits deep, pulling the root up with one's teeth, and jumping out—according to one of my informants—even when men are standing around the opening with sticks in their hands, one will be turned into a man-eating tiger and spend the remainder of his life in the jungle composing verses and springing down upon unwary persons. Certainly, one who can believe that a man can leap out of so deep a hole and dodge the blows of his fellows at the top, will experience no difficulty in believing the rest of this story.

A second form of white magic is what is defined as productive magic. It has to do with increasing a crop, rendering a family prosperous, or adding children to the family circle. Certain plants of the ginger family *(Zingiberaceae)* growing in Burma are supposed to be endowed with the power of bringing a good crop production. Consequently, they are set out at the entrances of the

---
[4] *Karen Thesaurus*, new ed., Vol. I, pp. 643, ff.

PAKU KAREN SCHOOL GIRLS
These maidens are carrying the smaller Toungoo baskets. They are wearing the usual Paku costume.

fields. A native reported to me an example of productive magic in connection with the finding of a spiral coil of heavy brass wire by his great aunt. The coil was from four to six inches in diameter and was unearthed by the aunt while digging a large yam in the jungle. The coil was carried home, but at first brought only misfortune. However, in the full moon of "Thadingyut" (Burmese for October) the aunt hit upon the happy idea of offering the blood of a red cock to the spiral coil, and in due time the family became prosperous. A failure to make the annual offering was followed by ill-fortune. The offering must not be made by an unchaste person or by one who had fallen out of the house during the year. The coil, which sometimes assumed human form, must not be approached too closely. It was believed to possess the power of foretelling the future when it appeared in human shape.

The red and yellow varieties of the flowering plant, cockscomb *(Amarantus)*, which grow abundantly in the hills, are reputed to have a beneficial effect on the crops. The red variety has the added virtue, according to various tales, of dazzling the eyes of pursuing spirits, which are so attracted by it that they forget any evil intent they may have had against persons or objects. A root taken from a red cockscomb found growing in a field three years after cultivation, if bound up in the turban of a husband, will prevent the wife from conceiving, according to Karen lore. The opposite result is attained by the women of Shwegyin by wearing the bones of the "Ta t'hkaw hkaw" (a one-legged female demon) as a necklace. They buy these bones from the Brecs.[5]

Black magic is bad magic or witchcraft. The Karen speak of it as "ta ho ta yaw" or sometimes as "ta ho ta lo," meaning to work evil on a person and thereby cause his death. It is difficult to learn very much about the practices involved in the art, for those who exercise it are prone to keep their methods secret, revealing them, if at all, to one or two intimates only and thus preventing their secrets from losing their potency. By blowing on a cup of water that is later to be handed to the intended victim, the worker of black magic imparts to it a baleful action that will cause him to sicken and die. A quid of betel blown upon in the same way may be thrown at the person intended to be harmed, and, if it strikes him, will produce the fatal result desired. Some sorcerers pretend to have the power of inducing a lingering disease, which after a year or two will terminate the life of their victims. Other methods

---

[5] See Chapter XXII on Supernatural and Mythical Beings, p. 233.

resorted to are reputed to stimulate the growth of tumors, thick membranes, or bones in the bowels of a person and thus effect his premature death. It was reported to me that one sorcerer demonstrated his destructive power by coaxing a squirrel to come near and hitting it with a betel quid upon which he had blown, whereupon the little animal fell dead. The man telling me of this experiment had not witnessed it, but learned of it from one who had. The practice of magic by the blowing method is attributed to a certain man, named Saw Hteu (a famous prophet), who was gashed severely by a wild boar in the chase. The prophet blew and spat on the wounds, which healed immediately. It was said that the mastery of this method could be gained only through instruction from its author. It is a method that can be used either for good or evil purposes. Those who apply it in doing harm are often called false prophets ("wi a' bla") and are greatly feared by those Karens who are still deep in ignorance and superstition. Dr. Wade thinks this blowing charm is of Talaign origin, which is very likely, for it is used by all the peoples in Burma and is probably a survival of the old demon-worship, which still remains powerful despite centuries of Buddhist teaching.[6]

A well-known method of wrecking vengeance on an enemy, but one that would be used only by the most craven wizzard, is that of invoking the action of the skull of a corpse that had been left unburied. During the daytime the skull appears to be harmless enough; but at night, if magical lore is to be credited, it takes on the complete similitude of a wretched man, a kind of retributive agent, ready to be sent on a mission of murder. Another familiar method of doing evil to a person is to take a piece of his clothing, a lock of his hair, or even some of the dust from his foot-prints and, after blowing the baleful breath on whatever has been taken, to make a little image of him, stick a feather in the bottom of it, and hang it on a tree. When the wind swings this manikin to and fro, the mind of the person it represents will begin to give way, becoming capricious and unsettled. The imparting of bad luck is also accomplished by secreting a fragment of a monstrous woman's skirt in the pillow of the hated individual. I heard of a wife who did this out of spite to her husband, who had taken unto himself another woman. The result of her action was all that could have been desired, for the man finally died.

---
[6] *The Karen Thesaurus*, new ed., Vol. I, p. 445.

Certain stones ("ler na") and some plants of the ginger family ("paw na") are credited with having the ability to consume food. If offered raw flesh and blood, they prefer the latter. The owners of such specimens can cause harm to any one against whom they have a grudge. In case one of the "ler na" is sent to a person, it takes on the appearance of the owner and produces the death of the recipient. Such stones, according to report, are usually picked up in swampy places, glow in the dark, and will eat into one's flesh like an acid. It seems to be customary to send one of these carnivorous stones to the intended victim when he is in a weakened condition on account of sickness. He is, therefore, in a physical state to experience such an hallucination as that referred to above.

To counteract the effects of the "ler na," a medicine is compounded from the gall-bladder of one who has suffered a violent death and been stolen from the grave at night. The remains of the gall-bladder are mixed with the charred dust scraped from the bamboos used in piercing the corpse when it was being burned. These ingredients are moistened with water and shaped into a ball, from which the patient takes doses when he finds the spell of the magic stone asserting itself. Other fragments of the medicine-ball are pulverized and scattered in the air about the patient. This internal and external treatment is supposed to afford both cure and protection from the menace of the "ler na."[7] Another method (called "po") of preventing witches and wizards from working their evil spells, is by inserting twigs of the indigo plant in the split ends of three sticks, spitting on the twigs, and offering a prayer for deliverance.

Much of the magic of the Karen prophets and "medicine-teachers" is concerned with recalling the "k'las" of sick persons. The multitude of demons and powers by which the tribesman believes himself to be surrounded, renders it next to impossible for him to tell which of these spirits is assailing him when he falls ill. Hence he calls in a diviner, unless he should undertake to consult the chicken bones or make marks on a bamboo, in order to determine for himself the cause of his sickness. When he has learned the cause, he makes offerings to placate the particular spirit concerned. In case his recovery is not as rapid as he thinks it ought to be, he calls in some "wi" to find out what the matter is and what he must do. The "wi" who was summoned to prescribe for a sick grandmother some years ago, inspected the chicken bones several times and, when

---

[7] Dr. Wade, *The Karen Thesaurus*, new ed., Vol. I, p. 463.

he got a satisfactory divination, placed some rice, cooked chicken, and liquor on a tray and drew it along the floor of the house to the top of the ladder at the entrance. He then ran a string from the tray down the ladder to the ground for the old woman's k' la or shade to come up on. The "k' la" did not return because, as the witch-doctor explained, it was held captive in a betel-box by some one. Thereupon, he asked for seven cubits of white cloth, wound it about himself, and lay down to sleep with a "dah" (large knife) and an axe on either side of him. With the shades of these tools in hand his "k' la" was to go and release the shade or spirit of the grandmother. On awaking, the witch-doctor reported that he had had a hard struggle and been shot at by the man who was restraining the old woman's spirit from returning, but that he had succeeded in releasing it. When the doctor unwrapped himself, so the granddaughter of the patient told me, the cloth was riddled with what appeared to be shot holes. The string on the ladder was broken, showing conclusively that the "k' la" had returned at last. A piece of this string was now tied around the patient's wrist to prevent her spirit from again escaping. Needless to say, the old woman recovered her health.

A ceremony is sometimes observed among the Karen to keep the "k' la" of a deceased person from aimlessly wandering about and to beguile it into remaining with the corpse, until it shall depart to the king of spirits. In this ceremony the coffined body is placed in the center of the floor. A slender rod of bamboo is inserted in a hole in the coffin lid, a thread reaching from the tip of the bamboo to the floor. This thread has small tufts of cotton and bits of charcoal tied to it in alternate order throughout its length. Under the loose end of the thread a small cup containing a hard-boiled egg is placed. A silver or brass ring hangs at the end of the thread just over the cup. In case the thread is drawn downward with some force so that it vibrates or breaks, the "k' la" is supposed to have returned from its wanderings, otherwise not. Colonel MacMahon relates that he watched an experiment of this kind, but that when he required everybody to go a considerable distance from the cup, nothing happened.[8]

Among the Karen and Burmese the abdomen is held to be the seat of the passions and the diseases, varying moods and bodily

---

[8] A similar ceremony is gone through at noon of the last day of the funeral rites. See *ante*, p. 237; Col. A. R. MacMahon, *The Karens of the Golden Chersonese*, p. 138; Cross, in the *Journal, American Oriental Society*, Vol. I.

conditions being attributed to the presence of wind ("k'li"), fire ("me"), or water ("paw leh"). The elders assert that fifteen hundred cavities in the abdomen contain wind, twelve contain fire, and one contains water. The prevalence of wind over the other elements produces pride, ambition, avarice, evil desires, and hilarity. When fire is in the ascendancy, one is incited to envy, malice, hatred, and revenge. When water predominates, issuing from its single cavity, it disseminates peace, love, kindness, patience, quietness, and other allied virtues. The various qualities are intermingled in one's character in proportion to the mingling of the several elements.[9]

Many of the charms worn by both the Karen and the Burmese are intended to prevent wind from gaining the ascendency in the abdomen. Among such charms are strings of dried berries of certain plants, strings of coins that have been blown upon, and knotted cords that have been put on the wearer by elders or prophets.

Something remains to be said about the "k' thi thras" or "medicine-teachers," who compound drugs from various roots and herbs with which they practice a sort of medical lore, in addition to their occult rites. There is no doubt but that they understand the medicinal action of certain plants. They will often point out a particular tree with the remark that its leaves are good for fever or some other ailment. On my request for some prescriptions a Karen doctor gave me a hundred of them. Dr. Wade has collected over forty pages of medical formulae of various kinds, among them many of real value. Dr. Mason mentions the name of a small creeping plant *(Hydrocotyle asiatica)* which, if applied as a poultice in time, will arrest, if it does not cure, leprosy.[10] How many of these Karen prescriptions are of Burmese, Shan, or Talign origin I am unable to say. I have been told several times that the Karen who still remain in their primitive condition, depend wholly on magic and offerings to cure sickness. My observation leads me to believe that the use of medicine increases, as the people come more and more into contact with other races.

The Karen believe that smells have a marked effect on the body, both for good and for ill. There is hardly anything that a Karen or, indeed, a Burman fears so much as he does the smell of cooking fat ("ta neu xo"). They believe that the odor somehow enters the body, especially if there is an abrasion of the skin,

---
[9] *The Karen Thesaurus*, new ed., Vol. I, p. 500.
[10] Dr. F. Mason, *British Burma, Its Peeople and Productions*, pp. 501, ff.

and causes all kinds of trouble, even sudden death. To avoid coming in contact with this smell, they usually do any frying that may be necessary out-of-doors and hold their hands over their noses to keep off the dread danger. For curative purposes smelling-salts are popular among both Karens and Burmans, when they can be bought in bazaar. Many of the medicines contain asafoetida and other pungent-smelling ingredients, which are thought to have an immediate effect on the patient. Bitter and acrid-tasting drugs are also in great favor.

Apart from such remedies the Karen "medicine-teachers" resort to disgusting concoctions of the scrapings from the horns of the sambur, the hair and genitals of certain animals, tigers' and leopards' whiskers, certain parts of human corpses, the body hair of human beings, dung of all kinds, the scrapings from the charred ends of bamboos used in piercing corpses on the funeral pyre, etc. The urine of one sex is sometimes prescribed as a liniment for persons of the opposite sex. The following is a prescription taken from the *Karen Thesaurus*, where it is described as "a grand febrifuge": "Take the umbilical cord cut from a new-born child, the undigested kernels from the dung of a dog, white and red onions, ginger and black pepper in equal quantities; mix thoroughly and make into pills the size of the end of the little finger; dose, one at a time to be taken in hot water." [11]

The formulae for other kinds of pills are even more disgusting than that just given. Draughts, lotions, liniments, smelling-compounds, liquids for bathing, hot and cold applications; herbs and other things to be hung over the patient, placed under his bed, or in an adjoining room, are among the strange mixtures that might be enumerated without interesting any but the curious.

---

[11] *The Karen Thesaurus*, new ed., Vol. I, p. 641.

## CHAPTER XXVII

## DIVINATIONS

Recourse is had to the bones of the fowl for prognosticating the future throughout many parts of southeastern Asia. In these regions the chicken is indigenous, and it may be that the custom of examining their bones came about in a natural way, as suggested by Sir J. G. Scott.[1] It would be natural for people entering a new country for the purpose of settling in it to take note of all indications as to its fertility, including the size and condition of the fowls. Perhaps this gives us the clue to the origin of the Karen practice of inspecting the holes of the thigh-bones of the fowl. The words designating this usage are "ka hsaw ki," which literally mean to break the fowl's bones. It may be that originally they actually broke the bones and examined their structure, strength, and condition to determine whether the fowls were well nourished or not, and that later the custom arose of inspecting only the holes in the bones. Why such a change should have taken place is without explanation, unless the people thought they had discovered a relation between the general healthiness of the bones and the pinholes along their sides.

The Karen people themselves connect the origin of this custom with the legends of their early golden age, before they had lost their book or "Mü kaw li" (Satan) had tempted their ancestors to disobey the eternal God, "Y'wa," and had then taught them divination. The story of the Lost Book is found among other peoples in this region of the earth and in brief is as follows: In the beginning "Y'wa" had seven sons, the eldest of whom was the Karen and the youngest, the white man. The father, being about to go on a journey, invited the Karen to accompany him; but the latter declined on the score that he had his field to clear. The Burman also refused to go. However, each of them gave "Y'wa" a gift, the Karen presenting him with a bamboo trough, such as the pigs feed out of, and the Burman, with a paddle.[2] The white brother was induced to accompany his father,

---

[1] Sir J. G. Scott, *Burma, A Handbook*, 399, ff.

[2] Another version of this myth says that the Karen gave "Y'wa" a "saw ku" or rain cover such as is worn when the people are transplanting rice in the rainy season.

and, when they got to the sea, they transformed the trough into a boat and the paddle into a mast and sail. By these means they soon reached the celestial shore. While there "Y'wa" prepared three books: one of silver and gold for the Karen, because he was the oldest; one of palm-leaf for the Burman, and one of parchment for their white brother. These were given to the white man, and he accepted them, but kept the silver and gold book himself, sending the parchment book to the Karen by the hands of the Burman. The Karen was busy clearing his fields and, paying little attention to the book, forgot to carry it home. When he burned off his clearing, it was lying on a stump and was nearly destroyed. The pigs and chickens ate the charred remains of it.[3] Thus, the wisdom contained in the book, which the ancestors of the race sorely needed after sickness and trouble came upon them, was nowhere to be found except in the pigs, chickens, and charcoal, and it was to these they turned in their distress. According to the account contained in the "Y'wa" legend, the serpent, "Mü kaw li," was directly responsible for leading them to these sources of wisdom.[4] Such is the mythical story of the origin of divination among the Karen.

If one asks Karens versed in the old poems, why the people consult these omens, they are apt to answer by quoting the following lines:

> "The book of the ages was rooted by the pigs.
> At first the women neglected it.
> The men also did not look at it.
> If both men and women had studied it,
> All the world would have been happy."

> "Our book of gold that "Y'wa" gave,
> Our book of silver that he gave,
> The elders did not obey.
> Lost, it wandered to the foreigner."

Among the forms of divination the one most in vogue is that of examining the chicken bones. It is used on all occasions. Nothing is undertaken by those retaining the old superstitions, whether of little consequence or great importance to them, without divination,

---

[3] There are two accounts of the loss of the book, which are about equally common. Besides the version which says that the book was left on the stump, is another relating that the book was left on the floor, near the entrance to the house. Here it lay unheeded, till at last it fell through the cracks and was picked at by the fowls and chewed by the pigs under the house, being finally entirely destroyed. Then, at last, the unhappy people began to feel the need of its guidance.

[4] See Chapter XXI on Religious Conceptions, p. 213.

FIELD-DAY, THARRAWADDY KAREN HIGH SCHOOL

usually by inspecting the fowl's bones and obtaining a favorable omen. Detailed accounts, which I have obtained of the interpretation of the arrangement of the holes in the thigh-bones of chickens, show that these vary more or less. The system of readings furnished to me by an old man of the Tharrawaddy district corresponds in general with data from other Sgaw sections. According to this system, the left thigh-bone ("mi") represents the jungle. If this bone has a larger number of holes than the right thigh-bone or has them arranged in a certain way, the omen is unfavorable. That is, the "k' la" or life principle will be influenced by this reading to depart from the body of the person concerned, thus causing his sickness or death. If, however, the bones are being consulted in regard to some undertaking, the reading above indicated would imply that it must be postponed until a favorable omen can be had. The right thigh-bone ("hsa") represents the house, and, when it affords the favorable reading, all is well for the undertaking or the person concerned. The bones are held reversed at the time of reading, the top being called the "hkaw" (literally, the foot), the other end being designated the "hko" (literally, the head). The right ("hsa") and left ("mi") are the reverse of the diviner's right and left.

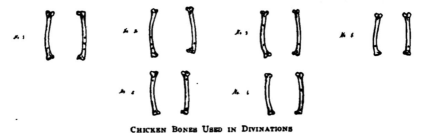

CHICKEN BONES USED IN DIVINATIONS

Six different arrangements of the holes were specified to me, as follows:

(1) In this arrangement the jungle bone ("mi") has three holes, while the house bone ("hsa") has only one. Hence, the diviner says: "Mi a, mi neu hsa," meaning that "the jungle has more and wins over the house. This bodes bad luck or sickness.

(2) This arrangement is the opposite of (1) and is reported as "Hsa a, hsa neu mi." This reading is a prognostication of good fortune.

(3) In this instance the bones show both a foot and a head hole

on the right and a head but no foot hole on the left. The reading is "Hsaw xi wa ti htaw," and the omen is good.

(4) In this instance both the right and left bones show a head hole, the explanation is "Hsaw xi wa hkwa," and the omen is fair.

(5) The bones show foot holes on both sides, the explanation being "Shaw xi ku hko mi." The omen is less than fair.

(6) In this instance the left bone shows only one hole in the middle, a most unfavorable omen. The reading is "Hsaw xi htaw deh pgha k' le." Thra Than Bya says that in case the bones have no holes at all it is a most unfavorable omen; for once in the remote past the signs read this way when a certain king was going to war, and the outcome of his campaign was an utter defeat. Hence, no one will now undertake anything, when he gets this reading of the bones.[5]

If the bones display any of the unfavorable omens, three more attempts are made in the hope of obtaining a better response. Supposing that the omen is being taken in order to ascertain the fate of a sick person and none of the four trials is successful, his relatives and friends will withhold the discouraging information, lest by telling it they should hasten the patient's death. I am unable to give translations of most of the phrases quoted above, for they seem to be in archaic language not readily understood at the present time. I am not sure that the six readings which I have mentioned exhaust the list.

Captain C. E. Poynder and Lieutenant E. W. Carrick have noted that in some of the Bwe and Padaung communities hairs or bamboo splinters are inserted in the holes of the chicken bones. According to Bwe practice, if these slant at the same angle the omen is regarded as being favorable. According to the practice among the Padaung people, if the inserted splinters slant upwards the sign is good, but if inwards it is bad.[6] Before inserting the splinters to see whether a journey may be undertaken, the diviner holds the bones up before him and addresses them, saying:

> "O, you supernatural chicken bones!
> We are now planning to go and return.
> If it is right for us,
> Show us a favorable omen.
> Do not let the reply turn out bad."

In certain localities the splinters are not inserted until the

---
[5] Rev. T. Than Bya, M. A. *Karen Customs, Ceremonies, and Poetry*, p. 42.
[6] Capt. C. E. Poynder, *Notes on Bwe Expedition* (Government Press, Rangoon) 1894-95, p. 1; Lieutenant E. W. Carrick, *Notes on Report of Bwe & Padaung Countries*, 1894-5, p. 11.

bones have been spat upon, rubbed with charcoal, scraped all over with a sickle, and the holes cleaned out. Sometimes the wing-bones are used, but not so generally as the thigh-bones.

Before preparing and eating the feasts in honor of the "Bgha," as has been pointed out elsewhere,[7] the gall-bladder of a pig is examined. If it is full and round, it is evident that the spirits will be pleased with the offering and that good fortune, health, and plenty will follow. This form of divination is common not only among the Karen, but also among the tribes of Malaysia and Borneo.[8]

On occasions of little consequence, and perhaps more often nowadays than formerly, the Sgaw resort to a form of divination in which a number of transverse marks are made at random with a piece of charcoal, which has been spat upon, on a stick of wood or a piece of bamboo. When the space allotted has been filled up, the marks are counted by twos. If it appears that an even number of marks has been made, the affair in hand will turn out well; if not, the same process is gone through a second time in the hope of securing a different result. In case this attempt also fails, the project is abandoned for the present. The use of the charcoal is reminiscent of the charred remains of the Lost Book.

A method that is sometimes used to discover the outcome of an illness may be described as follows. The diviner holds a fresh egg to his mouth, spits upon it, and says: "May this egg show us what is the cause of the illness. If due to the 'Bgha,' may the egg have white streaks on its yolk; if due to the 'th' re ta hka,' may it have red streaks on its yolk; if due to witchcraft, may the red streaks be mixed with blood." After rubbing the sick person with the egg, the elder breaks it open in the palm of his hand and carefully examines the yolk for one of the signs he has mentioned. If he observes any of these, he prescribes the offering to be made to the spirit concerned. If, however, the yolk discloses no particular marks, he repeats the operation and this time prays to "Pa'k' sa Y'wa" (Father God) to aid him: " 'Pa k sa Y'wa,' this man is sick. We do not know the reason for it. But you are in heaven and care for all of your children. As you have prophets, give them a word to say." Again the egg is rubbed over the sick person, broken open, and examined. A peculiar appearance of the contents, described to me as consisting of two points connected by fibres going around

---

[7] See Chapter XXIV on Feasts to the "Bgha," pp. 251, 252.
[8] For Borneo, see Hose & MacDougall, *The Pagan Tribes of Borneo*, Vol. II, 60, ff.

the yolk, is supposed to show that a "ta na" (one of the violent evil demons) has caused the illness and that he will be hard to appease. If the streaks are black, the patient is thought to be doomed to die.

In practicing these various forms of divination the Karen, like other primitive peoples, feel that they are peering into the realm of the unseen but powerful forces that dominate the universe. To the Karen the omens obtained are real revelations, without which they dare not venture into the future. When they fail in their undertakings despite favorable omens, they believe that some other power, opposed to the one invoked, has held sway. Their concern then becomes to win the favor and assistance of this more influential power in their next venture.

## CHAPTER XXVIII

## TABU

As among the Polynesians and South Sea Islanders, so also among the Karen people, certain foods, animals, persons, places, days, names, etc., are temporarily or permanently prohibited under penalty of a curse falling upon those who disregard the tabu. Among the Karen such prohibitions ("ta dü ta htu") are most commonly associated with marriage, adultery, births, widows and orphans, portents, signs of bad luck, crops, certain domestic animals, the "Bgha" feasts, the names of persons, high waters, and the gathering of herbs for dyestuffs. The people's fear of offending powerful spirits and thereby bringing calamity upon themselves, is at the root of most, if not all, of these tabus, which serve to illustrate the fact that primitive man does not recognize broad principles of conduct, but depends on precepts covering specific experiences in his life. When asked why they do not do the tabued acts, most Karens content themselves with the reply, "Ta t' ghe ba" (It is not good). The observance of these prohibitions, which are usually accompanied by certain sacrifices or offerings, is a matter of custom that has descended from former generations.

It is evident that most of the tabus are related to the domestic life and the occupations of the people. Only in a few instances are they concerned with interests distinctly tribal. It was formerly the custom among the Red Karen for the mothers of prospective chiefs of the tribe, and for the chiefs themselves, to abstain from the use of rice and liquor.[1] The tabu on the eating of rice by these persons is difficult to explain; but we know that the Red Karen use rice less extensively than the inhabitants of the plains, yams and other roots constituting an important part of their diet. The suggestion has been made that the tabu on liquor drinking by the chiefs and their mothers, was for the purpose of promoting the clearness of mind so desirable in the leaders of the tribe; but it is truer to say that they believe that by ascetic practices one may gain unusual powers—perhaps magical—either for oneself or, in the case of the chief, for his people. When the Red Karen chiefs ob-

---

[1] *Upper Burma Gazetteer*, Vol. I, Part II, p. 808.

served their tabus they prospered, but when they neglected them they suffered adversity, it is alleged.

Marriage of a Karen with a person of another race was formerly strictly forbidden. This exclusiveness kept the racial stock pure and unmixed. In recent times the prohibition has not been rigorously enforced. Hence, the barriers between the Karen on the one hand and the Burmese and Shan on the other have been somewhat weakened, betokening—it must be confessed—a moral looseness that was unknown before. The village elders have always maintained that marriages outside of the tribe ("taw leu hko") were not good, although such unions have not been lately tabued. Marriages between members of the same tribe or of the same village, providing the parties concerned are not more closely related than cousins, are permitted. To marry a relative closer than a cousin would be incest, and all the tribes forbid such unions. On the day of a wedding in a village the inhabitants are forbidden to labor.

Adultery and fornication are under strict tabu, except in the Red Karen tribe,[2] the belief among the other tribes being that these sins are offensive to the "Bgha"[3] and destroy the productiveness of the fields, the "Lords of the earth" withholding their favor from the crops when they find that such deeds have been committed. In making their annual feast to these deities, the Bwe tribe formerly required those who had been guilty of uncleanness during the year to confess their sins and did not permit them to come near the sacrificial altars.

A number of prohibitions are connected with birth. One of the Sgaw precepts forbids pregnant women to eat the flesh of the curious monkey-tiger *(Ictides ater)*, bitter herbs, and the long smooth pod called alligator's tongue. Before the men adopted the modern fashion of wearing their hair short, the husband of a woman who was with child was not permitted to trim his locks, for fear of shortening the life of his expected offspring. During the first six days following a birth the custom of the Paduang denies to the father the right of associating or even speaking with any one, except his own family. He alone cares for the mother and child during the period named.[4] The purpose of thus secluding the father is to prevent the transmission of the danger and weakness

---
[2] See Dr. Mason's account in the *Journal, Asiatic Society of Bengal*, 1866.
[3] This is true in those localities where the "Bgha" are regarded as the family penates. In other localities, as among the Bwe, the offended powers were the "lords of the earth."
[4] Lieutenant E. W. Carrick, *Report on Bwe Expedition*, 1894-95, p. 23.
[5] E. B. Cross, J. A. O. S. (1854) Vol. IV, 293, ff. and D. C. Gilmore, Journ. Burma

of child-bearing to other members of the village. MacMahon states that the Bwe husband of a newly delivered mother complies with the custom of cutting fresh bamboo joints, in which he draws and heats the water for bathing the infant, over a fire kindled by himself in the open. He then carries the water to his wife's room up a new ladder, which he has made. After his wife has washed the child or he himself, in case she is too weak to do so, he hangs the bamboo joints under the house and leaves them there for six days before they may be used again.[5] On the day of the birth of a child, or even of a domestic animal, members of the village are forbidden to work. This is the tabu of births ("ta dü ta ble").

In the early times widows and orphans, as well as persons found to be holding improper relations, became tabu and were expelled from the village, in order to keep other inhabitants from falling under the vengeance of the evil-working demon, whose attention might be diverted from his first victims. The driving of these unfortunates into the jungle to live there by themselves, may be described as a kind of primitive quarantine.[6] Precaution of a different kind was at the bottom of the requirement that a visiting stranger should enter and leave the village-house by the same ladder. It was also required that the visitor must descend the ladder while facing inwards. Leaving the house by a different way from that by which one had entered, created suspicion of hostile intent among the inhabitants and might lead to hostilities. Like other neighboring peoples, the Karen observe a tabu in regard to women's garments, which must not come in contact with a man. Garments that are put out to dry must be hung away from the common paths in some inconspicuous place. Probably this custom originated in the fear that the supposed weakness of woman might be communicated to the men. For the same reason, evidently, the Brec tribe prohibits married men from taking part in making the coffin for a woman who has died in child-birth.

Tabus connected with portents, such as eclipses of the moon, earthquakes, the cries of apes, and certain strange sounds in the jungle, have a religious significance for the Karen and are accompanied by the prohibition of work for one or more days. The witnesses of these portents are seized with fear, drop their work, and stand about in helplessness. This, undoubtedly, is the normal behavior of primitive people under such circumstances. They as-

---
[5] MacMahon, *The Karens of the Golden Chersonese*, p. 319.
[6] See Chapter XIV on Social Conditions, pp. 133, 134.

cribe the portent to some angry demon, who may at any moment impose a worse calamity upon them if they fail to observe this warning. The tabu of labor, until their fears have subsided, is clearly the precept that would suggest itself to people of deep-seated superstitions. According to Karen legend, the dogs that cause the eclipse of the moon by eating that luminary, are colder than water; while the one that swallows the sun, is hotter than fire. In order to prevent excessive heat or cold and the sickness and death that would follow, the people must abstain from work on the days when an eclipse occurs. The Karen name for the tabu of the eclipse is "ta dü ta yu mü ta yu la." [7]

The portent of the earthquake is produced by the mythical giant, "Hsi Ghu," when the beetle that feeds on the refuse of human beings, tries to deceive him into believing that the human race has disappeared from the earth. In his wrath the giant shifts the planet from one shoulder to the other, and the people shout to him in consternation: "We are still here. We are still here." When, in times past, the giant caught the beetle in this trick, he struck it in the face, and the beetle has had a flat nose ever since. At the time of an earthquake the people refrain from their work for a day, in order to help restore the equilibrum of the planet and to mollify "Hsi Ghu." This practice is called the tabu of the earthquake or "ta dü haw hko hu." [8]

When the apes howl it is a portent that the goddess "Ta La." who dwells on Mount "Thaw Thi," [9] one of the higher peaks of the mountain range separating the Toungoo district from Karenni, is uttering curses, which are greatly feared. In Shwegyin the people ascribe the falling of the leaves in the latter part of February to her imprecations and refrain from work for three days. They believe that if they failed to observe this "ta dü hpa taw" (the long tabu), their crops would be ruined.

The portent of strange sounds in the jungle betokens a combat between two celestial beings, one of whom, "Kwe De," hurls his spear at the other. The whizz of the weapon as it speeds through the air and its thud on striking the ground, evoke the cry, "Htaw law," from those who hear these startling sounds. They must stay at home that day, lest they should be in danger from these mythical spears.

---
[7] See Chapter VII, p. 54.
[8] See Chapter XXII, p. 230.
[9] See Chapter XXV, p. 262.

A number of tabus are associated with signs of bad luck. Many of these signs are incidental to going on journeys. For example, if one sneezes on rising to start on a journey, or on the way hears the cry of a barking deer, or sees one of these animals or a snake crossing his path, or hears of somebody's death, or sees a civet-cat near his path, he must give up his excursion until another day. Otherwise, he will meet with an accident, fall sick, or experience some misfortune in his family. It was once the custom of those who were setting out on a trading journey to repeat the following words:

> "I am going to ——— to trade.
> O Snakes, do not cross my path.
> O Barking-deer and Rabbits, do not hinder me.
> I am going across my land and along my path.
> There are many other paths on the earth.
> O white Civet-cat, do not hinder me."

If divination shows that one's illness is due to having taken the wrong road on a recent journey, that road rests under a tabu for a period of from four to seven days. The branch of a tree is laid across the forbidden trail where it leaves the main path, and no one will enter it until the tabu is lifted. This is called the tabu of the road ("ta dü kleh"). When a death occurs in a village, the death tabu ("ta dü ta thi ta pgha") is observed until the burial ceremonies are over. Children and persons of weak constitution are kept from witnessing the removal of a corpse from the village, inasmuch as their "k'las" are said to be easily enticed away by that of the dead person. On an elephant hunt it is forbidden to mention the name of the beast, lest its spirit should hear and take alarm, thus destroying the chance of success in the chase. Instead it is called "ta hpa do" or "the great one." Other signs of ill luck surely bring their tabus. If one does not return from work on hearing the wildcat's cry, one will die. No one should live in a house whose owner dies, or by which a green pigeon flew while the house was building.

The observance of certain tabus are regarded as conducive to the production of good crops or of prosperity in other forms. When the people have made the offering, "theh a hku," they must refrain from going into their fields for seven days. Otherwise, the demons will follow them and spoil their crops. This tabu is known as "ta dü hkü ta dü theh." During the dark and the full of the moon, in February and July, respectively, when people say that "it is hot," meaning that conditions are unfavorable, they avoid work for the purpose of improving the conditions and keeping their crops from being ruined. Failure to observe this custom brings disappointment ("t' kle t htwa"), for one's labor will be worse than useless. On the plains, where they prepare a dirt threshing-floor after the Burman style, it used to be prohibited to drive a cart across it or to walk on it with shoes on. In other sections, where the threshing is done on a great mat, no one may step on it but the members of the family who take part in the work. The succulent shoots of vegetables, which are grown with the paddy, must not be cut with a sharp knife or other instrument, inasmuch as cutting would endanger the "k'la" or life principle of the paddy and scare away the demons that preside over the fields. Both the vegetables and their shoots, the latter being largely used for greens, must be plucked with the fingers. Another tabu prevents the eating of flesh during harvest-time. Any family who should transgress this precept would find, it is believed, that their supply of rice had vanished from the storage bin.

The following examples of tabus relating to domestic animals may be cited. If a sow or bitch has a litter composed only of females, they must all be killed. When less than three chicks are hatched from a nest of eggs, they must be killed. So also must the chick whose down dries fast to the feathers of the mother hen. A crowing hen is likewise doomed to death. These phenomena are supposed to be signs of weakness in the creatures concerned, for which some offended demon is responsible. Such weakness must not be allowed to spread.

Certain tabus contribute to preserve the integrity of the family through the female line. One of these prevents any outsider from entering a house where the family is celebrating the "Bgha" feasts. Indeed, a tabu debars from such gatherings the men who have married into the family, while those who are privileged to attend must remain in the house during the performance of the rites.

On the plains, where the Karen villagers build separate houses after the manner of the Burmans, persons are forbidden to drive their carts through the village road close enough to the houses to bump against the supporting posts. This tabu, which, in the eyes of a Westerner, partakes of the nature of a town ordinance, is enforced upon the offender by the imposing of a fine, namely, four annas in money or a fowl, payable to the heads of the household concerned. In the hills the money is put in a hole in the bamboo ladder leading into the house or, in lieu of a money payment, the fowl is hung under the house. Some persons, who have received the fine in the latter form, have shown a prejudice against eating it. I have been told that the British Government officials have upheld this tabu, when the collection of the fine has been resisted by the offending party.

Perhaps there is no more widespread tabu among the Karen people than that of personal names.[10] I have known some individuals for years without knowing their names and have used the common expedient of calling them by the name of their eldest son. A man who served as our cook for years in the Baptist school at Tharrawaddy I knew only as "Ba Gyaw's father;" although I did finally discover his own personal name. For a boy to mention his father's name is almost equivalent, according to Karen ideas, to the son's wishing his parent's death; for the spirits, learning the latter's identity, might destroy him. Instead of speaking of his wife, a man will talk of the mother of his children, or of his oldest child whose name he may think it safe to mention. Not long ago a young man of good education, who was engaged in filling his blank application for a marriage certificate, was confronted with the fact that he was unable to give his mother's name. Not infrequently parents bestow opprobrious names on their children, in order to deceive the demons into thinking them too unworthy to be molested.

During the month of July, when the streams are in flood, the people observe the tabu of the rising and falling of the waters ("ta dü ta htaw ta law"). They refrain from labor, make an offering of a fowl all of one color on the path near a stream, and utter the following prayer: "O Lord of the great water and the small water, of the oceans and the lakes. We are offering you a large sweet fowl and sweet rice. Flow in your own banks as usual, so that we shall not be drowned or fall into the water to be devoured by crocodiles and dragons. Watch over us on our journeys, eat our offerings, and do not molest us." They then examine the fowl's bones and the gall-bladder of a pig, and, if the omens are favorable, they swim the stream three times. In case no mishap occurs, they believe that their offerings have been acceptable and that they will prosper. If the omens are not propitious the first time, they try

---

[10] See Chapter XVIII on Birth Customs and Childhood, p. 170.

A CHRISTIAN KAREN VILLAGE SCHOOL, THARRAWADDY DISTRICT
A number of Burman boys from neighboring villages attend this school in addition to the Karen children.

a second time and if necessary a third, in order to obtain a favorable response.

The Karen esteem the gall-bladder of a certain variety of fish as a valuable medicine, but assert that during the early days of August this medicinal organ becomes enlarged and "hot" (that is, flabby). They, therefore, consider it necessary to desist from work, in order to restore the gall-bladder to its normal condition and efficacy. During the other months this medicine is thought to be strong and useful in certain severe illnesses.

The time for gathering the herbs of which dyestuffs are made, is determined by divination. If, however, some one happens to pick them on a day found to be unfavorable, he becomes subject to a tabu, lest colds and coughs should spread throughout the village. To prevent this epidemic, the erring person must cut a sheaf of tall grass and set it up in the ashes of his fireplace, and when the other villagers come in they must spit on it. An elder then takes up the grass, saying: "May all coughs and colds be prevented. May we not catch them." Next, he leads the people out into a field, where he plies their heads and the stumps in the field with the sheaf until it is broken, meantime calling out: "Beat here. Beat there. Beat the tails of the demons and woodpeckers. Do not bring us illnesses, coughs, or colds." When he has finished, he leaves the frayed grass against a stump, and they all return to their houses. Finally, the elder asks in a loud voice: "Is every one well?" and they all shout back: "All are well." This is repeated three times, after which they all shut their doors and refrain from work during the rest of the day.

While all of these numerous tabus have helped to nourish the ancient superstitions of the Karen, it is well to remember that some of them, in the absence of other social and moral sanctions, have exercised a beneficial influence. Among the latter are the tabus against marriage outside of the tribe, and especially outside of the race. These tabus have been instrumental in maintaining the integrity of the various tribes and of the people as a whole, and in enabling the Karen to live largely apart from the corrupting influences of neighboring peoples. Other tabus have served to magnify the importance of the religious rites and to enforce a stricter morality than prevails among some primitive races. It is obvious that these benefits have been secured at a great economic cost, when one considers the large number of holidays which falls to the lot of the conscientious Karen. These holidays, however, have contributed in no small degree to sociability among the people, for they could spend them only in sitting at home in conversation and gossip with their friends over the hospitable betel-box. The rapid progress of the race in recent times has been accomplished by the breaking down of the validity of these tabus—a thing that is to be commended. Nevertheless, the civilizing agencies will have failed of performing an essential service, if they do not succeed in speedily creating a healthy public opinion and new social and religious sanctions in their place, in order to overcome the present tendency towards moral slackness.

TWO KAREN CHRISTIAN PASTORS
The younger man (on the right) is the pastor and manager of the school shown above. The other is the son of the first convert in the Tharrawaddy District.

## CHAPTER XXIX

## GROWTH OF CHRISTIANITY AMONG THE KAREN

If one were planning to start a movement to transform the life and religion of a race, one would not be expected to choose a savage bandit—a cutthroat who had taken part in the murder of at least thirty persons—to promote his enterprise. But such was the first Karen, under the providence of God, whom Dr. Adoniram Judson, the founder of the American Baptist Mission, undertook to teach.[1] Dr. Judson purchased this man, Ko Tha Byu, who was about to be sold into slavery in payment for a debt, in the hope of gaining access to the Karen, of whom he had hitherto had only fleeting glimpses. Notwithstanding the fact that the bandit was then in middle life, seemed to be hopelessly stupid, and yielded at times to his diabolical temper, Dr. Judson was rewarded for his months of patient effort in trying to teach this most unpromising pupil by seeing his mind begin to open. Ko Tha Byu became eager to learn and gained the ability to read the Burmese Bible. His whole life underwent a gradual transformation. When the Rev. George D. Boardman went to Tavoy for the purpose of establishing a mission station, he took Dr. Judson's pupil with him and baptized him there on May 16, 1828. In this obscure way was begun the movement that has resulted in the remarkable growth of Christianity among the Karen can, therefore, be regarded as complete, which does not contian missions during the last hundred years. No account of the Karen can, therefore, be regarded as complete which does not contain some mention of the widespread influence of the Christian religion among them, raising them from a humble position to one of importance and transforming them to such an extent as to cause their Burman neighbors to marvel greatly at the change.

---

[1] The Rev. Adoniram Judson, D.D., was the first missionary of the American Baptist Foreign Mission Society. He landed in Burma, July 13, 1813, and began his labors among the Burmese under great difficulties. His zeal as a Christian apostle, his remarkable linguistic attainments, and the terrible imprisonments he endured, have given him a place among the foremost missionaries of modern times. While he always maintained a friendly and helpful attitude toward the Karen people, he devoted himself almost entirely to the Burmese. His compilation of the Burmese grammar and dictionary and his translation of the whole Bible into Burmese, are among his great contributions to the Christianizing of the country.

Immediately after his baptism, Ko Tha Byu set out for the Karen villages in the hills. He was shortly to confirm a tradition, then current among the people, to the effect that one day their long absent "white brother" would return to them from across the great waters, bringing the Lost Book which they had looked for with unabated expectation.[2] His message of good news was received with wonder and surprise by the elders in the jungles. Delegations accompanied him to Tavoy to see the "white brother" and listen to his teaching. Among those who came was a prophet, who a few years before had bought from a white sailor in Tavoy a book that he had since regarded as a fetish. On examination this book proved to be a Book of Common Prayer; but the elders accepted the message of their white brother, Mr. Boardman, as the fulfilment of their own prophesies, and a number of them were soon baptized. They wished to learn to read, and Ko Tha Byu became their teacher. Later he traveled in the Moulmein district, and it was there in 1832 that Dr. Wade, while engaged in reducing the Karen language to writing, first learned to his great surprise that the old poems of the Karen contained the "Y'wa" tradition.[4]

In 1833 Ko Tha Byu removed to Rangoon to carry the good news to his countrymen in the Burmese territory of Pegu. By the end of the first rainy season the report had spread throughout the jungles of this region, and groups of Karens came in from a wide area, some to learn more about the mission of the white brother and others to receive immediate baptism and admission into the Christian Church. The movement grew apace and attracted the attention of the Burmese authorities, who forbade the Karen to come to Rangoon and imprisoned those whom they caught, among these being the influential young chief of Bassein, Ko Shwe Waing, who was only released through the good offices of the English resident, Mr. Edwards.[5]

Determined to carry back to his people a few copies of certain religious books which had been prepared for the Karen, the young chief succeeded in smuggling them out of Rangoon. He traveled by unfrequented jungle trails and, on reaching home, hid the books

---

[2] *The Karen Apostle, or Memoir of Ko Tha Byu,* by Dr. Mason, gives an interesting account of this first Karen convert. Unfortunately this book is now out of print.

[3] Letter of the Rev. George Dana Boardman in the *Missionary Magazine,* Boston, Mass., Jan., 1830, p. 22.

[4] Journal of the Rev. Jonathan Wade, *Missionary Magazine,* May, 1833, pp. 196, ff.

[5] Rev. T. Than Bya, *The Karens and Their Progress,* p. 21.

in a bundle of old clothes. Long after nightfall, stealthily by ones and twos, men and women came to his house. Guards were posted outside of the village, and the bundle was brought out and unwrapped until, by the dim light of a wick burning in an earthen cup filled with oil, the books were disclosed, including a Bible that was regarded as the now recovered Lost Book. At the sight of this unspeakable treasure some of those present bowed down and worshiped, others wept, some touched and caressed the sacred book, some kissed it, and some gazed long and curiously at its title. They crowded around the volume so thickly that the chief lifted it high above his head, in order that all might see, and all gazed at it with bated breath. They had been permitted to witness the return of their book, and they believed that they were no longer to be members of a despised nation.[6]

The years just preceding the annexation of Pegu by the British Empire, were hard ones for the Karen Christians. Their faith was severely tested by persecutions. Thra Klaw Meh, pastor of a Bassein church, and the converts of his village were imprisoned for their acceptance of the new religion. Their friends collected a handsome sum for their ransom, and all but the pastor were released. He was ordered to give up preaching, but, refusing to do so, was subjected to torture for days and finally was disemboweled and shot. Others were much persecuted, many suffering martyrdom both before and after the Second Burmese War.[7] Until Pegu was annexed by the British Government in 1853, no missionaries were allowed to remain permanently in Lower Burma. Hitherto the work for Bassein had been directed by the Rev. E. A. Abbott and his associates from Sandoway, in Arracan, and that for Rangoon and vicinity had been supervised from Moulmein. But as soon as the country was opened to resident missionaries, Dr. J. H. Vinton removed to Rangoon and established the headquarters of the mission there, near Mission Road, where his descendants are still supervising the activities of some ten thousand Karen Christians. The Rev. E. A. Abbott removed to Bassein and put the mission work of that district on a permanent and self-supporting basis. He has

---

[6] Thra Than Bya, then a little boy, went with his mother to see the Book on this notable occasion.

[7] In the Rangoon district Thra Ng Lay escaped martyrdom only through the accession of a new governor, whose first official act was to release him on the eve of his execution day. However, persecution did not deter such men or their descendants from becoming preachers. Both Thra Klaw Meh and Thra Ng Lay have had sons in the ministry, and their grandsons have since been in the Theological Seminary at Rangoon, preparing for the same calling.

KAREN THEOLOGICAL STUDENTS
The one on the left is the grandson of Thra Klaw Meh, Karen martyr, and the other of Thra Ng Lay, who narrowly escaped martyrdom.

been succeeded by several able missionaries, including Dr. C. A. Nichols, the present superintendent, under whose direction certain industries have been started, including a saw-mill, a rice-mill, and a launch-building plant. Twelve other important centers for work among the Karen were established by the American Baptist Mission. The founding and conduct of churches and schools have been carried on in and from all of these centers. In 1853 Dr. Francis Mason finished his admirable version of the Bible in Sgaw Karen. Meantime, Dr. Jonathan Wade was engaged in preparing dictionaries and a grammar of the Sgaw and Pwo dialects. The Bible was also translated into Pwo Karen by the Rev. D. L. Brayton. A Karen Theological Seminary was organized by the Rev. J. G. Binney in 1845 at Moulmein. This institution was later removed to Rangoon and still later to its present location in Insein, where the Rev. D. A. W. Smith, D.D., served for many years as its president. The Baptist college at Rangoon, now called Judson College, has served the Karen young people, both men and women, since its organization in 1875.

Careful statistics do not appear to have been kept during the early years of the Baptist Mission, and it is, therefore, difficult to discover how many of the Karen became Christians. In 1856 eleven thousand, eight hundred and seventy-eight communicants were reported, but this number includes many estimated returns. From that time on there has been an almost steady increase in the membership of the Baptist Mission, which numbered in 1919 fifty-five thousand, three hundred and fifty-three communicants enrolled in Karen churches, representing a nominal Christian community of two hundred thousand souls.[8] In this same year there were nineteen thousand, four hundred and twenty pupils in the Karen mission schools, including both the Anglo-vernacular and the village-vernacular schools, the converts contributing 375,426 rupees or $125,142 toward the maintenance of these. Not only do the Karen Christians contribute to the support of their schools, but also to that of their churches and pastors. For this purpose they expended 38,596 rupees or $12,856 in 1919. In the same year they gave to benevolences outside of their own fields 152,203 rupees ($50,734) for home and foreign missionary work and 184,627 rupees ($61,532), making a total of 375,426 rupees or $125,122 for all purposes.

---

[8] *Annual Report*, American Baptist Foreign Mission Society, 1919, p. 195.

Apart from the generous sums of money which the Karen Christians give, many of the men who have been trained in the schools have manifested the spirit of self-sacrifice by going out to the more distant tribes and some even into China, despite their small pay, in order to carry the Gospel and its civilizing influence to the people in those regions.

The Roman Catholic Mission began its labors among the Karen in the forties of the last century at Myaungmya, near Twante, in Palaw township, Mergul district, and at Bassein. About two thousand persons were baptized. It was not, however, until the arrival of Bishop Biganget that the work of converting the Karen was undertaken in earnest, and it has been continued ever since. In 1919 there were seventeen stations under the charge of resident priests and approximately twenty-five thousand, three hundred and fifty converts, including infants.[9] At many of these stations schools are conducted, which together enroll a large number of Karen children.

The Church of England Society for the Propagation of the Gospel entered the field at Toungoo in 1871, taking over some three thousand members of the Baptist Mission. The work has been carried on from that city, where two separate missions are maintained. Early in 1919 the Anglican Bishop of Rangoon wrote that "the total number of Christian people (in the Toungoo region) is about five thousand. Of these sixteen hundred are communicants. About six hundred are under instruction with a view to baptism. The Karens contributed about £250 to the funds of the two missions during the year."[10] About fifty boys and the same number of girls are boarders in the Toungoo schools. The number of pupils in village schools is not available.

While the figures given above supply a certain index to the success of the missions among the Karen people, it must be remembered that they do not illuminate particular features that have become an important part of modern mission work. The most significant of these features are the education of the children, the training of the men to become intelligent leaders in their communities, and the inculcation among the women of better ideals as homekeepers, all contributing to the elevation of the people. If these results are not measurably attained by the mission work at the

---

[9] Notes on the Roman Catholic Mission in South Burma by the secretary of the Diocese, dated Moulmein, March 3, 1919.

[10] Letter of the Bishop of Rangoon, dated Rangoon, February 12, 1919.

A CHRISTIAN VILLAGE SCHOOL, PROME DISTRICT
There are more than a thousand village chapels in Karen villages throughout Burma, built entirely by the villagers themselves.

THE CHAPEL AND SCHOOLHOUSE OF THE AMERICAN BAPTIST MISSION HIGH SCHOOL, THARRAWADDY DISTRICT
One-fourth the cost of this building was contributed by the Karen Christians of the district.

present time, it is regarded as falling short of its proper aims. When the people have realized sufficient growth and stability in Christian character and have gained the breadth of vision to enable them to assume leadership in their religious affairs, it will be time for the white teachers to allow them to undertake the responsibility. In the past it has been too much the custom to place undue emphasis on creed and dogma. The development of character through Christian experience is the primary object to be attained, and without the formation of admirable character no abiding result can be achieved. The Baptist Mission—I can not speak for the others, although they may maintain similar ideals—demands total abstinence and the surrender of all animistic religious practices as prerequisites for church-membership. The Baptist denomination is convinced that these requirements have been the means of social and economic progress, although the enforcement of them has tended to limit the growth in numbers. No doubt, much may still be done in the way of character-building among the members of the churches; but when we consider the environment of the people and the fact that they have had less than a century of Christian development, may we not say that they have made remarkable progress.

## CHAPTER XXX

## THE PROGRESS OF THE KAREN RACE

Although the Karen tribes have probably lived in Burma and Siam for more than a thousand years, in company with the Burmese, Shan, Siamese, and Chin, occupying no territory that they did not share with other people except the hills of Toungoo and Karenni, they have remained curiously isolated. Politically subordinate to the ruling races in the countries in which they had settled, except in the last named localities, they were subjected to oppression and exploitation, which they could resent only to the extent of local raids against poorly defended villages or of occasional assaults upon stray foes caught in the lonely jungle or in outlying districts. The inevitable result of these conditions was mutual hatred of the races, which was intensified on the side of the Burmese by their feeling of contempt for the subject race; while the enforced clannishness of the Karens drew sustenance from the conviction that their "golden age" lay in the past, and that the customs and precepts which they had inherited from the matchless elders of that age were not to be changed. There was nothing in the religion or life of the Burmese that appealed to the Karen, even if it had been offered to them—certainly nothing from which they could expect any amelioration of their condition. Progress was almost impossible to people so situated, who could only look vaguely into the future for the deliverer, the "white brother," whose coming was foretold in their traditions.

The acquisition by the British East India Company in 1827 of the provinces of Arracan and Tenasserim, on the western and southern coasts of Burma, respectively, made little impression on the Karen at the time, although it was the beginning of a new era in their history and that of Burma—one in which the ideals of justice and fair play were to become increasingly operative. Christian missionaries were beginning their labors in the country at the same time, thus making possible the spiritual emancipation to which the Karen had looked forward. The significance of these events lay in a double revelation, which the missionaries first imparted.

SCHOOLGIRLS AT CALISTHENICS, THARRAWADDY KAREN HIGH SCHOOL

SCHOOLBOYS LINED UP FOR DRILL
This school of about five hundred pupils has both Karen and Burman pupils working side by side, as in many schools in the country.

That the Karen were eager for a change of administration is shown by several circumstances. In the first expedition of the English forces against Ava in 1826 they served as guides and were commended for their good faith by Major Snodgrass.[1] In the provinces that fell under British control they found themselves sympathetically dealt with and soon began to take on new ways; but in the province of Pegu, where the old regime of Ava still held sway, they continued to suffer from oppression. They were prohibited from visiting their teachers in Rangoon, and the Burmese viceroy of the city threatened, even as late as 1851, to shoot instantly the first Karen whom he should find capable of reading.[2] In the Second Burmese War (1852) they are reputed to have again acted as guides to the attacking force, which took the Shwe Dagon Pagoda, the most formidable military work near Rangoon, by assault in the rear.[3] The Burmese knew that the Karen regarded the English as their deliverers and took vengeance on them accordingly, burning all their villages within fifty miles of Rangoon, seizing or destroying their stores of rice, and putting men, women, and children to death in barbarous ways.[4] No wonder that a large number of the oppressed and persecuted people migrated from the delta of the Irrawaddy to Moulmein, or across the Arracean hills into those provinces where they could dwell in security. Even under British rule conditions were not what they might have been, for there were frequent miscarriages of justice on account of the employment of Burmese officers in subordinate and local positions.[5]

Nevertheless, the new order of things in Burma has brought progress in many respects. The continual raids and forays, which previously devastated numerous Karen villages, have been stopped. The administration of justice has been taken out of the hands of private individuals and placed in those of accredited officials. Marked progress in education has been made. A new literature in the vernacular has come into circulation. Christianity has made a strong appeal to the Karen. Finally, in the World War the people again showed their loyalty to the British Empire by offering their services in its defense. Such of these topics as have not been

---

[1] Major Snodgrass, *Narrative of the Burmese War*, pp. 140, 142.

[2] Calista V. Luther, *The Vintons and the Karens*, p. 30.

[3] I have repeatedly heard the statement that Karens served as guides in this war, but I can not verify it by reference to any work at hand.

[4] Calista V. Luther, *The Vintons and the Karens*, pp. 89, 90, 92, n.

[5] For instances of miscarriage of justice, see Mason, *Burma*, pp. 610-618; Smeaton, *The Loyal Karens of Burma*. I regret that similar instances are not hard to find, even at the present day.

treated elsewhere in this volume will be briefly discussed in the following paragraphs.

The cessation of open hostilities between the Karen and the Burmese has largely mitigated the old animosity existing between them. Where members of the two races live in close proximity, however, some friction is still produced. Nevertheless, the Karen's dislike of their neighbors is not so great as to prevent many of those living on the plains from adopting Burmese ways and speech. They do this not out of admiration for things Burmese, but because of the prevalence of Burmese culture and in order to avoid the appearance of rusticity that marks those who fail to conform. Some not only wear the dress of the Burmese and speak their language —always with more or less of an accent—but also, except the Christians, go to the pagodas and participate in Burmese feasts. A number of wealthy Karens, who have moved into the larger Burmese towns along the railway line and live there in Burmese style, have to all appearances lost their racial identity. In many cases those who have copied the manners of their neighbors, experience a decided weakening of their old religious faith and its moral restraints, being led into evil ways by Burmans of the less respectable classes, with whom they fraternize.

The first experiment of the British in the administration of justice among the Karen, was not successful. It consisted in appointing certain influential Karen chiefs to serve as magistrates for their people. This plan was unsatisfactory because some of the appointees were reluctant to assume authority, and also because the different tribes were much intermingled. It was, therefore, decided to try the cases of Karens, like those of the members of the other races, in the ordinary courts. While this method is correct in principle and an improvement in practice, it has not always been administered by representatives of the English nation or in the spirit of British justice. A closer supervision of the courts is needed to curb the prejudices sometimes manifested by the local magistrates.

The progress of the Karen in education has been very marked. Their "Lost Book" having been restored to them by their "white brother" in the person of the Christian missionary, they have been most eager to learn to read it. This has been true from the early years of missionary activity. Before the British had established orderly government in Burma, one American missionary had pupils in her school in Moulmein almost every year who came over two

A KAREN TEACHER AND LAHU BOYS
The man in the long garment is a Sgaw Karen, who is a missionary in the North Shan States among the Lahu people. He has brought three pupils to Lower Burma with him.

hundred miles through the jungles by night, "not daring to travel by day," for the sake of learning to read the Bible in their own tongue.[6] The number of mission and Government schools began to increase rapidly, being scattered in all parts of the country. Every Christian church had its accompanying school, and in recent years many, if not most, of the non-Christian villages have come to have their schools also. The early Christian teachers, realizing the dangers lurking in the new conditions, began aright by teaching self-control, as well as the usual subjects, infusing the whole educational movement with moral purpose. The result has been more than gratifying. "It is not often given," says Mr. D. M. Smeaton, late Chief Commissioner of Burma, "to witness such a remarkable development of national character as has taken place among the Karens under the influence of Christianity and good government." Another observer adds: "Where only a few years ago were tribal wars, child-stealing, house-burning, and savagery, now are quiet, orderly villages, each with its preacher and teacher, chapel and school."[7]

The *Fifth Quinquennial Report on Public Education in Burma*, covering the years 1913-1917, inclusive, gives the number of Karen children in school as 34,896, an increase of twenty-five percent over the total for the previous five-year period. This number is about three percent of the total Karen population. The figures for the Burmese are not given. Judging, however, from the number of Buddhist school children, which is 531,541 and includes the children of some Karens and most of the Shan, while excluding those of a few Burmans, the Burmese have under six percent of their population in school. The Shan have 5,730 school children, or about one-half of one percent of their population.[8]

From their village school the children, boys and girls, go to the mission boarding-school at the district or mission headquarters or to some neighboring Government school, where they learn English and, if they progress so far, prepare for college. A considerable number of Karen young men and a few young women are college graduates and are leading useful lives in various communities, as may be seen by looking over the list of officers in Government positions in the Education, Forest, Police, Military, and subordinate branches; while others are doing well in business and the

---
[6] Calista V. Luther, *The Vintons and the Karens*, pp. 82, 83.
[7] H. P. Cochrane, *Among the Burmans*, pp. 278, 279.
[8] *Fifth Quinquennial Report on Public Education in Burma* (for the years 1912-13 to 1916-17), p. 28.

professions. Perhaps the most prominent Karen, the Hon. Dr. San C. Po, is a physician, graduate of an American medical college, who has served for several years in the Legislative Council of the province of Burma, being the first member of his race to be thus honored.

With the progress of Christianity and education has come literature. As soon as the Karen language had been reduced to writing, the missionaries began to prepare books for the people. In this work they have been assisted by a number of educated Karens. Thus far these translators have provided in the vernacular the Bible, a few plays of Shakespeare, *Pilgrim's Progress,* the *Arabian Nights,* and short stories and pamphlets in large number. Dr. Wade, with the aid of Saw Kau Too, has compiled *The Karen Thesaurus,* a vernacular encyclopedic dictionary of language and customs in four volumes, which is a work of great value. Christian literature, in the form of commentaries and text-books of various kinds, has been largely supplied by Dr. E. B. Cross, Dr. D. A. W. Smith, and the Rev. T. Than Bya, D.D. An admirable collection of hymns has been brought together, including both some of the English favorites and some original hymns composed by Karens as well as by missionaries. The largest number in the collection by one writer is by Mrs. J. H. Vinton. Of the seven or eight vernacular newspapers and monthly periodicals all but one or two are under native management. The *"Dawkula" (Karen National News)* is a biweekly, the others being monthlies, of which the *Karen Morning Star,* founded by Dr. Francis Mason at Tavoy in 1841, has had a continuous existence and is the oldest vernacular periodical in southeastern Asia.

The American Baptist Mission Press at Rangoon has been from its establishment the headquarters for Karen printing. Karen type were first manufactured here and the first pages struck off in the new characters. Here also the linotype machine has been adapted to vernacular use. Other Karen presses are in operation at Bassein and Toungoo.

At the time of the Third Burmese War (1885), when the Karen were suffering from brigandage which threatened to devastate the whole country, certain leaders of the race began a movement to develop a national spirit among the people, who had always been clannish and provincial. Some progress was made immediately after the war through the formation of Karen levies, without which the province could scarcely have been brought back to a state of good order. At length the Karen National Association ("Daw k' lu," meaning literally "the whole race") was organized. All the districts in which the Karen live were represented at its first meet-

REV. THRA MAUNG YIN, OF BASSEIN
He held the rank of honorary havildar in the Karen battalion of the Burma Rifles, 1917-1920, and was most highly commended by his commanding officers for his wholesome influence as a religious teacher.

ing, a few non-Christians attending, although the leaders were Christians. The aim of the association was simply to promote the economic and educational interests of the people, as well as to plan for their representation at public functions, such as on the occasion of viceregal visits. Funds have been raised for these purposes, but, unfortunately, through mismanagement, have not proved to be permanent. During the World War the association served as a mouthpiece for the expression of the loyalty of the race and did some active work in recruiting. It furthered the sending of deputations to meet the Montague Commission and later sent a rather ill-advised delegation to England to promote the national interests, which have been so much emphasized as a result of the world conflict.

The military activities of the Karen have been largely confined in the past to village raids. There have been times when there was a prospect that a real leader might arise to unite a large group of villages into a kind of state and carry on warfare on a large scale. One such attempt was made by a Karen, of Martaban or Shwegyin, who assumed the Burmese title of "Nün Laung" or Coming Prince—a favorite title with rebellious members of the Burmese court who tried to ursurp the throne. This adventurer organized a religio-political movement among his compatriots throughout the region from Siam to Bassein. They expected him to fulfil a prophecy to the effect that the Karen would drive out the foreigners and establish a new dynasty at Pegu. However, this rebellion was soon put down and its leaders were driven into Karenni, where they disappeared.[9]

The Karen levies, which did so much to re-establish peace throughout the province of Burma after the Third Burmese War, and, for the most part under their missionaries as officers and with but little military organization, captured some of the dacoit leaders after scattering their followers, rendered a service deserving of more credit than it received at the time. Local and racial feeling was still running too high, and official circles did not always understand the situation fully.[10]

Soon after these services, which were rendered by most of the Karens gratuitously and with arms which they had paid for, malicious rumors were circulated that these men were of doubtful loyalty. The result was that they were divested of their arms and given no compensation whatever. It still remained true, however, that they had saved their homes, protected the honor of their

---

[9] *British Burma Gazetteer*, Vol. I, p. 488; *Imperial Gazetteer, Burma*, Vol. I, p. 335; Lieut. Gen. A. Fytche, C. S. I., *Burma, Past and Present*, Vol. I, Ch. 3, quoted in an article entitled "The Karens" in the *Rangoon Gazette* of June 6, 1917.

[10] For an account of the capture of Bo Hline, the notorious dacoit, in Toungoo, see the closing chapters of Cumming's *In the Shadow of the Pagoda*. These chapters are quoted in Dr. Bunker's *Soo Tha*, pp. 248-276. The murderers of Mr. Barbe, the deputy commissioner of Bassein, were apprehended by the Karen levy in that district.

wives and daughters, and rendered an important service to the Government, the fruits of which have not yet disappeared. After all their long suffering and patient endurance this experience was a hard one, to which they should not have been subjected.[11]

KAREN MILITARY POLICE
These men were a part of a squad who shot some notorious dacoits in the Insein District, 1917. They are all from Toungoo District.

Meantime, a battalion of the Karen Military Police had been organized and was rendering service to the Government. It remained a separate unit until 1899. At that time an unfortunate affair, in which liquor played a prominent part, resulted in the dispersion of the battalion, the companies that were retained being sent into different sections of the province. These surviving companies have not failed to give a good account of themselves, for example, in scattering within the last few years the dacoits in the Okkan region of the Insein district and also in the Bassein district.

---

[11] This statement is based on correspondence between members of the American Baptist Mission and the Secretary to the Government carried on at the time.

At the outbreak of the World War in 1914 the loyalty of the Karen people manifested itself in the large number of applications to enter military service in defense of the Empire. Some of the applications were made through the author. None was accepted at the time, for the Government had not yet adopted the policy of recruiting in Burma. Later, when this was done, the response on the part of the Karens was not equaled by that of any of the neighboring races. However, the number of Karens taken into the service was limited. In the Burma Rifles, the one regiment recruited in the province, of a total of sixteen companies three were Karen; one, Shan; one, Arracanese, and the others, Burmese. Karens were in all the other regiments in about the same proportion.[12] In the Sappers and Miners, the first unit to leave the country for duty abroad, the highest native officer was a Karen. There was also a small group of Karens in the company which did itself credit in Mesopotamia. An officer of that company told me that other officers, in calling for detachments, often asked that Karens might be sent. In one Karen company so many of the men were detailed for instruction service in other companies that regular drill was much interfered with. These incidents suggest that the enlisted men among the Karens were rendering an honorable and appreciated service in the war.

Should one inquire as to the future of the Karen people, my answer would be that not as a separate people, living apart and seeking special advantages for themselves, will they make the most progress; but, forgetting racial feeling as far as possible and throwing themselves into the life of the land in which they find themselves and adding their quota to the general good, they will not only raise themselves, but also the level of the common life which they must share with their neighbors. In this way they will truly find themselves and contribute to the growth and progress of a country that is capable of untold advancement.

---

[12] The following statement is taken from a letter of Feb. 16, 1919, from the officer in charge of recruiting at Meiktila: "In all other units Burmans and Karens are mixed up together, but probably the proportion would be about the same as in the Burma Rifles. There are also Karens in the Military Police."

# APPENDIX A

## GLOSSARY OF KAREN WORDS

NOTE. The vowels in this glossary are to be pronounced after the usual continental method. *Eh* is pronounced as *e* in *met*, and *eu* as *e* in *her*. The Greek *x* is used for the guttural which is pronounced as *ch* in *loch*, and *th* is as in *thin*. Asperated consonants are indicated by placing the *h* in front of the letter as *hk, hp, ht*, etc. The half vowel is shown by the apostrophe following the letter, as *k', t'*, etc. In pronouncing, slip over this half vowel as in the first syllable of cajole or the coloquial pronounciation of t'morrow.

*Bgha*, family demon.
*bgha a hko*, leader of the bgha feast.
*bla e*, bat dung; powder.
*blaw*, young men's club room, or guest room.
*Brec*, name of a Karen tribe.
*Bü deu htaw li*, the paddy has headed out (lit., conceived).
*bwe*, seeds of the coix plant.
*Bwe* (for *Bghai*), the name of a Karen tribe.
*dah* (Burmese), long knife.
*daw do*, a relation by marriage.
*daw t' ka*, race of giants who feed on the k'las of mortals.
*deu*, room or section of a village-house.
*deu mü lwa hpa*, three stars just east of the Pleiades.
*De nya*, a lily, the lily month (May).
*du la*, a plot selected for cultivation in the hills.

*Ghw Le Be*
*Ghaw Ser Paw* } two Pwo Karens who stole the original drums.
*Ghaw Kwa Htu*
*Ghaw Kaw Se* } names of the two original bronze drums.
*Gai hko*, the name of a Karen tribe.

*Hi*, house.
*hi hpo xeh*, tiny model of a house used in bgha rites.
*hkaw*, the foot.
*hkli*, the crossbow.
*hkli p' ti*, a kind of long bow.
*hko*, the head.
*hko hti*, the fontenal.
*hko peu*, a headdress or turban.
*hko peu ki*, a woman's woven headdress.
*hko saw*, a hut-shaped receptacle for the bones of the dead.
*hko so law*, a receptacle as above, but pagoda-shaped.
*hk' ye*, trumpet-shaped fish trap.
*Hkü de*, demon of the dry season.
*Hkü Te*, king of hades.
*hpa k' pu*, a fireplace.
*hpa hpaw mü*, midnight.
*'pa ti*, uncle.
*hpaw*, a flower.
*hpaw baw*, yellow cockscomb.
*hpaw ghaw*, red cockscomb.
*ni ba*, musical pipes.
*Hpi Bi Yaw*, name of the goddess of the crops.
*hpo*, child; little.

*hpo khwa*, a son.
*hpo mü*, a daughter.
*hpo nya mo*, } part of wedding ceremony, (lit., children tease mother, children tease father).
*hypo nya pa*, }
*hpo tha hkwa htaw*, to become adolescent (spoken of a boy).
*hsa*, a star; also the right thigh bone of a fowl used in divination.
*hsa a hsa neu mi*, a good omen derived from reading the chicken bones.
*Hsa bü hpaw*, the Milky Way.
*Hsa deu mü*, the Pleiades.
*Hsa hki hko*, the constellation Sagittarius.
*Hsa k' hsaw*, the Great Bear, (lit., the elephant).
*Hsa kwa hka*, Orion.
*hsa t' so*, a constellation.
*Hsa hta hko*, three stars south of the Pleiades.
*Hsa tu ghaw*, the morning star.
*Hsa tu ha*, the evening star.
*hsa meh htaw*, a comet.
*Hsa mo la*, a star near the moon.
*Hsa yo ma*, the three stars of Orion's belt.
*hsa yu*, } shooting stars.
*hsa hpo tha*, }
*hsaw*, a fowl; also a basket for catching fish.
*hsaw xi wa ti htaw*, a good omen obtained from reading the fowl's bones.
*hsaw xi wa hkaw*, a less favorable omen.
*hsaw xi ku hko mi*, a rather unfavorable omen.
*hsaw xi htaw deh pgha k' la*, an unfavorable omen.
*hsaw o*, the crowing of the cock; early morning.
*hse*, a Karen garment; a smock.
*hse plo*, a man's garment.
*Hsi hsa*, the tenth month.
*Hsi mü*, the ninth month.
*hso hko*, a platform for receiving guests.
*hta*, a hand loom; a song.
*hta do*, an epic poem.
*hta mo pgha*, a great poem.
*hta na do*, poems chanted over the dead.
*hta hpo*, lyric poems, or narrative poems of light character.
*hta plü*, poems of the dead.
*hta thi kwaw*, extempore poems of betrothal.
*hta thwe plü*, poems chanted at funerals addressed to the spirit.
*hta yeh law plü*, poems for the king of hades.
*htaw law*, a cry which one utters on hearing strange noises in the jungle.
*Htaw meh*, Monday.
*hteh*, a plow.
*hteu*, a bag.
*Hte kü*, the second month.
*hti*, water.
*hti hsaw*, a scoop for catching fish in shallow water.
*Hti k' saw k'sa*, the lords of water and land; the lords of the earth.
*hti pu law*, place in the house for the water-joint.
*hti th' mu*, charmed water.
*hti seh meh ywa*, the river of running sand, or the sandy river.
*hto bo*, a pole for poling a boat.
*hto tu*, a harrow.
*htwi maw seh*, a hunting dog.

*K'la*, the shade or spirit of a person.
*k'la pyeh*, a booth.
*k'li*, the wind.
*K'paw ta thu*, a demon who causes total eclipses.
*k'sa*, lord, (a person or a title).

# APPENDIX A.—GLOSSARY—CONTINUED

*k'taw*, a shield.
*k'thi*, medicine.
*k'thi baw tho*, a magical tiger medicine.
*k'thi thra*, a doctor (lit., a teacher of medicine).
*ka hsaw zi*, the inspecting of fowl's bones for divinations.
*ka law ta*, an offering for demons.
*Ka ya*, the Red Karen tribe.
*Kayin* (Burmese), the Karen people.
*ki ku*, a creeper, the leaves of which are used in certain rites.
*klaw*, a mat.
*klo* (couplet, *klo ogh tra ogh*), bronze drums.
*klo a deu*, the base tube of a Karen xylophone.
*klo ka paw*, }
*klo ma ti*, } three kinds of Karen bronze drums.
*klo ghaw ple* }
*kü*, a basket.
*kwa*, the cry of the wildcat.
*kweh*, the wedding horn.
*kyee zee* (Burmese), a triangular gong.

*La*, the moon; a month.
*La hkli*, the fourth month.
*La hkü*, the ninth month.
*La naw*, the eleventh month.
*La nwi*, the seventh month.
*La plü*, the twelfth month.
*La zo*, the eighth month.
*Law*, demons of the rainy season.
*Law hpo*, demons who bring about the reproduction of the grain.
*ler na*, stones having magical power.
*li*, grandchildren.
*Li naw*, Sunday.
*lo*, to transmit life.
*longyi* (Burmese), a loin cloth or skirt worn by men and women.

*Ma*, a wife.
*ma hpo tha*, little wife or concubine.
*maw*, a small bamboo cup.
*maw ksh*, a giant creeper, the seeds of which are used as playthings.
*Maw law, kwi*, the king of the crocodiles.
*me taw*, rice cooked in joints of bamboo.
*me u*, fire.
*Meh la ka*, the Southern Cross.
*meu do*, a large bamboo trap.
*mi*, the left thigh bone of a fowl used in divinations.
*mi a mi neu hsa*, an evil omen obtained from reading the fowl's bones.
*Mü daw hpa*, Friday.
*mo*, mother.
*mo a si*, an offering made to bring a good crop of paddy.
*mü*, the sun.
*mü gha*, aunt.
*mü haw law*, early evening.
*mü heh htaw*, sunrise.
*mü heh htaw hpa htaw*, the sun is high.
*Mü Hka*, the king of spirits.
*mü hse wa htaw*, dawn, (lit., the sun's garment whitens).
*Mü htaw k'hou*, Saturday.
*mü htu*, noon.
*Mü kaw li*, the evil power or devil.
*mü law nü*, the sun is set.
*mü re law*, the sun declines.
*mü yaw ma*, late evening, (lit., the sun is deep down).

*mü pgha*, a married woman.
*Mü za*, celestial spirits that preside over births.
*Mü za do*, one of the principal demons of the Karen.
*Mü za hklew*, a divinity presiding over the banyan tree.
*mwi*, a blood-brother; a friend.

*Na*, a sword.
*na nya hti meh*, a sword shaped like the tail of an eel.
*na theh hko*, a sword with two edges and a sharp point.
*na zu hko*, a blunt-pointed cutting sword.
*naw blü tha*, sling-shot pellets.
*Naw k'plaw*, the evil demon opposed to Y'wa (God).
*naw raw*, wild indigo.
*ni*, a woman's skirt; a day; a year.
*ni-thaw*, the couplet meaning a day.
*ni-la*, the couplet meaning a year.
*nya*, fish.
*nya u*, fish paste, (lit., rotten fish); Burmese, *ngape*.

*P'yo*, a great dragon or a demon in the form of a great dragon.
*pa*, father.
*Pa k' sa*, Father God (used of Y'wa).
*paw*, (Burmese, pauk), a kind of fish-trap.
*raw ku*, a xylophone.
*paw leh*, the sea.
*paw na*, plants having magical powers.
*pgha*, a person; also means old.
*pgha a pgho*, a wonder worker or magician.
*pgha ba bgha*, one who has offended the family demon.
*Pgha k' nyaw*, the Karen term for themselves, (lit., men).
*pgha htaw leu hko*, one who marries outside the tribe.
*pgha tha pgha*, an old man; an elder.
*pgho*, an impersonal all-pervasive force; (Melanesian, *mana*).
*pgho ghaw*, the peacock pheasant.
*Pghaw ghaw*, the twin peak of Mt. Thaw Thi, the sacred mountain.
*po*, the method of preventing witches from working evil charms.
*po dwa*, open bamboo pipes.
*pru-u-u*, a call for children, fowls, spirits, etc.
*pu*, a fish-trap.
*pula*, betel-leaf vines trained to run up tall trees.
*Pu Maw Taw*, mythical owner of the first bronze drums.

*Seh*, a rough basket.
*sgheu*, the fructifying principle in life.
*so*, power to resist an evil charm; personality; a generation.
*soh*, a charm made out of a wild boar's tusk.
*so so za za*, generation upon generation; eternally.
*Sgaw*, the name of a Karen tribe.

*T"ba*, negative particle.
*t'kaw*, a measure of distance; the distance one can hear a call.
*t'hka*, a pace.
*T"hke mo baw*, the demon that causes partial eclipses.
*t'hkwa*, a cousin.
*t'hkli*, a yard.
*t'hpi*, the stretch of the thumb and forefinger.
*t'hta*, a hand's breadth.
*Thwe kaw*, the third month.
*t'kle t' htwa*, a disappointment brought about by disregarding a tabu.
*t'kwi leu*, a stone's throw.
*t'le*, a post set up at funerals over the receptacle holding the bones.

# APPENDIX A.—GLOSSARY—CONTINUED

*t'leu*, a fish-trap made by placing a jar in the water.
*t'lo pa*, a mediator who arranges weddings.
*t'mü tu leh*, a half-day's journey.
*t'na*, a harp.
*t'ni leh*, a day's journey.
*T'nu*, the destroying angel who exterminates the wicked.
*t'pla*, a cubit.
*t're t' hka*, ghosts of tyrants, etc., who harass mortals.
*t'so*, a unit of measure.
*t'sü mü*, the length of the forefinger.
*t'ze*, the jew's-harp.
*t'zo*, Karen armor.
*t'yaw*, a decoction of the bark of a tree used for washing the hair.
*t'yaw lo ke-a k'la*, rites intended to recall the k'la or spirit of the dead.
*ta*, the nominal prefix.
*ta aw bgha*, the feast to the household demons.
*ta aw bwaw a tha*, a feast as above to prevent illness.
*ta aw saw ke saw na*, the feast at which all relatives must be present.
*ta aw k'teu*, a final feast before giving up the worship of the demons.
*ta di law kweh leh*, an offering to the king of hades.
*ta do hkaw*, the rhinoceros.
*Ta do k'the, ta do k'hsaw*, the Great Elephant addressed as a demon.
*ta dü ta htü*, tabu, chiefly prohibition of work.
*ta dü haw hko hu*, tabu to be observed at the time of an earthquake.
*ta dü hkü ta du theh*, the tabu after offerings for good crops.
*ta dü hpa htaw*, the long tabu.
*ta dü kleh*, the tabu on traveling.
*ta dü ta ble*, the tabu connected with births.
*ta dü ta yu mu ta yu la*, the tabu connected with eclipses.
*ta dü ta htaw ta law*, the tabu connected with the rising and falling of a stream.
*ta dü ta the to pgha*, the tabu connected with death.
*ta ho ta yaw* } witchcraft or bad magic.
*ta ho ta lo* }
*ta hkü hka*, the cool season.
*ta hpa do*, the great one, used of the elephant by men hunting lest the spirits should hear its name mentioned.
*ta hpi htaw a k'la*, to recall a human spirit from under the water.
*ta hseh hsu ma beu*, a raid.
*ta k'heu*, things that will win.
*ta ko hka*, the hot season.
*ta kweh k'la hpa do*, the great ceremony of recalling the human spirit.
*ta le mi*, lighting the dead on their way.
*ta leh kaw*, a game at funerals, (lit., stretching the neck).
*'a lü*, a sacrifice or offering.
*ta lü hpa do*, a great sacrifice to the lords of the earth.
*ta lü hpo*, the small sacrifice to the lords of the earth.
*ta lü klu htu hti*, an offering to the water witches.
*ta lü law pa law*, offerings to the celestial spirits that preside over births.
*Ta mü za*, the spirits of those who have been notoriously evil.
*ta na*, malevolent supernatural beings.
*ta neu zo*, the smell of burning fat.
*ta plü aw ka*, the fleeting existence of babies who die soon after birth.
*ta se kle*, the game of jumping bamboo poles.
*ta su hka*, the rainy season.
*ta t' ghe ba*, lit., it is not good (spoken of things tabued).
*ta t' ka*, ghosts of persons left unburied.
*ta t'hkaw hkaw*, a one-legged female demon.
*ta t' su*, a canopy erected over a bier.
*ta taw law ta*, offerings to the demons.
*ta taw the hka keh*, offerings for the spirits of notoriously evil persons.
*ta to kü*, pounding pestles (a funeral game).

*ta wi ta na*, evil spirits.
*ta xeh*, a sickle.
*ta yaw ke a k'la*, recalling human spirit from the clutches of a wizard.
*ta yaw kha*, the dry season.
*taw*, a paddy basket, (Burmese, *taung*).
*taw*, a paddy basket, (Burmese, *taung*)
*taw kwe taw*, }
*taw klaw taw*, } a ceremony performed at funerals of very old men.
*taw leu hko*, to marry outside the tribe.
*Taw Meh Pa*, the mythical ancestor of the Karen race.
*Teu kweh*, the rainbow.
*teu*, a bag.
*Th' le*, the first month.
*th' reh t' hka*, spirits of those who have died violent deaths.
*th' waw*, a village.
*tha*, soul.
*th' ma*, a crocodile.
*the na*, a monarch of hades.
*theh a hkü*, to make offerings for the field.
*ta th' mo*, to make offerings for the field.
*Thi hko mü xa*, the lord of the demons, of heaven and earth.
*thi keh*, a bamboo pole or standard used in the bgha feast.
*thit se* (Burmese), laquer.
*Thi thwa*, Thursday.
*tho*, a blood brother.
*Thwe kaw*, the third month.
*To kyaw*, Wednesday.
*to me to pi*, paste made of glutenous rice.
*To mü*, Tuesday.
*tu*, traps in which weights fall on the victims.

*U*, to embroider.
*ugh de de*, to thrust the finger into one's naval to prevent the rainbow demon from injuring one.

*Wa*, bamboo.
*Wa hkaw*, a spring trap; a spear made of bamboo.
*Wa hklu*, a kind of large bamboo.
*weh*, a basketwork paddy-bin; elder brother or sister.
*weh hpo hkwa*, older brother.
*weh hpo mü*, older sister.
*wi*, prophet; soothsayer.

*Xeh*, a sickle.
*xaw htu*, a plant used for poisoning the water in fishing.

*Y'wa*, the Great Spirit of the Karen; God.
*ya*, wild plantain or banana.

# APPENDIX B.

## BIBLIOGRAPHY

Annual Report, American Baptist Foreign Mission Society, 1919.
Baptist Missionary Magazine, The.
Bunker, Rev. Alonzo, D.D., Soo Tha, A Tale of the Karens, New York, 1901.
Bunker, Rev. Alonzo, D. D., Sketches from the Karen Hills, New York, 1903.
Carrick, Lieut. E. W., Report on the Bwe Expedition, Rangoon (Gov't), 1894.
Cross, Rev. E. B., D.D., On the Karens, in Journal, American Oriental Society, Vol. IV, (1854).
Gilmore, Rev. D. C., D.D., A Karen Grammar, Rangoon, 1901.
Gilmore, Rev. D. C., D.D., The Karen Traditions, in Journal, Burma Research Society, Vol. I, Pt. II, 36. Phonetic Changes in the Karen Language, Vol. VIII, Part II, 122.
Karen Morning Star, The.*
Karen Recorder, The, Rangoon, Burma, 1915-1917.
Logan, J. R., On the Ethnographic Position of the Karens, in Journal, Indian Archipelago, Vol. II, (1854).
Lone, Ko San, Sketch of Rev. Jonathan Wade, D.D., and Karen Tradition. Rangoon, 1907.*
Lowe, Lt. Col. James, The Karen Tribes or Aborigines of Martaban, in Journal, Indian Archipelago, Vol. IV, 413 (1854).
Luther, Mrs. Carlista Vinton, The Vintons and the Karens. Boston, 1880.
MacMahon, Lt. Col. A. R., The Karens of the Golden Chersonese. London, 1876.
Mason, Rev. Francis, D.D., British Burma, Its People and Productions. Rangoon, 1860, Revised edition by Theobald Hertford, 1882.
Mason, Rev. Francis, D.D., The Karen Apostle, A Memoir of Ko Tha Byu. Boston, 1861.
Mason, Rev. Francis, D.D., Religion and Mythology of the Karens, in Journal, Asiatic Society of Bengal, (1858), Vol. XXXIV, Pt. I; Physical Character of the Karens, Vol. XXXV, (New Series, CXXXI) (1866); On Dwellings, Works of Art, etc., of the Karens, Vol. XXXVII, (1868).
Mason, Rev. Francis, D.D., The Story of a Workingman's Life (Autobiography) New York, 1870.
O'Riley, E., Esq., Journal of a Tour in Karen Nee, in Journal, Indian Archipelago, Vol. II, (N. S.) (1858) 391; Notes on Karen Nee, in Vol. IV, (N. S.) (1859) 25.
Poynder, Capt. E. W., Report on Bwe Expedition. Rangoon (Government publication), 1894.
Rangoon Gazette, The, June 6, 1917; Sept. 27, 1919.
Smeaton, D. M., The Loyal Karens of Burma. London, 1887.
To Rev. Ba, "The Union of the Karen Tribes," in Minutes of the Second Annual Meeting of the Karen Trading Society, etc. Rangoon, 1912.*
Than Bya, Rev. T., M.A., Karen Customs, Ceremonies, and Poetry. Rangoon, 1906.*
Than Bya, Rev. T., M.A., The Karens and Their Progress, 1854-1914. ▼Rangoon, 1914.*
Vinton, Rev. J. B., D.D., and Rev. T. Than Bya, Karen Folk-lore Stories, Rangoon, 1908.*
Wade, Rev. Jonathan, D.D., The Grammar of the Sgaw and Pgho Karen Language. Tavoy, 1842.**
Wade, Rev. Jonathan, D.D., The Karen Thesaurus, Vols. I-IV., Tavoy, 1847.** New edition in press, Vol. I. Rangoon, 1915.
Wade, Rev. Jonathan, D.D., A Dictionary of the Sgaw Karen Language, (Karen into English). Rangoon, 1896. Revised by Rev. E. B. Cross, D.D.**
Wade, Rev. Jonathan, D.D., The Anglo-Karen Dictionary, (Completed by Mrs. J. G. Binney). Rangoon, 1883.**

### General Works Dealing with Burma

Burma Archaeological Survey, Annual Reports.
Cochrane, Rev. H. P., Among the Burmans. New York, 1913.
Cochrane, Rev. W. W., The Shans. Rangoon, 1912.
Colquhoun, N. R., Amongst the Shans. New York, 1885. Introduction on History of the Shans by Prof. de Lacouperiet.

Crawfurd, J., Journal of an Embassy from the Governor General of India to the Court of Ava. Vols. I and II. London, 1834.
Cumming, E. D., In the Shadow of the Pagoda. London, 1893.
Fifth Quinquennial Report on Public Education in Burma.
Forbes, Capt. C. J. F. S., Burma and Its People. London, 1878.
Frazer, Sir J. G., The Golden Bough, Vols. I-XI. Oxford, 1911.
Frazer, Sir J. G., The Old Testament and Folk-lore. Oxford, 1919.
Graham, W. A. Siam, A Handbook of Practical, Commercial, and Political Information. London, 1913.
Hanson, Rev. O., Litt. D., The Kachins. Rangoon, 1911.
Heger, F., Alte Metalltrommeln aus Sudost-A'sien, Leipzig, 1902.
Hose and MacDougall, The Pagan Tribes of Borneo, London, 1912.
Imperial Gazetteer, Burma, Vol. I.
Jevons, Introduction to Religion.
Laufer, Berthold, The Si Hia Language, A Study in Indo-Chinese Philology, in Teoung-Pai, 2nd. Series, Vol. XVII, No. 1. Leyden, 1916.
Laufer, Berthold, "Review of Mythology of all Races," in Journal, American Folklore, Vol. XXXI. No. CXX.
Lowis, C. C., "The Tribes of Burma," in Ethnological Survey of India, Rangoon, (Gov't), 1910.
Nieuwenhuis, Dr., Quer Durch Borneo. Leyden, 1907.
Parker, E. H., China and Religion. New York, 1905.
Parmentier, H., "Anciens Tambours de Bronze," in Bulletin, l'Ecole d' Extreme-Orient, Hanoi, 1918.
Richardson, Dr., "Tours in the Shan Country," in Journal, Asiatic Society of Bengal, (1837).
Sangermano, Father, Description of the Burmese Empire, 1783-1808. (Reprint) Government of Burma. Rangoon, 1885.
Scott, Sir J. G., "Indo-Chinese Mythology," in Mythology of All Races, Vol. XII. Boston, 1918.
Scott, Sir J. G., Burma, A Handbook of Practical, Commercial, and Political Information. London, 1911.
Scott, Sir J. G., and Hardiman, J. P., The Upper Burma Gazetteer, 4 vols. (Government). Rangoon, 1901.
Scott, Sir J. G., ("Shwe Yoe"), The Burman and His Life and Notions. London, 1883.
Skeat and Blagdon, The Pagan Tribes of the Malay Peninsula. London.
Snodgrass, Major, The Narrative of the Burmese War. 2 vols. London, 1827.
Spearman, Col. H., British Burma Gazetter, 2 vols., Rangoon, (Gov't) 1880.
Yule, Col. Sir Henry, Narrative of the Mission to the Court of Ava in 1855. London, 1858.
Wayland, Rev. Francis, D.D., Life of Adoniram Judson. Boston, 1853.

## OTHER GENERAL WORKS

Carpenter, J. E., Comparative Religion. New York, 1913.
Codrington, R. H., The Melanesians. Oxford, 1918.
Cole, Fay Cooper, The Wild Tribes of the Davao District. Chicago, 1913.
Davies, Maj. H. R., Yunnan, The Link between Burma and the Yangste. London, 1913.
Deniker, J., The Races of Men. New York, 1906.
Foy, W., "Uber Alter Bronzetrommeln aus Sudost-Asien," in Mitteilungen der Anthropologischen Gesellschaft in Wien, Vol. XXXIII, 1913.
Indian Imperial Census, The, Part I. 1911.
Ross, John, The Original Religion of China.

---

\* Denotes works in Karen.
\*\* Denotes works in both English and Karen.

# INDEX

ABBOTT, Rev. E. A., Baptist missionary in Bassein, 298.
Administration, judicial, of the British, 307.
Adultery, condemnation of, in Karen laws, 148; sacrifice and ostracism for, 192; tabu against, 287.
After-life, the. See Immortality.
Agriculture, economic aspect of, 92-93, 130; use of magic in, 271-273; tabus and, 290-291. See Cultivation.
Alcoholic drink. See Beverages.
Alphabet, the Sgaw, 32; the Pwo, 33. See Language.
Altar the, use of, in sacrifices, 78, 235, 241, 259. See Ritual, also Sacrifices.
Amiability, of the Karen, 30.
Ancestor worship, practice of, 248, 250.
Anderson, Dr., on the manufacture of Karen bronze drums, 124-126.
Anglican Mission, the, 301.
Animism, 210-211. See Demonology; also Religion.
Antidotes, use of, against poisoned arrow-tips, 98.
Appearance, physical. See Physique.
Arabian Nights, the, translation of, into Karen, 310.
Armor, Karen use of, 160.
Art, Karen, 126. See Bronze Drums.
Astronomy, Karen knowledge of, 53-54.
Auspices, and the prophets, 245; the use of, 275. For occasions of, see Ritual, Sacrifices, Divination.
Ava, oppressive rule of, in Burma, 306.

BAG-PIPE, the, 166.
Banyan tree, the, sacred character of, 224.
Baptist Mission, the American, foundation of, 296; interest of natives in, 297; activities of, 298-300, 310.
Basketry, Karen, 113-114.
Beauty, appreciation of, 30. See Dress, Ornaments.
Beliefs. See Religion, Superstitions.
Betel plant, the, use of, 72-73; cultivation of, 84-86.
Betrothal. See Marriage.
Beverages, variety of, 71-72. See Drunkenness.
"Bgha," the, feasts to, 248-257; customs incidental to the feasts, 257-260; tabus and, 261, 291.

Bible, the, identification of with the Lost Book, 298; translation of, into Karen, 300, 310.
Biganget, Bishop, Roman Catholic missionary, 301.
Binney, Rev. J. G., founder of the Karen Theological Seminary, 300.
Birth-marks, on Karen children, 19; Karen explanation of, 21.
Blankets, Karen, 41.
"Blaw," see Guest-chamber.
Blood-brotherhood, strength of bonds of, 25; kinds of, 136; ceremonies of, 136-138; obligations of, 137-138.
Blow-gun, the, mode of manufacture, 96-97.
Blythe, Rev. E. W., on sacrifices to the "Bgha," 259.
Boardman, Rev. G. D., missionary at Tavey, 296, 297.
Bow, the, mode of manufacture of, 98.
Boxing, among the Karen, 175.
Box trap, the, 99.
Brayton, Rev. D. L., translator of the Bible into Pwo Karen, 300.
Brecs, the, a Karen tribe, 4; stunted growth of, 16; drunkenness among, 29; poverty of, 36, 42; customs observed at childbirth, 169; tabus of, 288.
British Government, the, conquers Burma of, 127, n; 141; Karen attachment to, 26, 305; annexation of Pegu by, 298; effects of, in Burma, 306-307; employment of Karens by, 309, 312, 313, 314.
Bronze drums, bearing on racial origin of the Karen, 9; original source of, 9, 115, 116-117; kinds of, among the Karen, 115, 118-119, 120; value of, 9, 116-117; descripiton of, 120-124; manufacture of, 124-126; use of, 194.
Buddhism, influence of, on Karen cults, 264.
Bunker, Dr. Alonzo, on Karen customs at childbirth, 169.
Burial, practice of, 204-206, 221; places of, 205-206. See Funerals.
Burma, habitat of the Karen, 1, 12, 14; British conquest of, 127 n.; 141, 304; arrival of Rev. Adoniram Judson in, 296, n., 1; progress of Christianity in, 296-303.
Burmese, the, habitat of, 1; and, the Karen, vii, 22, 76 n., 87, 304, 306, 307; alphabet and Karen writing, 31; influence on Karen life and practices, 37, 42, 111, 114, 167, 171, 262; umbrella, 43; costume, 47; purpose of charms worn by, 277; persecution of early Karen Christians, 297, 298.

Bwe tribes, the, habitat, 3; numbers, 4; peculiar practice in counting, 33; funeral customs, 208; great sacrifice of, 237-238; the priests of, 247.
Bya, Rev. Thra Than, cited on Karen betrothals, 177; on the propitiation of demons, 242; on divination, 283; translations into Karen, 310.

CALENDAR, the Karen. See Time.
Captives, disposal of, 157. See Slavery, warfare.
Carpenter, J. E., on primitive religious ideas, 210 n., 1.
Carrick, Lieut. E. W., on the Karen art of divination, 283.
Caste, among the Karen, 129.
*Census Report*, enumeration of the Karen, 3-4.
Characteristics. See Mental, Physical.
Charms, potency of, 233, 268; the use of, 271, ff. See Magic.
Chastity, 134, 139, 142; enjoined in laws of the elders, 30; of marriages, 192, 225, 288.
Chief, his authority in the village, 128-129, 143, 241.
Childbirth, methods employed at, 168-169; and demonology, 169-170, 224; tabus observed at, 287.
Children, protection of, against demons, 169-170; naming, 170; treatment and care of, 170-171; pleasures of, 172-175; betrothal of, 176-177; funerals of, 208.
China, the original home of the Karen, 6, ff.; linguistic influence of, on the Karen, 31-32.
Christianity, foundation for, in the "Y'wa" legend, 212; Karen readiness for, 217; abandoning heathen practices for, 260-261; influence of, on Karen religious cults, 264; introduction of, by first Baptist Mission, 296; spread of, among the Karen, 296-300, 309-310. See Religion.
"Climbing the fruit tree." See Funeral games.
Cloth, mode of manufacture, 108-111; quality of, 111-113.
Clothing. See Dress.
Clouds, Karen mythical explanation of, 231.
Codrington, Bishop R. H., on an impersonal power in men and things, 210, n. 1.
College, the Baptist, 300.
Concubinage, 134.
Confession, practice of, at the great sacrifice, 286.
Congo, region of the, musical instruments of, 166, n. 4.
Constellations, the, Karen myths about, 53-54.
Converts, number of Karen Christian, 300.
Cooking, Karen utensils, 67, 70. See Diet, Meats.

Cotton, cultivation, 84; ginning, 108; mode of preparation for spinning, 108; spinning, 110. See Dyeing, Weaving, Cloth.
Courtship, serenading in, 139-141; and the bethrothal, 177-178.
Crawfurd, John, on boxing among the Karen, 175.
Creation, the Karen view of, 10; "Y'wa," tradition of, among the Karen, 211-213.
Cremation, practice of, 204. See Funerals.
Crime, condmenation of, in Karen law, 144, ff.
Crops, rice, 75, ff., 93; subsidiary products, 84-86; yield of, on the plains, 92. See Agriculture, Production.
Cross, Rev. E. B., on Karen mythology, 223; contributions to Karen literature, 310.
Crossbow, the, use of poisoned darts, 97; proficiency with, 98.
Cultivation, primitive methods of, in the hills, 75, ff.; mode of, on the plains, 87, ff. See Agriculture, Crops, Ritual.
Cults, religious, the "Maw Lay" cult, 29, 264; other, 264-265.
Customs, Karen, pre-natal and natal, 168-170, 171. See Marriage, Funerals, Ritual, Sacrifices.

DANCING, 167.
Davies, Maj. H. R., on the Karen language, 8.
"*Dawkula,*" the, or the *Karen National News*, 310.
Death, Karen fear of, 194; relation of, to the "k'la," 218-220. See Funerals.
Decoration. See Bronze drums.
DeLacouperie, Prof., on origin of the Karen, 14, n.
Democracy of Karen government, 143-144.
Demonology, classification of demons, 223, ff.; diversity and ubiquity of demons, 225, ff.; sacrifices to demons, 235, ff. See Animism, Mythology, Sacrifices.
Devil, the, in Karen religion, 213; and the fall of man, 215-216; influence of, over the first woman, 249; the temptation by, 279.
Dialects. See Language.
Diet, Karen, character of, 66, 68, 71.
Diseases, prevalence of, 16; susceptibility of the Karen to, 19: For treatment of, see Sickness.
Diviniation, Sir J. G. Scott on origin of, 279; mythical origin of, 279, 280; practice of, 279-280; art of, 282-285. For occasions of, see Ritual.
Divorce, practice of, 191-192.
Domestic animals, 64-65, 102.
Dress, Karen, the "hse" or smock, 35-40; Shan and Burmese influence on, 36, 37; diversity of pattern and colors in, 35-38; female, 38-41; head-dress, 43.
Drugs. See Medicine.

# INDEX

Drums. See Bronze drums.
Drunkeness, prevalence of, 29; relation of, to crime, 72.
Dualism, in the Karen religion, 213, 217. See Devil.
Dyeing, 110.

EARRINGS, Karen use of, 46.
Earthquake, Karen myth of, 230; Karen explanation of, 289; tabus during, 289.
East India Company, British, annexation of Burmese provinces by, 304.
Eclipses, Karen explanation of, 54, 231, 289; tabus during, 288-289.
Education, progress in, 27, 307, ff.; influence of, on Karen occupations, 95, 309, 310; mission schools, 300, 301.
Elders, the, position of, in the village, 127-128; authority of, 143-144; healing offerings made by, 247; on cavities in the abdomen, 277; first hear the Christian message, 297.
Elephants, use of, 87; hunting of, 102-104.
Esthetic sense, 30.

FALL of man, the Karen account of, 214-216.
Family, the, Karen regard for, 135-136; the "Bgha" of, 248; feasts to the "Bgha," 254, ff.
Famine, 145.
Fear, prevalence of, among the Karen, due to Burman oppression, 22; and superstition, 288-289.
Feasting, 249, ff. For occasions, see Funerals, Marriage, Sacrifices.
Feud. See Vengeance, Warfare.
Fire, mode of making, 70-71.
Firearms, introduction of, into Burma, 159; use of, by the Karen, 159. See Weapons.
First Burmese War (1824-6), 127, n. 1.
Fishing, implements of, in the hills, 104-106; various modes of, 104-107.
Food, Karen, mode of preparing, 68-70; serving and eating, 70. See Diet.
Forays. See Warfare.
Fornication, condemnation of, in Karen laws, 148; penalties for, 192; an offence against the Bgha," 258; tabu on, 287.
Fowl, the, mythical explanation of use of, in sacrifices and divination, 258-259, 279-280; use of chicken bones in divination, 282-283. For occasions of use of, see Ritual, Sacrifices.
Foy, W., on old bronze drums, 115, n. 1.
Frazer, Sir J. G., on fear of loss of one's "k'la," 219, n. 14, on the scapegoat, 235, n. 3.
Funerals, Karen, festive character of, 193-194, 208-209; preparing the body, 195-197; diversity of rites at, 197, ff.; poetry used in, 197, 198-200; games used in, 200-202; ceremonies at, 202-204.

GAME, abundance of, in Burmese hills, 96.
Games, of children, 171-175; funeral, 200-202.
Gates, Mr. F. H., on Karen use of shields, 160.
Gilmore, Dr. D. C., on origin of Karen race, 6; on Karen language, 9, 32; on Karen myth of the fall of man, 213, ff.
Ginning, method of, 108.
Gobi Desert, the, 5-6.
God, conception of, in the Karen religion, 212; the "Y'wa" legend, 212-213; and the fall of man, 213-216.
Government, the Karen, 127-129; democracy of, 143-144; the British, 306-307.
Great sacrifice, the, of the Sgaw Karen, 235-236; of the Bwe Karen, 237-238.
Guest-chamber, of the Karen village-house, 62, 138-139.
Guitar, the, 163-164.

HABITAT, of the Karen, 1-2.
Harp, the Karen, 162; the Burmese, 162, n. 2.
Harris, Rev. E. N., and the Karen hymn-book, 161.
Head-dress, Karen, 37, 40, 43.
Health, of the Karen, 19. See Diseases.
Heger, Mr. Franz, on manufacture of bronze drums, 124-126.
"Hkli Bo Pa," a Christian Karen cult, 265.
Homosexuals, 21.
Honesty, Karen reputation for, 27, 82, 144, 149.
Horn, see Wedding-horn.
Hose and MacDougall, quoted on resemblances between the Karen and the Kayans of Borneo, 14-15, n.
House, the Karen, character of, 56, 63, 64, 257-258; construction of, 57-58; interior of, 60-63.
"Hpi Bi Yaw," mythical goddess of the crops, 84, 93, 226.
"Htaw Meh Pa," mythical founder of the Karen race, 5, 12-14, 46, 259.
Hunting, Karen delight in, 96; mode of, 96; weapons employed in, 96-98; use of dogs in, 102; elephants, 102-104; lack of sportsmanship in, 104.
Hymns, Karen love of, 29; Karen, 310. See Music.

IMMORTALITY, condemnation of, in Karen laws, 148; attitude toward, 192; Karen ideas of, 222, 230, 233. See Fornication.
Incantations, on removal of village, 63-64; in agricultural sacrifices, 75-83; in connection with blood-brotherhood, 137; in preparation for a foray, 153-154; natal, 169-170; wedding, 188-189; funeral, 195, 197, 205; in propitiation of demons, 225, ff.; at feasts to the "Bgha," 250, 251; in ritual of divination, 283, 284.
Indo-Chinese peninsula, habitat of the Karen, 1.

Industry, effect of tabus on Karen, 286, ff.; 295. See Occupations.
Intellect, Karen, 26, 27. See Education.
Intermarriage, prevalence of, 176.
Irrawaddy, delta, habitat of the Sgaw Karen, 1; native melodies of, 29.
Irrigation, 93.

JEWS, the, supposed influence of, on the Karen, 10-12.
Jew's-harp, the, 162-163.
Judson, Dr. Adoniram, on religious cults among the Karen, 264; founder of American Baptist Mission, 296 n. 1; his first disciple, 297.
Judson College, at Rangoon, 300.
Justice, Karen practice of, 129, 143-144, 236; Karen laws, 144-151; British practice of, in Karen districts, 306, 307.

KAREN, the, as a race, 1, ff.; origin of the word, 7-8; relations of, to their neighbors, vii, 22, 56, 87, 104, 106, 111, 114, 124, 159, 168, 262, 297, 298, 304, 305, 307; loyalty to British rule, 305, 306, 314. For Origin, Religion, Customs, Occupations, etc., see appropriate heads.
Karenni, the. See Red Karen.
Kinship, Karen ideas of, 135-136. See Family.
"K'la," the, Karen conception of, 193, 218-221; seat of, 221, 245; importance of, 169, 193, ff., 232; and the soul, 218; in sickness, 239, ff.; sacrifices to, 243-245; and the use of magic, 275-276.
Kondagyi village, bronze drum from, described, 121-124.
Ko Pisan (Ko San Yo), founder of a Christian cult among the Karen, 264-265.
Ko Shwe Waing, early convert to Christianity, 297.
Ko Tha Byu, first native Christian missionary, 296-297.

LAND, distribution of, 129. See Agriculture, Cultivation.
Language, Karen, classification, 8; bearing of, on origin of Karen race, 6-8; characteristics of, 8-9, 31-33; the written, 31; and Chinese, 32; family relationships expressed in, 135-136. See Literature, Poetry.
Laufer, Dr. Berthold, on origin of the Karen people, 6, 10-11.
Laws, Karen, traditional character of, 143-144; mode of preservation of, 144; subject-matter of, 144-151. See Justice.
Lightning. See Thunder.
Logan, J. R., on origin and racial affinity of the Karen, 14, n.
Loom, the Karen, 111, 112, 114; the Burmese, 112.

"Lords of the land and water," in Karen demonology, 225; the great sacrifice to, 235, ff.; the small sacrifice to, 239.
Lost Book, the, legendary account of, 279-280; supposed recovery of, 297, 298, 307.
Lowis, C. C., 12, n. 18.

MacMAHON, Col., A. R., on Karen dancing, 167; on Karen magic, 276; on Bwe tabus, 288.
Magic, Karen ideas on, 210, 267; Karen practice of, 267, 270, ff.; practitioners of, 268-269; white magic, 271-273; black magic, 273, ff.
Malaria, prevalence of, 16.
Manners, Karen, 30.
Marriage, practice of monogamy, 134; matchmaking, 176-181; wedding ceremonies, 181-190; permanence of Karen, 190-191; and demonology, 224; and tabus, 287, 294.
Martyrs, among early Karen Christians, 298.
Mason, Rev. Francis, D.D., on the theories of Karen origin, 5, 10, 12, 14; on the veracity of the Karen, 27; on the order of the months in the Karen calendar, 50; on the breed of pigs, 65; on bronze drums, 116; on blood-brotherhood, 136-137; on Karen slavery, 141; on the preservation of Karen laws, 143, 144; on forays and peace pacts, 158; on natal practices of the Karen, 169; rendering of a Karen poem on God, 212; on the legend of the ancestors of the human race, 217, n. 11; on Karen mythology, 222; on Mount "Thaw Thi," 262, 263; on Karen medicine, 277; translation of the Bible, 300; foundation of "Dawkula," 310.
Match-making. See Marriage.
Mat-making, 113.
Matriarchy, possible survival of, among the Karen, 133, 190, 249.
Maw Lay, the, music of, 29; cult of, 264.
Mawnepgha Karen, the, belonging to the Sgaw group, 1; domestic animals of, 65.
Measurement, Karen standards of, 51-53.
Meats, variety of, in use, 66; preparation of, 69-70. See Diet, Food.
Medicine, Karen resort to, 270; the medicine-teacher, 269, 270, 277; native practice of 277, 278. See Magic.
Medicine-teacher, the, 269, 270, 277, 278.
Meh, Thra Klaw, martyrdom of, 298.
Mental characteristics, 22, ff.
Midwife, the Karen, 168.
Migrations, legendary of Htaw Meh Pa, 5; supposed routes of, 12-14.
Mind, the Karen, 22, ff.; 27.
Missions. See Baptist, Roman Catholic, Anglican.
Missionaries, in Burma, 296, n. 1; 297, 298, 300, 301, 303, 304.
Monogamy. See Marriage.

# INDEX

Monotheism. See Religion.
Mopgha Karen, the, dress of, 38.
"Mü kaw li." See Devil.
Murder, penalties for, in Karen law, 149-150.
Music, Karen love of, 29; occidental, 29, 161; native, 29, 161; proficiency in, 161.
Musical instruments, Karen, 162, ff.
"Mü xa," the, spirits that preside over births, 223-224, 248.
Mythology, character of Karen, 223; demons in Karen, 223, ff.; of Karen origins, 5-6; and bronze drums, 117; relating to Karen funerals, 193-194; of the fall of man, 213, ff; concerning the cultivation of rice, 226; concerning the king of hades, 227-228; of Atlas, 230; and Mount "Thaw Thi," 6, 262, ff.; of "Y'wa" and the Lost Book, 279-280. See Demonology.

NABAAIN village, bronze drum from, described, 120-121.
Names, Karen, of children, 170; superstitions in regard to, 292.
Nationalism, rise of, 310-311; 312.
Necromancy. See Magic.
Negrito blood, admixture of, 17.
Nestorianism, supposed influence of, on the Karen, 10-11.
Newspapers, Karen, 310.
Nichols, Dr. C. A., Baptist missionary in Bassein, 300.
Nicknames, Karen, 170.
Nieuwenhuis, Dr., on the rice-pounder dance in Borneo, 201, n. 5; on fear of loss of one's "k'la," 219, n. 14.
Numerals, Karen, 33.
Nwedaung village, manufacture of bronze drums in, 124.

OCCUPATIONS, Karen, agriculture, 75-95; fishing and hunting, 96-107; cloth-making, 108-113; mat-making and basketry, 113-114; subsidiary, 86-87, 95, 309, 310.
Offerings, for the sick, 239-243; to the e"k'la," 243-245. See Sacrifices.
Omens, variety of, 178, 190, 229, 290; and tabus, 290. See Divination, Ritual.
Oranges, growth of, 85.
Ordeal, of tree climbing, 236.
Origin, of the Karen people, the legendary founder of the race, 5-6; various hypotheses of, 6, ff.; Karen monotheism and the lost tribes of Israel, 10; Karen migrations, 12-14.
O'Riley, Mr. J., on the probable route of Karen migrations, 13-14.
Ornamentation. See Bronze drums.
Ornaments, Karen, diversity of, 43, ff.; grotesqueness of, 44-45; worn by men, 46-47.
Orphans, ostracism of, 134, 288; magical powers of, 269-270, 288.

Ostracism, ancient practice of, 133-134, 288; for adultury, 192.

PADAUNG Karen, the, ornaments of, 44; the bag-pipe of, 166; natal practices of, 169; art of divination of, 283.
"Paddy." See Rice.
Paku Karen, the, belonging to the Sgaw group, 1; dress of, 35; domestic animals of, 65.
Pao, the. See Taungthu.
Parker, E. H., 12, n.
Passions, the Karen explanation of, 276-277; charms used to control, 277.
Patriarch. See Chief.
Peace pact, the Karen, 157-158.
Pegu, annexation of, by British Empire, 298.
Pegu Hills, the, Karen dress in, 35, 40; the Karen village in, 56, 126; Karen fishing in, 107; bronze drums in, 118; funeral rites in, 197, 206-207; feasts to the "Bgha" in, 249, ff.; persecution of Karen Christians in, 297, 298, 306.
Persecution, of early Karen Christians, 297, 298.
"Pgho," the divine essence, 210.
Philippine Islands, similarities between tribes of, and the Karen, 15; musical instruments of, 166, n. 4.
Physique, Karen, height, 16; color, 16-18; features, 18; hair, 18; general traits, 19-20.
Pig, kind of, among the Karen, 64; sacrificial character of, 259, 279-280, 284. See Sacrifices.
Pilgrim's Progress, translated into Karen, 310.
Pipe, the bamboo tobacco, 164-166.
Po, Dr. San C., a prominent Karen, 310.
Poetry, ditties of Karen children, 173-174; rhyming contests, 177; of betrothals, 177, ff.; wedding, 182-183, 188; funeral, 197, 198-199, 200, 208; religious, 211-212, 263. See Literature.
Poison, use of, 97-98, 107; antidotes, 98; possession of, condemned by Karen law, 150.
Politics. See Government.
Polygamy, practice of, 134.
Population, Karen, 3-4.
Portuguese, missionaries in Burma, 11; introduce firearms into Burma, 159.
Pottery, Karen, 67, 70.
"Pounding the pestles." See Games, funeral.
Poynder, Capt. C. E., on the Karen art of divination, 283.
Practices, Karen. See Customs.
Prayer, Karen, at the great sacrifice, 235-236; at the small sacrifice, 239; in sickness, 240, ff., 294; to the "k'la," 243-245; at feasts to the "Bgha," 250, 251, 257; to demons, 240, ff., 293. See also Incantations, Sacrifices.
Precepts. See Laws.
Press, the Karen, 310.

Property, regard for private, 129, 131; community of, 130.
Prophets, the, business of, 245-247, 275-276; selection of, 247.
Pü Maw Taw, mythical owner of the first bronze drums, 117.
Pwo, the, a group of the Karen, 173; relation to the Sgaw, 33.
Python, the White. See White Python.

RAINBOW, the, in Karen demonology, 227, 228.
Rangoon *Gazette*, on the classification of bronze drums, 118.
Red Karen, the, a Bwe tribe, 4, 31; dress of 37; ornaments of, 44; bronze drums of, 117; special tabus of, 286.
Reincarnation, relation of, to the "k'la," 168, 218, ff., 222.
Religion, Karen, monotheism, 10-12, 212-213; three conceptions of, 210-211; and ostracism, 134; the soul and the "k'la," 218, ff.; Mount "Thaw Thi," 263; religious cults, 264-265. See Christianity, Ritual.
Rhinoceros, the, in Karen demonology, 225.
Rice, importance of, 66; preparation of, 67-68; fermentation of, 71-72; cultivation of, 75, ff.; sacred character of, 222, 226.
Ritual, Karen religious, at annual removal of village, 63-64; in connection with agriculture, 76, ff., 93-95; and bronze drums, 118-119; at feasts to the "Bgha," 133, 249, ff.; of blood-brotherhood, 136-138; of the foray, 152-154; 157-158; at childbirth, 167-170; at betrothal, 178; of the wedding, 188-189; of the funeral, 64-65, 195, 197, 205; origin of, 216; of propitiation, in sickness, 224, 225, 234, 240, ff., 243-245; of divination, 283. See also Incantations, Prayer, Sacrifices.
"River of Running Sand," the. See Origin.
Roman Catholic Mission, the, 301.
Ross, John, 12, n. 16.

SACRIFICES, Karen religious, mythical origin of, 226, 227; classification of, 234, ff.; festival character of, 237; to the "k'la," 243-245; to the "Bgha," 251; animals used in, 259; to demons of the flooded rivers, 292. See also Incantations, Prayer, Ritual.
Satan. See Devil.
Sayings, of the elders, 12, n. 17; 144-150.
Schools. See Education.
Scott, Sir J. G., on lack of humor among the Karen, 23; on natural origin of the practice of divination, 279.
Second Burmese War, (1852-3), 127, n. 1; 298, 306.
Sects. See Cults.
Seining, mode of, among the Karen, 106-107.
Serpent, the Devil as a, 215.

Sgaw, the, a group of the Karen, 1-3; language of, 31, ff.; great sacrifice of, 235-236, small sacrifice of, 239; practice of divination, 284; pre-natal tabus of, 287.
Shakespeare, translation of, into Karen, 310.
Shan, the, neighbors of the Karen, 1, 4, 12; influence of, on the Karen, 36, 37, 43, 67, 114, 116, 159; bronze drums manufactured by, 9, 124.
Shwegyin district, Karen dress in, 40; the betel plant in, 84; marriage customs in, 177, 187; funeral rites in, 206; household deities in, 248, 250; religious cults in, 264.
Shyness, Karen, 23.
Siam, habitat of the Karen, 1, 2, 304; rite of removal in, 64; drunkenness among the Karen in, 72; funeral practices in, 197-198, 204; feast to the "Bgha" in, 250.
Sickness, interpretation of, 193, 241, 270; propitiation of the spirits in, 193, 234, 239-243, 249, ff.; use of magic in, 270, 274, 275; use of medicine in, 277, 278; divination in, 282, 283.
Sin, the original, in Karen legend, 213-216; penalty for, after death, 230, 233; confession of, 236.
Skeat and Blagden, on the blowpipe, 97, n. 1.
Slavery, prevalence of, 141, 142, 157.
Slingshot, the, 88.
Small sacrifice, the, of the Sgaw, 239.
Smeaton, D. M., on the benefits of Christianity, 309.
Smells, Karen superstitions regarding, 277-278.
Smith, Rev. D. A. W., president of the Karen Theological Seminary, 300; author of commentaries and text-books, 310.
Snodgrass, Maj., 306.
Skeat and Blagden, on the blow-gun, 97, n. 1.
Society for the Propagation of the Gospel, in Toungoo, 301.
Soul ("Tha"), the, Karen conception of, 218.
Space, Karen conception of, 51-53.
Spices, use of, 66, 69.
Spinning, 108-110.
Spinning-wheel, the, 108-110.
Sportsmanship, Karen, 104, 107, 175. See Hunting, Fishing.
Spring trap, the, 99-101.
Statistics of the Baptist Mission in Burma, 300.
Stealing, see Honesty, Theft.
Superstitions, Karen, regarding the "k'la," 218-221; regarding smells, 277-278; and tabus, 286, 288, ff. See also Customs, Demonology, Tabus.
Stars, the, Karen acquaintance with, 53-54.
Strangers, entertainment of, 62, 139; attitude of Karen toward, 257-258; restrictions on, 288.
"Stretching the neck." See Games, funeral.
Suicide, attitude of Karen toward, 150.
Swa, the, 116, n. 2.

Swords, Karen, 150.
Symbolism, in propitiatory sacrifices, 242-243.

TABU, what associated with, 286; description of various tabus, 261, 286-294; effects of tabus, 294-295.
Taunghthu tribe, the, belonging to the Pwo group, 1, 3.
Taxes, Karen, 129.
"Thaw Thi," Mount, the Karen Olymphus, 6, 224, 231, 262-264; the worship on, 263.
Theft, penalties for, in Karen law, 27, 149.
Theological Seminary, the, foundation of, 300.
*Thesaurus, Karen, The*, on the value of bronze drums, 116; on Karen swords, 159; on Karen conceptions of the divine force, 210; on Karen mythology, 223; on native medicine, 278; compilation of, 310.
Third Burmese War (1885), 127, n. 1; 306, 310.
Threshing, modes of, 82, 90; tabu of the threshing-floor, 291.
Thunder, Karen mythical explanation of, 231.
Time, Karen measurements of, 48-50. See also Astronomy.
Tobacco, Karen use of, 72, 74.
Toungoo district, habitat of the Bwe Karen, 1, 31; domestic animals in, 65, 102; agricultural products of, 84-85, 86; baskets of the Karen in, 114; bronze drums of, 118; warfare in, 152; Mount "Thaw Thi," 262-263; Anglican Mission in, 301.
Trade, in rice, 92; in firearms, 159.
Traditions. See Mythology.
Trapping, 98 ff., 105, ff. See Hunting, Fishing.
Tribes, of the Karen, 3, 127.
Twins, Karen explanation of, 170.

UPAS tree, the, poison from, 97.

VEGETABLES. See Crops.
Vengeance, Karen ideas of, 25, 147, 150, 152, 274.
Village, the Karen, construction of 56-60; stockade of, 60; Burmese influence on, 63; appearance of, 60-63; annual removal of, 63-64; government of, 127-129, 143-144, 247; community life in, 130.
Vinton, Dr. J. B., on the "River of Running Sand," 5, 6, n.
Vinton, Dr. J. H., on Tribal Resemblances of the Karen, 15; in Rangoon, 298.

Vinton, Mrs. J. H., author of Karen hymns, 310.
Voices, Karen, 29. See Music.

WADE, Dr. Jonathan, on paired words in the Karen language, 31-32; comparison of Pwo and Sgaw dialects by, 33; on blood-brotherhood, 136; of the proper rendering of the word "soul," 218, n. 13; on Karen magic, 274; on Karen medicine, 277; reduces Karen language to writing, 297; author of dictionaries and grammars of Pwo and Sgaw dialects, 300; compiler of the *Karen Thesaurus*, 310.
Waer, the, habitat of, 116, n. 2.
Warfare, Karen, character of, in olden days, 152; the foray, 152-157.
Wealth, Karen ideas of, 129-130.
Weapons, Karen, for hunting and trapping, 96-102; for fighting, 158-159; introduction of firearms, 159; use of armor, 160. See Firearms.
Weaving, 110-111.
Wedding, the Karen, preparations for, 181-182; procession, 182-184; feasting at, 186-189; tabus, 190; in the Pegu Yomas, 184-186.
Wedding-horn, the, 166.
Weirs, Karen use of, 107.
White, Mrs. U. B., note on Karen music by, 161, n. 1.
White Python, the, myth of, 38, 193-194, 263.
"Wi." See Prophets.
Widows, ostracism of, 184, 288.
Wife purchase, remnant of, among the Karen, 187.
Witchcraft. See Magic.
Women, Karen, timidity of, 23; dress of, 38, ff.; ornaments of, 43, ff.; beauty of, 44; position of, 64-65; 131-133, 168, 190, 249, 288; use of betel and tobacco by, 73, 74.
Woodpecker, the, a bird of ill-omen, 190, 229.
World War, the, Karens in, 306, 314.
Worship, Karen. See Religion, Sacrifices.

XYLOPHONE, the, 164.

YOUNG, Rev. W. H., 4, n.
Yu, the, and bronze drums, 116, n. 5.
Yunnan, original home of the Karen, 9, 12; the crossbow in, 97, n. 2; source of bronze drums, 116.
"Y'wa," the legend of, 211-213; the abode of, 263; and the Lost Book, 279-280. See also Religion, Christianity.

LaVergne, TN USA
24 August 2010
194502LV00003B/19/P